"My dear friends Christopher and Melissa, a very talented duo, have done the photography for six of my cookbooks. They now have poured their talent and passion into a cookbook all their own, *Canal House Cooks Every Day*. This cookbook is a collection of deliciously simple recipes, formatted according to seasons, and the extensive collection of beautiful pictures—each one full of flavor and bold colors—is worth the price of the book alone!"—*Lidia Bastianich*

"In a world where home cooks feel compelled to re-create the stainless steel sterility and vertical towers of excess that belong only in restaurant kitchens, one is ravenous for the kind of comfort, grace, and authenticity defined by the marriage of honest food to life in all its seasonal vagaries and delicious rituals large and small. Christopher Hirsheimer and Melissa Hamilton's glorious *Canal House Cooks Every Day* satiates that hunger: it is delectable in its flavor, its warmth, and its heartfelt invitation to share a year of cooking, eating, celebrating with friends and family, and the pleasures of simple, real food."
—*Elissa Altman*, *Poor Man's Feast*

"Jonathan Waxman of Barbuto gave me my first copy of a Canal House cookbook and I was immediately struck by what was not in the book— all the noise, fuss and bother that complicates what is a joyful, simple task—preparing food. In *Canal House Cooks Every Day*, Hamilton and Hirsheimer have arrived at the point where all good cooks desperately hope to arrive—a kitchen in which the purity of recipe and style reflects the true essence of the ingredients and lives well-lived."
—*Christopher Kimball*,
Founder, *America's Test Kitchen*

"Christopher Hirsheimer and Melissa Hamilton understand food so intuitively, cook it so superbly, and present it—whether in the form of words or images or (if you're really, really lucky) an actual plate in front of you, straight from their kitchen—so accessibly that sometimes you just have to wonder why anybody else even bothers."
—*Colman Andrews*, Editorial Director, TheDailyMeal.com

"I get goosebumps every time I receive a new seasonal Canal House cookbook. This collection is the consummate guide to cooking seasonally. The raw illustrations and photographs are exquisite. Christopher and Melissa have come to define the immediacy of delicious food, made to order, now!"—*Mario Batali*

"Combine kitchen stove commonsense with food that's drop-dead gorgeous in its simplicity, and you have *Canal House Cooks Every Day*, a book that gives us hope that we can cook like that, too!"
—*Dorothy Kalins*, Director, Dorothy Kalins Ink, and founding editor, *Saveur*

"Any poseur can write six minutes of music so complex you can't bear to hear it. Only a genius can take three chords and one hook and make a 3-minute rock classic. Melissa and Christopher's recipes are the culinary equivalent of classic hits. You can dance to them. And you will. Year after year."—*Jesse Kornbluth*, HeadButler.com

"...*Canal House Cooks Every Day* offers recipes full of heart and simple goodness. Melissa and Christopher create inspiring dishes with passion and a deep understanding of the simple pleasures in life."
—*John Besh*, chef & cookbook author

CANAL HOUSE COOKS
every day

To Anne,
Eat well, be happy!

Melissa & Christopher

CANAL HOUSE COOKS
every·day

Hamilton & Hirsheimer

**Andrews McMeel
Publishing®**

www.andrewsmcmeel.com

Kansas City · Sydney · London

Andrews McMeel Publishing, LLC
an Andrews McMeel Universal company
1130 Walnut Street, Kansas City, Missouri 64106

www.andrewsmcmeel.com

thecanalhouse.com

12 13 14 15 16 TEN 10 9 8 7 6 5 4 3 2

ISBN: 978-1-4494-2147-2

Library of Congress Control Number: 2012936742

Production & Design by CANAL HOUSE

ATTENTION: SCHOOLS AND BUSINESSES
Andrews McMeel books are available at quantity discounts with bulk purchase for
educational, business, or sales promotional use. For information, please e-mail
the Andrews McMeel Publishing Special Sales Department:
specialsales@amuniversal.com

for the children

***

frani & verity
nash, lillie, henry & molly — ch

olivia & eliot — mh

The sky through the window of seat 26k of a 777 flying to Istanbul, Turkey

ITHACA

When you set out on your journey to Ithaca,
pray that the road is long,
full of adventure, full of knowledge.
The Lestrygonians and the Cyclops,
the angry Poseidon — do not fear them:
You will never find such as these on your path,
if your thoughts remain lofty, if a fine
emotion touches your spirit and your body.
The Lestrygonians and the Cyclops,
the fierce Poseidon you will never encounter,
if you do not carry them within your soul,
if your soul does not set them up before you.

Pray that the road is long.
That the summer mornings are many, when,
with such pleasure, with such joy
you will enter ports seen for the first time;
stop at Phoenician markets,
and purchase fine merchandise,
mother-of-pearl and coral, amber, and ebony,
and sensual perfumes of all kinds,
as many sensual perfumes as you can;
visit many Egyptian cities,
to learn and learn from scholars.

Always keep Ithaca in your mind.
To arrive there is your ultimate goal.
But do not hurry the voyage at all.
It is better to let it last for many years;
and to anchor at the island when you are old,
rich with all you have gained on the way,
not expecting that Ithaca will offer you riches.

Ithaca has given you the beautiful voyage.
Without her you would have never set out on the road.
She has nothing more to give you.

And if you find her poor, Ithaca has not deceived you.
Wise as you have become, with so much experience,
you must already have understood what these Ithacas mean.

— *Constantine Cavafy*
(translated by George Barbanis)

recipe index x

foreword xvi

introduction xviii

spring 1
April — May — June

summer 94
July — August — September

autumn 176
October — November — December

winter 264
January — February — March

index 346

metric conversion table 357

acknowledgments 359

recipe index

⟨ soups ⟩

cold **avocado** & **cucumber** soup 108

restorative **beef** broth 276

warm **beet** soup 183

cold **carrot** soup 140

chicken soup with ditalini 186

chicken broth with spinach &
   little meatballs 193

spinach tagliatelle & peas in golden
   chicken broth 46

cleansing ginger-**chicken** soup 277

chilled **corn** soup 108

cold white **corn** soup with
   lobster & avocado 128

duck soup with cabbage, ham &
   chinese rice noodles 173

roasted red pepper & tomato **gazpacho** . . 107

lobster stew 255

stinging **nettle** soup 7

chilled **potato** & **celery** soup 140

roasted **pumpkin** soup 189

white **sweet potato** soup with
   pickled scallions 280

turkey & **potato** soup 228

everyday **vegetable** tonic 276

watercress soup 330

⟨ salads ⟩

artichoke, pea & **fava bean** salad 23

asparagus vinaigrette 56

shaved **asparagus** & **arugula** salad
   with bruschetta 33

pickled **beets** with horseradish cream . . . 27

canal house year-round **caprese** salad . . . 72

chopped **celery** salad 284

chanterelle salad 162

roast **chicken** & **bread** salad 324

marinated **chicken** salad with
   radicchio & iceberg 186

waldorf **chicken** salad 314

corn, string bean & **potato**
   succotash salad 164

canal house **crab** louis 101

cool **cucumber** & **mint** salad
   with sichuan pepper 103

escarole salad with lemon & parmigiano . . 228

ruby red **grapefruit, avocado**
   & **escarole** salad 280

green lentil & **smoked ham hock** salad . . 165

potato salad "buttered" & lemoned 103

old-fashioned layered **potato** salad 102

hearts of **romaine** with mimosa dressing . . 299

string beans vinaigrette with french feta . . 101

composed **summer salad** with
   lemony aïoli 115

sliced **tomatoes** with arugula 130

tomatoes with tonnato sauce 111

treviso with mustard vinaigrette 324

eggs

how to **boil** an egg 70

"**buttered**" eggs 71

buckwheat **crêpes** with ham & cheese . . . 314

deviled eggs 71

chorizo & potato **frittata** 10

ham & cheese **omelet** 13

open-faced zucchini **omelet** 72

open-faced **sandwiches** 38

soft **scrambled eggs**
   & chanterelles 160

pasta, rice & grains

asparagus on pasta with a poached
   egg & lemon butter 18

lasagne **bolognese** 244

pappardelle **bolognese** 241

butternut squash & candied bacon
   on fresh pasta 250

cannelloni 248

deconstructed **carbonara** 201

spaghetti alla **carbonara** 45

curd rice 296

raviolini with **fava beans** & **parmigiano** . . 81

green **lasagne** with tomato sauce
   & fresh ricotta 244

buttery **lobster** capellini 33

pappardelle & **mushrooms** 245

rigatoni with **passato** &
   parmigiano-reggiano 188

fresh **pasta** 236

pappardelle with **peas** & **scallions**
   bathed in cream 7

rice salad 81

risotto cakes with anchovies (or not) . . . 10

shrimp risotto 46

hot **spaghetti** tossed with
   raw tomato sauce 128

spaghetti with tomato sauce & ricotta . . . 44

spinach pasta 238

spinach taglietelle & peas in
   golden chicken broth 46

spinach taglietelle with tomato sauce
   & ricotta 250

spinach taglietelle bolognese 241

pizza

pizza **dough** 304

escarole, fontina &
   black olive pizza 305

potato & **onion** pizza 305

prosciutto, lemon & **green olive** pizza . . 304

white clam pizza 305

fish & shellfish

canal house **crab** louis 101

potted **crab** 316

birthday **halibut** with beets &
  asparagus vinaigrette 56

buttery **lobster** capellini 33

lobster stew 255

fried fish & french-fried **potatoes** . . 322

grilled **salmon** 139

wild **salmon** crudo with arugula salad . . . 76

smoked **salmon** butter 316

smoked **salmon** with chèvre on crax 77

poached wild **salmon** with fresh
  english peas & morels 76

sausage & **clam** stew 188

pickled **shrimp** & **celery** 254

shrimp roast 296

sole meunière with peas, parsley & chives . . 20

birds

chicken en gelée sandwiches 158

chicken roasted over potatoes & lemon . . 184

chicken thighs with pancetta &
  caperberries 299

fennel & ginger–rubbed **chicken**
  with cauliflower 12

marinated **chicken** salad with
  radicchio & iceberg 186

pan-fried **chicken** thighs with
  little zucchini 38

poached **chicken** with tarragon &
  chive mayonnaise 31

roast **chicken** 158

roast **chicken** & bread salad 324

roast **chicken** smothered with chanterelles . 158

roasted **chicken** in a pot with
  spring onions 82

the fry queen's fried **chicken** 112

waldorf **chicken** salad 314

duck breasts with apples & caraway 168

confit of **duck** legs with potatoes
  sarladaise 172

roast **goose** with ten legs 258

grilled **quail** with braised chestnuts &
  kabocha squash 194

galantine of **turkey** & **pork** with peas . . 40

roast **turkey** 220

day-after-thanksgiving
  turkey sandwich 228

meat

braised **beef brisket** with onions
  & currants 300

beef tenderloin with parsley-tarragon
  butter 284

whole **beef tenderloin**,
  peppered & grilled 134

roast **beef** sandwich with avocado
  & tomato 130

roast prime rib of **beef** 256

bratwurst with fingerling potatoes 210

bratwurst with sautéed caraway cabbage . . 210

sliced **brisket** with onions on a
soft potato roll 300

corned beef & cabbage 338

rolled **flank steak** with pesto 78

baked **ham** with golden bread crumbs . . . 306

ham & **bacon** with mustard &
brown sugar sauce 272

sliced **ham** on baguette 306

cold leg of **lamb** with cannellini & lemon
mayonnaise 166

roast leg of **lamb** for easter 26

lamb shoulder chops with rosemary
potatoes 216

march **meatball** madness 328

pork chops with roasted beets
& escarole salad 333

pork cutlets with pickled pearl onions
& pancetta 334

pork stewed in guajillo chile mole 198

galantine of **turkey** & **pork** with peas . . 40

roast **pork** with salmoriglio 9

rabbit stew 340

sausage & **clam** stew 188

pimentón & caraway **short ribs**
with egg noodles 312

two **steaks** feed four 134

skirt steak with buttered spinach &
french fries 214

hoisin-ful **spareribs** for the fourth of july . . 102

breast of **veal** braised with green olives
& tomatoes 50

"brunette" de **veau** 343

vegetables & legumes

asparagus—the magestic stalks of spring . 15

asparagus with lemon-butter sauce 17

roasted **asparagus** 17

fire-toasted corn tortilla with mashed
avocado 279

avocado mash on multigrain toast 279

pickled **beets** with horseradish cream . . . 27

borlotti beans with sautéed baby kale . . . 283

butternut squash & candied bacon
on fresh pasta 250

cannellini with smoked ham & rosemary . . 43

caponata 136

cauliflower with bread crumbs,
pancetta & prunes 213

fricassée of **chanterelles** 162

chestnut & **pearl onion** stuffing 222

cranberry beans in olive oil 166

fritto misto 143

the **garden** giveth 84

kabocha squash, yukon gold potatoes
& **cipolline** 196

roasted **kabocha squash** 196

crushed **potatoes** with pancetta,
peas & scallions 330

brian's mashed **potato** trick 221

sister frances's **potatoes** 27

roasted **spring onions** 23

tomato "rollmops" 127

tomato tart 156

tomatoes all dressed up for summer 127

tomatoes take a warm oil bath 130

tomatoes with tonnato sauce 111

the splendid summer **tomato** sandwich . . 127

olive oil–poached **zucchini** &
raw **tomatoes** 144

sautéed **zucchini** with scallions &
fresh mozzarella 144

desserts

apple galette 230

apple tart 174

apricot & almond upside-down cake . . . 88

mixed berry cobbler 92

sugared berries with crème anglaise 116

thick & chewy brownies 106

thin & crisp chocolate chip cookies . . . 344

chocolate sponge cake 310

fallen chocolate soufflé cake 311

little chocolate turnovers 289

strong coffee granita 148

old-fashioned baked vanilla custard . . . 344

gianduia 203

gianduia & caramel tart 204

little gianduia turnovers 289

ginger spice cake with dried cherries . . . 262

ice creams: cassis, coffee, peppermint
crunch, strawberry 87

puff pastry jam tartlets 290

kabocha squash pie 226

lemon meringue tart 29

pink lemon granita 148

marmalade cake 261

vin santo–roasted pears 203

agee's pecan pies 223

chocolate-covered boozy prunes 290

pumpkin chiffon pie 227

red velvet cupcakes with meringue
frosting 308

roasted rhubarb 52

birthday strawberry pavlova 57

strawberries romanoff 62

strawberry shortcake 62

classic tuiles 116

classic vanilla ice cream 86

poached white peaches in lemon
verbena syrup 118

drinks

amante 52

apricot cooler 91

apricot sparkler 91

bellini 121

limonada 270

lemonade 121

melon water 147

milk punch 252

rummy apricot 91

tisane of fresh or dried lemon verbena . . . 146

winter margarita 270

canal house essentials

anchovy & lemon butter 316

apples cooked with cumin 258

apricot syrup 88

balsamella 240

blue cheese with black pepper 316

browned flour 220

buckwheat crêpes with ham & cheese . . . 314

buttermilk love cakes 272

cheese straws 252

compound butters: fresh herb butter,
   lemon butter, fresh horseradish butter,
   pimentón butter 135

cornbread 201

cranberry-port gelée 221

dill sauce 329

golden bread crumbs with pancetta
   & prunes 213

green sauce with mint & parsley 26

ian's healthy pancakes 273

irish soda bread 339

little yorkshire puddings 256

melba toasts 316

no-knead bread 286

open-faced sandwiches 38

parsley sauce 339

potted crab 316

preserved lemons 294

preserved strawberries & jamón serrano
   on little toasts 60

ragù bolognese 241

red currant jelly 91

rhubarb syrup 52

simple puff pastry 155

simple syrup 147

quick tomato sauce 328

simple tomato sauce 240

strawberry conserves 60

tartar sauce 322

tetrazzini sauce 329

turkey gravy 220

turkey stock 221

celebration menus

Easter Dinner 26–29

Birthday Lunch 56–57

The Garden Giveth 84

Fourth of July 102–106

Thanksgiving 220–228

Christmas 252–262

Hair of the Dog 270–273

Pizza Party 302–305

Valentine Sweets 308–311

March Meatball Madness 328–329

St. Paddy's Day 338–339

FOREWORD

by
Julia Child
as dictated from beyond to
Amanda Hesser

My husband Paul and I once had a home in Provence. We called it *La Pitchoune*, or "The Little Thing." Paul hung a pegboard there for me that held rows of my pots, and there was a block for my many knives. It wasn't a particularly French kitchen but it was *my* kitchen, a little place where I could be the cook that I am. Where I could futz around the small space and whip up *potées* and *gratins* and *daubes*, good rich food for our many friends and visitors. Nothing fussy. After years in Paris, I had come to love the easy-going cooking of the provinces.

Every cook needs to find her kitchen. I was so besotted by my chefs at Le Cordon Bleu, and their sense of order, the cool and stiff French *batterie*. But it must be the American in me that needs a little space and practicality, a *soupçon* of humanity. I liked my pots hanging, with outlines of where each belonged. Simca bought me a cleaver I couldn't live without, and I adored cradling one of those handsome round copper bowls for whipping egg whites. It was like holding a baby.

Whether it was *La Pitchoune* or my more generously sized kitchen in Cambridge, or for that matter the many television-show sets I worked on, my idea of a kitchen traveled with me. I came to realize over the years that this didn't mean just my stuff, but also my style. My kitchen and my cooking were intertwined. My balloon whisk wasn't only constantly being used, it was constantly providing me with comfort when I spied it hanging near the sink.

I've been an enthusiastic admirer of Christopher Hirsheimer and Melissa Hamilton since they were at *Saveur* magazine in the 1990s, two forthright women on a mission to cook. They were part of a dream-team that created a wonderful magazine that felt both worldly, yet unique to them. I loved the realism of their photos. I wanted to lick the pages!

The cooking they celebrated back then was a relaxed, natural cooking from around the globe. They made Vietnamese food as enticing as a French crown roast. And now, at Canal House, it's as if they've found their home, their center, like I did when I went to France in the 1940s.

In Christopher and Melissa's thrice yearly books, they offer you glimpses of their kitchen, a little spare and flooded with light. There are slabs of marble and knife-slashed wood, and two humble-looking stoves. And there are the worn oval platters that seem to come from an old hotel, or maybe a bistro.

And their partnership—women gathering to cook and to share their recipes—reminds me so much of my years with Louisette and Simca. We'd pile into the kitchen at Roo de Loo in Paris, with its coal stove, which I called the "monster," and work fish through the *tamis* for *quenelles* and hand-whisk meringues, taking notes and chatting away. In our case, Paul was our photographer and we were cooking to perfect our understanding of French cuisine.

In Christopher and Melissa's case, Christopher is the photographer and Melissa the illustrator, and there is no particular cuisine they are after. They cook what suits them—ripe tomato sandwiches, pan-fried pork chops to go with bitter greens, ribbons of pasta with fresh peas and scallions, and tart grapefruit marmalade cake. And that is what we should all be doing, and we should all be doing it in a place that feels like our own. For them, Canal House is clearly the spot. I hope you will find yours. *On y va!*

—— JC / AH

— WE COOK EVERY DAY —

Welcome to the Canal House — our studio, workshop, dining room, office, kitchen, lair, lab, and atelier devoted to good ideas and good work relating to the world of food. We write, photograph, design, and paint, but in our hearts we both think of ourselves as cooks first.

How did we get here? Neither of us set out to make careers in the food world. Actually, there wasn't much of a "foodie" world when we both started. But our deep interest in it led us down paths that unfolded before us.

We had worked with each other as food editors in the magazine world. We traveled the globe in search of essential and authentic recipes, sliding into banquettes in famous restaurants, meeting big deal chefs, and even cooking in far-flung home kitchens. It was great and exciting. But our work took us away from our families, our homes, and our gardens, away from what really matters.

We live in little towns across the river from each other, one in New Jersey, the other in Pennsylvania. So we decided to join forces. We share similar backgrounds, having both grown up in big families where food came first. In a time that now seems like eons ago, our aproned grandmothers nurtured us with wholesome, comforting food—buttermilk pancakes drenched in salty butter and maple syrup. Our mothers were glamorous. They loved parties and cocktails and restaurants and brunch with Bloody Marys—food was exciting. Last night's Chinese takeout would show up at breakfast reheated with two poached eggs on top. Both of us have deep food memories and large legacies to uphold.

We found our loft studio in an old redbrick warehouse downriver from where we live. A beautiful, lazy canal runs alongside the building. One hundred years ago mules plodded along the towpath, hauling barges up and down the state. In warm weather, we throw open the studio's French doors and the voices of the people walking or fishing below float up to us. We plant herbs in our window boxes and grow tomatoes in pots on our wrought-iron balcony. In the winter we build fires in the Franklin stove to keep cozy when it's snowy and gray outside.

The Canal House has a simple galley kitchen. Two small apartment-size stoves sit snugly side by side against a white tiled wall. An old wooden carpenter's worktable with a little sink at one end is our long counter and pots hang from a rack suspended above it. We have a dishwasher, but we find ourselves preferring to hand-wash the dishes so we can look out of the tall window next to the sink and see the ducks swimming in the canal or watch the raindrops splashing into the water.

The town around us is a small American river town. A noon whistle still blows and church bells chime—no kidding! There is a drugstore around the corner. Across the street is an old hardware store, and the best bar in the world is right down the alley.

And every day we cook. Starting the morning with coffee or cups of sweet milky tea, we tell each other what we made for dinner the night before. We cook seasonally because that's what makes sense. We want stews and braises and rich thick soups in February when it's snowing and blowing. In midsummer, we buy boxes of tomatoes to dress as minimally as we do in the heat. And at the height of the season, we preserve all that we can, to save a taste of summer.

But this book really started because of lunch. We needed to eat. So we began making lunch for ourselves, simple meals that we could put together quickly, or that were an encore of last night's leftovers that we brought from home. We'd stop work in the middle of the day, set the long wooden table in the center of the studio with paper napkins, and take time to sit and eat together. The whole experience was so pleasing that we wondered why more people didn't do it. Then we got the idea to take a quick picture of what we were eating and we posted it on our website every day with no more than a descriptive caption. We just wanted to encourage people to cook. Those pictures and meals were the beginning of this book.

Canal House Cooks Every Day captures a year of cooking at Canal House. The recipes reflect the seasons and what inspires us to cook for ourselves, our families, and our friends every day. It may be that asparagus just came into season, or a craving we have, or what happens to be languishing in the fridge; and sometimes, like everyone else, we're motivated purely by what we can quickly pull together. Lunch and dinner can be as simple as spreading crackers with preserved lemon butter and adding silky smoked salmon and fresh chives, or floating delicate little meatballs in a rich chicken broth with a big handful of tender spinach leaves. But we also make time to cook seriously delicious food like braised chicken and wild mushrooms with fine egg noodles, or beef brisket smothered in onions for dinner—which we'll serve the next day for lunch, sliced on a soft potato roll. And we always cook for the holidays: Easter lunch, a Fourth of July picnic, Thanksgiving, Christmas, Saint Patrick's Day.

It came naturally to write down what we make. As you cook your way through a few of the recipes in this book, you'll see that who we are comes right through in these pages. It is a collection of our favorite recipes—home cooking by home cooks for home cooks. With a few exceptions, we use ingredients that are readily available and found in most markets in most towns throughout the United States. All the recipes are easy to prepare (some of them a bit more involved), and all are completely doable for the novice and experienced cook alike. We want to share with you, as fellow cooks, our love of food and all its rituals. The everyday practice of simple cooking and the enjoyment of eating are two of the greatest pleasures in life.

Christopher & Melissa

spring

❧ April Recipes ❧

pappardelle with peas & scallions bathed in cream ～ 7

stinging nettle soup ～ 7

roast pork with salmoriglio ～ 9

chorizo & potato frittata ～ 10

risotto cakes with anchovies (or not) ～ 10

fennel & ginger-rubbed chicken with cauliflower ～ 12

ham & cheese omelet ～ 13

asparagus—the majestic stalks of spring ～ 15

roasted asparagus ～ 17

asparagus with lemon-butter sauce ～ 17

asparagus on pasta with a poached egg & lemon butter ～ 18

sole meunière with peas, parsley & chives ～ 20

artichoke, pea & fava bean salad ～ 23

roasted spring onions ～ 23

roast leg of lamb for easter ～ 26

green sauce with mint & parsley ～ 26

sister frances's potatoes ～ 27

pickled beets with horseradish cream ～ 27

lemon meringue tart ～ 29

poached chicken with tarragon & chive mayonnaise ～ 31

buttery lobster capellini ～ 33

shaved asparagus & arugula salad with bruschetta ～ 33

It's early spring here in the Northeast, and it's cold outside. The ground has begun to soften and has some give underfoot, but it's still hard and frozen below the surface, the way a piece of meat feels when it's defrosting but still has a ways to go. The trees are bony underneath the sheerest slips of pale green and dark pink. Clumps of wild garlic are crowning.

We've gathered a group of friends together for a feast in honor of an old friend who's visiting from the West Coast. We'll build the first outdoor fire of the season in the wide open fire pit that sat dormant for months. All winter we picked up limbs that came down, branches that fell, and sticks that littered the yard, and piled them into the pit. We'll tend the fire with our iron rake, transforming the wood into a bed of glowing coals. We're set to spit-roast a whole lamb, a twenty-five pounder, feeding the heat with pruned clippings of fruitwood, mostly apple, and some cherry.

It's just warm enough to be outside again, but the weather is toying with us, first throwing us bone-chilling rain, then furious snow flurries, and it makes the fire smoke. Undaunted, we just stand closer to the fire to keep warm. The more it smokes, the more perfumed the lamb.

Everybody wants to pitch in with preparing the meal, so some of us swab the lamb with branches of rosemary dunked in lemony olive oil or give the beast a quarter-turn every now and then. The dripping fat, hissing as it hits the coals, sets our tempo. Inside, the others have paired up and chat while shelling fava, trimming artichokes, peeling potatoes, roasting beets, boiling eggs, and setting the long table for the feast.

More guests than expected show up and we're worried that the young lamb roasting outside won't be enough. We have a private powwow and before anyone else notices, one of us is off to buy an extra leg from the butcher up the road. We roast it in the house in front of the fireplace, suspended from a string attached to a nail that is driven into the mantel. The roast spins around, winding up and winding down in perpetual motion.

The table is laid. The lamb is plentiful and most delicious. The spit-roasted meat is almost wild-tasting, the way it always is when cooked outside; the leg is meaty and perfectly rosy throughout. We sit, toast, eat, and drink, and everyone is caught up in this magical suspended moment. Like the smoke from the fire, it hangs and swirls and lasts on your skin and in your hair and in your memory, long after the meal is over.

PAPPARDELLE WITH PEAS & SCALLIONS BATHED IN CREAM

Lillie Anderson comes to visit Canal House from time to time. She is only twelve years old, but she's caught the cooking bug! Pasta is her specialty. Last year she made rigatoni with ham and peas, but now a year older and wiser, she has a greater appreciation for subtlety. So it's a swirl of pappardelle bathed in cream, with lots of peas, some scallions, and a generous grating of parmigiano-reggiano. Lillie suggests you serve it with plenty of cracked black pepper.

Cook 1 pound pappardelle or fettuccine in a large pot of salted boiling water over high heat until just cooked through, about 8 minutes. When the pasta is nearly finished, add 1 pound frozen peas and 1 bunch chopped scallions and cook for 1 minute. Set aside about ½ cup of the pasta cooking water, then drain the pasta in a colander. Return the empty pot to the stove. Add 2 tablespoons butter (preferably salted) and 1 cup heavy cream to the pot and warm over medium-low heat. Add the drained pasta, peas, and scallions, 1–1½ cups grated parmigiano-reggiano, and lots of cracked black pepper. Stir everything together, adding a bit of the cooking water to thin and loosen the sauce. Season with salt, if you like, and adjust the seasonings. — *serves 4–6*

April 1st, 33°
light snow falling

STINGING NETTLE SOUP

It must be an odd sight, the pair of us walking along the lush green banks of the canal wearing our elbow-high, pink rubber dishwashing gloves. But it means only one thing: It's stinging nettle season. And wear the gloves we must or suffer the weed's sting as we collect and prepare the sawtooth leaves for our soup. Miraculously, nettles lose their sting once they are cooked and their deep herbaceous flavor is uniquely delicious. If you're not the foraging type, look for stinging nettles at farmers' markets during the spring.

Bring 6 cups chicken stock, 1 large diced, peeled russet potato, and 1 small chopped onion to a boil in a large pot over high heat. Reduce the heat to medium and simmer until the potatoes are very tender, about 15 minutes. Increase the heat to medium-high. Wearing rubber gloves to avoid getting stung, chop 1½ pounds stinging nettle leaves. Add the leaves to the pot by the handful, stirring them in. Simmer until the nettles are completely wilted, about 2 minutes. Purée the soup in a blender or food processor until smooth. Strain it for extra-smooth consistency. Season with salt and pepper. Serve the soup in warm soup bowls, garnishing each serving with a pat of butter and a generous sprinkling of chopped fresh chives and their blossoms. — *serves 4–6*

April 5th, 40°
clear as a bell

VARIATION: Substitute 1½ pounds spinach for the nettles.

ROAST PORK WITH SALMORIGLIO
serves 6–8

When we have the time, we like to "dry brine" pork roasts, including crowns, loins, and bellies. It makes the meat more flavorful and juicy. Wet brines that soak the meat in a bath of salted water (and sometimes additionally seasoned with sugar and spices) do the same thing, of course, but we find them cumbersome—it's always a dilemma finding a large enough pot and then room in the fridge.

FOR THE ROAST PORK
1 boneless pork shoulder or butt,
   3–4 pounds
½ cup salt
½ cup sugar
Small handful fresh oregano leaves
Small handful fresh thyme leaves
6 anchovy filets
Pepper
2 tablespoons olive oil

FOR THE SALMORIGLIO
1–2 cloves garlic, minced
Small handful fresh oregano leaves, finely
   chopped
Small handful fresh parsley leaves, finely
   chopped
Juice of 2 lemons
1 cup extra-virgin olive oil
Salt and pepper

For the roast pork, place the meat in a wide dish and coat it with the salt and sugar. Cover it with plastic wrap and refrigerate for at least 1 hour or as long as overnight.

April 7th, 49°
overcast

Preheat the oven to 300°. Uncover the pork and brush off any residual salt and sugar. Put the oregano, thyme, anchovies, and a pinch of salt and pepper in a pile on a cutting board and finely chop everything into a paste. Rub the paste all over the meat.

Heat the oil in an enameled cast-iron or heavy wide pot with a lid over medium heat. Add the seasoned pork and brown it all over, about 10 minutes. Add ¼ cup water to the pot. Cover the pot and transfer it to the oven. Roast the pork until it is fork-tender, about 3 hours.

For the salmoriglio, put the garlic, oregano, parsley, and lemon juice into a medium bowl and stir in the olive oil. Season to taste with salt and pepper.

To serve, slice the meat and arrange it on a warm serving platter with some of the juices from the pot. Pass the bowl of salmoriglio at the table, for spooning some of it over each serving.

CHORIZO & POTATO FRITTATA
serves 4

We usually have a package of Spanish chorizo in the fridge. Because it keeps well, it's easy to pull something together to eat, like this layered potato-egg dish, one of our favorite standbys. The chorizo releases its reddish, spicy pimentón-flavored oil, giving the frittata a smoky richness we find irresistible.

4 tablespoons extra-virgin olive oil
1–2 cloves garlic, sliced
4 medium russet potatoes,
   peeled and sliced

7–8 ounces Spanish chorizo, sliced
Salt and pepper
2 eggs
1 cup half-and-half

April 8th, 47°
pouring rain

Preheat the oven to 500°. Heat 2 tablespoons of the oil in a large nonstick, ovenproof skillet over medium heat. Add the garlic and cook until fragrant, about 1 minute. Arrange some of the potato slices in the bottom of the skillet in a single layer, then scatter some of the chorizo on top. Season with salt and pepper. Continue layering with the remaining potatoes and chorizo, seasoning as you go. Drizzle the remaining 2 tablespoons of oil on top. Cover the skillet, reduce the heat to low, and cook until the potatoes are tender, 20–30 minutes. Tip the skillet occasionally, spooning some of the oil over the potatoes as they cook.

Whisk together the eggs and half-and-half, and pour over the potatoes and chorizo. Gently shake the skillet so the eggs will run between the layers to the bottom. Increase the heat to medium and cook until the eggs are beginning to set, about 5 minutes. Put the skillet in the oven and cook until the frittata is set, 5–10 minutes. Carefully invert the frittata onto a cutting board, cut into wedges, and serve warm or at room temperature.

RISOTTO CAKES WITH ANCHOVIES (OR NOT)

When you have leftover risotto, make these little cakes and lay an anchovy on top. We're fond of their salty flavor. If you prefer, sprinkle the cakes with coarse sea salt instead.

April 11th, 66°
scattered clouds

Mix together 3 cups cold risotto and ½ cup grated parmigiano-reggiano. Moisten your hands with water, then form 8 cakes, about 1 inch thick. Put ½ cup flour, 2 beaten eggs, and 1 cup panko in three separate wide bowls. Dredge one cake at a time, first in the flour, then dip in the eggs, then dredge in the panko. Set aside. Pour enough olive oil into a heavy large skillet to reach a depth of ½ inch and heat over medium heat until hot. Fry the cakes until golden brown and crisp, 2–3 minutes per side. Drain on paper towels. Serve each risotto cake garnished with an anchovy filet. — *makes 8*

FENNEL & GINGER–RUBBED CHICKEN WITH CAULIFLOWER
serves 4

We restock our pantry a couple times a year through mail order so we always have specialty spices on hand for dishes like this. Garam masala, or "hot spices", is always on the list. The mixture that makes up this Indian seasoning varies from region to region, but always includes ones thought to warm up the body—cloves, cinnamon, nutmeg, mace, and black pepper.

1 whole chicken

2 teaspoons garam masala

Salt and pepper

2 tablespoons olive or vegetable oil

½ teaspoon fennel seeds

1 small onion, minced

1 tablespoon grated, peeled fresh ginger

2–3 cloves garlic, grated

1 head cauliflower, cut into tiny florets

¼ teaspoon cayenne, or to taste

1 lemon, halved

1 bunch scallions, chopped

April 12th, 51°
heavy rain & wind

Cut the chicken, separating the thighs, drumsticks, and wings. Cut each breast in half. There will be 10 pieces. Season them all over with garam masala and salt and pepper.

continued

Heat the oil in a heavy large skillet over medium-high heat. Working in batches, brown the chicken all over, about 15 minutes. Transfer the chicken to a large plate.

Reduce the heat to medium and pour off any excess fat from the skillet. Add the fennel seeds to the skillet and toast for about 1 minute. Add the onions, ginger, and garlic and cook, stirring and scraping the bottom of the skillet with a wooden spoon to keep it from sticking, for about 5 minutes.

Add the cauliflower, cayenne, and a big pinch of salt to the skillet and stir. Arrange the chicken over the cauliflower and pour any juices collected on the plate into the skillet. Drizzle ½ cup water into the skillet, then cover and cook until the chicken is cooked through and the cauliflower is tender, about 15 minutes (remove breast pieces early if they cook faster). Add the juice of the lemon and the chopped scallions. Serve with yogurt or rice and/or big floppy flatbread like chapatis, if you like.

HAM & CHEESE OMELET

April 13th, 50°
dreary overcast

Lightly beat 3–4 eggs and a splash of milk together in a small bowl. Melt 2 tablespoons butter in a nonstick medium skillet over medium heat. Pour in the eggs and let them set slightly. Then, tilting the skillet, use a spatula to lift the edge of the omelet, allowing the uncooked eggs to run underneath. Repeat on the opposite side. Once the eggs have set on the bottom, yet are still loose on top, sprinkle a small handful of grated cheese (Gruyère, a good Cheddar, or your favorite) and a small handful of chopped ham down the center. Let the omelet cook a bit longer, until the bottom is pale golden brown. Using the spatula, fold the omelet into thirds toward the center (as you would a business letter). Tip the omelet out of the skillet onto a warm serving plate with the seam side down. Rub a little softened butter over the omelet and scatter a handful of chopped fresh chives or scallions on top. Season with salt and pepper. — *serves 2*

✒ ASPARAGUS — THE MAJESTIC STALKS OF SPRING ✒

Every year it seems to happen the same way. We wait and anticipate the arrival of spring, but she can be slow and fickle—it's warm one day, then cold and showery the next. She just doesn't want to commit. At our favorite farmers' market the pickings are still pretty slim in April. Nothing is growing yet and we wonder if anything ever will. Then one day the town buzz is: Asparagus are up! We drop everything and head for the market. If it's true, we'll be eating asparagus nonstop for the next few weeks.

∼ On the way, a fresh green smell wafts through the open car window, and we notice that the trees are finally wearing the sheerest slips of green. In the store we spot a big basket of red rhubarb, and as we turn the corner around the potato bin, we see four large pails filled with tall curving green spears with tight purple tips—the first asparagus of the season. We choose the straightest and fattest, matching the lengths. We buy too many, of course; we just can't help ourselves. This is an ancient rite of the vernal equinox—eating a spring tonic.

∼ Asparagus from commercial producers are prewashed, but these handsome devils (1) grown on a small farm, and the ones we harvest from a friend's garden nearby, need extra care to rid them of their grit. We plunge the *zaftig* beauties into a sinkful of cold clear water and give them a gentle swish to loosen any silty sand trapped in the tight, finlike leaves that line the length of each spear. We let them soak for a short while, swish them some more, then lift them from the water, leaving any sand to settle at the bottom of the sink. Some stalks get stored in the fridge in an open plastic bag until our next meal, their bottoms wrapped in wet paper towels. The rest we'll have for lunch.

∼ We always peel and trim fat asparagus (2). Peeling off the tough skin allows the spears to cook evenly from the delicate tip through the sturdy stalk. We lay the asparagus spears flat on a cutting board to keep them from snapping. Then we begin, starting just below the tip, one spear at a time, and shave off the green skin in long thin curls with our little rattly swivel-blade vegetable peelers. Fat asparagus don't snap at their most tender spot like skinny ones do, so we eyeball the spear and trim off the tough woody bottom with a sharp knife. We throw the trimmings onto the compost pile or feed them to the chickens running around next door.

∼ Then we discuss the merits of steaming (4) versus boiling (5). Someone once gave us a poncy asparagus steamer fitted with a tall wire basket, and we decide to give it a go. We line up a dozen spears, rummage through the drawers for kitchen string, and tie a bundle together. We cook them both ways to compare the taste. The steamed are delicate with lots of green grassy flavor, but so are the boiled. We're not gadget hounds so we decide to stick with the simplicity of boiling. We whisk up a sauce of luscious lemon butter, then stand at the kitchen counter and eat them with our fingers, dipping the juicy, meaty spears into the sauce one by one—chain eating. Later in the season we'll toss shaved asparagus (3) in a vinaigrette with pecorino, roast whole spears (6), fold chopped spears into tender risottos, and fry up lacy fritto misto, but right now this is the true taste of spring.

ROASTED ASPARAGUS

A good, aged balsamic vinegar—one that is composed of wine vinegar and reduced *must* and contains no artificial colorings or additives—makes these asparagus sing.

April 15th, 34°
clear & blustery

Preheat the oven to 400°. Put 16–25 peeled, trimmed fat asparagus all pointing in the same direction into a baking dish in a single layer. Rub them all over with 2 tablespoons extra-virgin olive oil. Season with salt and pepper. Roast the asparagus until tender, 20–25 minutes. Remove the dish from the oven. Use a vegetable peeler to shave thin shards of parmigiano-reggiano over the hot asparagus. Drizzle with 1 tablespoon aged balsamic vinegar. —— *serves 4*

ASPARAGUS WITH LEMON-BUTTER SAUCE
serves 2–4

We first tasted a version of this very light hollandaise sauce at Ballymaloe Cookery School, in Ireland. The real trick is to use good salted Irish butter, now readily available at many local supermarkets. We find that this sauce isn't as finicky as most delicate butter sauces.

FOR THE LEMON-BUTTER SAUCE
2 large egg yolks
8 tablespoons (1 stick) cold butter, cut
   into 8 pieces
Juice of ½ lemon
Pinch of cayenne or to taste
Salt

FOR THE ASPARAGUS
1 pound (about 12 spears) fat asparagus,
   peeled and trimmed
Salt
2 lemon wedges

April 16th, 48°
light rain

For the lemon-butter sauce, whisk together the egg yolks and 1 tablespoon water in a heavy medium saucepan. Heat over low heat, whisking constantly to prevent the yolks from "scrambling". Add the butter one piece at a time, whisking until it has melted into the sauce before adding the next. (If the sauce begins to separate, remove the pan from the heat and whisk in another piece of cold butter to cool the sauce down. It should come back together.) Continue whisking in the butter this way until it has all been incorporated into the sauce.

Remove the pan from the heat and whisk in enough lemon juice to suit your taste. Season with cayenne and salt. Keep the sauce warm by setting the pan in a larger pan of hot water over low heat. To prevent a skin from forming, whisk the sauce frequently or cover it with a sheet of plastic wrap laid directly on the surface.

For the asparagus, steam or boil it in a wide pot of salted water until tender, 4–5 minutes. Drain.

Put a big spoonful of the lemon-butter sauce onto each plate. Lay the asparagus on top of the pool of sauce and season with a little salt and a squeeze of lemon juice.

ASPARAGUS ON PASTA WITH A POACHED EGG & LEMON BUTTER
serves 2

Although this dish looks elegant, there's really nothing fancy about it. In fact, it came to-gether quickly one day for lunch. We were rummaging around in the refrigerator trying to figure out what to make. Buried in the back behind God knows what was a package of fresh pasta sheets. And with asparagus season going full tilt, we had a bunch of it in the vegetable drawer. The rest of the ingredients we always have on hand. How gratifying it is to turn simple ingredients into something so satisfying.

4–6 tablespoons butter
Juice of ½ lemon
1 pound (about 12 spears) fat asparagus, peeled and trimmed
2 eggs
Splash of vinegar

4 sheets fresh pasta, each about 4 inches long
1 small hunk parmigiano-reggiano
Maldon sea salt or fleur de sel, optional
Salt and pepper

April 18th, 61° scattered clouds

Bring a large pot of salted water to a boil over medium-high heat to cook the asparagus and pasta. Also, bring a medium saucepan of salted water to a simmer to poach the eggs. Melt the butter in a medium skillet over medium-low heat and swirl in enough of the lemon juice to suit your taste. Keep warm over low heat.

Cook the asparagus in the pot of boiling water until tender, 4–5 minutes. Lift the asparagus out of the water with a slotted spatula and drain on a clean dishcloth.

Crack the eggs into 2 small cups. Add the vinegar to the saucepan of simmering water. Give the water a good circular stir, then tip 1 egg at a time into the center of the swirling water. Simmer the eggs over medium-low heat until the whites are white and the yolks remain soft, about 3 minutes. Transfer the eggs to the dishcloth to drain.

Cook the sheets of pasta in the pot of boiling water until tender, 2–3 minutes. Using a slot-ted spatula or a long-handled strainer, divide the pasta between 2 warm plates, letting most of the water drip off before putting it on the plate.

Warm the asparagus in the lemon butter, then divide the spears between the plates. Put a poached egg on each plate. Spoon the lemon butter over the asparagus and pasta. Using a vegetable peeler, shave some parmigiano over each plate. Season with sea salt, if using (it adds a particularly nice crunch), or with the salt you've got on hand, and with pepper.

SOLE MEUNIÈRE WITH PEAS, PARSLEY & CHIVES
serves 2

It was a miserable day. A cold rainy spring day. A Sunday. We were working on a project that had to be completed by Monday. Before meeting at the studio, we decided to stop at the indoor farmers' market to pick up something to cook for lunch. The fishmonger happened to have the most beautiful, pristine filets of gray sole. We shelled out the big bucks and bought two. English peas had just come into season, so we bought a bagful from the produce lady. We lit a fire in the wood-burning stove when we got to the studio to take the chilly dampness out of the air. And for lunch we prepared the sole simply, done meunière style, served with a pile of buttery parsleyed peas. It's funny, but whenever we serve this dish, we think of the lunch we made that wet day and how those simple flavors buoyed us.

1 cup shelled fresh or frozen peas
2 filets of sole, about 6 ounces each
Salt and pepper
½ cup flour
8 tablespoons salted butter, preferably Irish

1 lemon, halved
Large handful of fresh parsley leaves, finely chopped
6–8 fresh chives, chopped

April 19th, 46°
a foul cold rain

Bring a small saucepan of salted water to a boil. Blanch fresh peas for 1–2 minutes or frozen peas for a few seconds or just long enough to take the chill off. Cool the peas in a bowl of ice water. Drain well, and set aside.

Season the filets with salt and pepper. Carefully dredge them in flour. Melt 2 tablespoons of the butter in a large nonstick skillet over medium-high heat until foaming. Cook the filets on the rounded side down first until pale golden brown, about 2 minutes. Using a fish spatula, carefully turn the fish over and cook the other side for 1–2 minutes. Transfer each filet to a warm plate.

Meanwhile, melt the remaining 6 tablespoons of butter in a medium saucepan over medium heat. Squeeze in some juice from half of the lemon while swirling the saucepan. Add more juice, if you like. Remove the saucepan from the heat. Stir in the peas and parsley, and season with salt and pepper. Spoon some of the peas and butter over each filet and scatter some chives on top. Garnish the plates with a wedge of lemon.

ARTICHOKE, PEA & FAVA BEAN SALAD
serves 6

We usher in springtime with this bright green salad of tender young things, often serving it alongside fat spears of chilled poached asparagus bathed in good olive oil.

12 baby artichokes	½ cup finely diced ham or prosciutto
2 lemons, halved	⅓ cup really good extra-virgin olive oil
Salt	½ cup grated parmigiano-reggiano
2 cups shelled fresh or frozen peas	1 bunch fresh chives, chopped
3 cups shelled fresh or frozen fava beans	Pepper

Pull off and discard the outer leaves of the artichokes until you get to the pale yellow-green inner leaves. Peel the stems. Trim off and discard the top half, then halve or quarter the artichokes lengthwise. Rub the artichokes with lemon juice as you work to keep them from discoloring. Put the artichokes in a medium pot, cover with cold water, add a generous pinch of salt, and boil them until tender, 5–10 minutes. Drain well. Put the artichokes in a large bowl and set aside.

April 20th, 50° calm & cloudy

Meanwhile, bring another medium pot of salted water to a boil. Put the peas (either fresh or frozen) in a sieve and lower it into the boiling water. Blanch fresh peas for 1–2 minutes or frozen peas for a few seconds. Cool the peas in a bowl of ice water. Drain well and add them to the artichokes. Blanch the fava beans in the pot of boiling water for 1–2 minutes. Drain, cool in the bowl of ice water, and drain again. Peel off and discard the tough outer skins and add the bright green fava beans to the bowl of artichokes.

Add the ham, olive oil, juice of ½ lemon, parmigiano, and chives to the bowl. Season with salt and pepper. Toss well. Adjust seasonings. Drizzle with more olive oil, if you like.

ROASTED SPRING ONIONS

These young onions make a good sidekick for roast chicken, fish, beef, or lamb, but they're meaty enough to be the hero accompanied simply by soft buttery polenta.

Preheat the oven to 500°. Arrange 6–8 whole spring onions with their stems attached in a single layer in a heavy roasting pan. Douse them with some extra-virgin olive oil and generously season with salt and pepper. Roast the onions until browned all over, 15–20 minutes. Reduce the oven temperature to 250° and continue roasting them until tender, 10–15 minutes. Remove the onions from the oven and drizzle with 2–3 small spoonfuls balsamic vinegar, turning them to coat. Season with a little more salt. — *serves 4–6*

April 22th, 51° mild

ROAST LEG OF LAMB FOR EASTER
serves 8

The rosy pan juices from this roast leg of lamb are perfectly flavorful *au naturel*, but for a rich brown gravy we add black coffee to the roasting pan to flavor the pan juices.

1 leg of lamb, 4–5 pounds, tail, pelvic, and
   thigh bones removed, shank bone and
   heel left attached, at room temperature
Salt and pepper
3 cloves garlic, chopped

3 anchovy filets
Large handful of fresh parsley leaves
2 cups black coffee
2 tablespoons flour
2 cups chicken stock, or more

Easter Sunday
April 24th, 82°
unseasonably warm

Preheat the oven to 350°. Season the lamb with salt and pepper. Make a pile with the garlic, anchovies, parsley, and a pinch of salt and pepper on a cutting board and chop it together to make a fine paste. Using the tip of a paring knife, make several 1-inch-deep slits all over the meaty parts of the lamb. Push the paste into the slits with your finger. Some of the paste will smear on the surface of the lamb, but that's fine.

Put the lamb on a roasting rack in a roasting pan. Pour the coffee into the pan. Roast the lamb until it is nicely browned on the outside, rosy pink on the inside, and the internal temperature reaches 130° for medium-rare, about 1½ hours. Add a splash of water to the pan as the lamb roasts if the pan juices begin to dry out. Transfer the lamb to a warm serving platter or cutting board, loosely tent it with foil, and let the roast rest for 15–20 minutes before carving.

To make the pan gravy, put the roasting pan with the drippings on top of the stove and heat over medium heat. Add the flour and cook, whisking constantly to prevent it from getting lumpy, until the flavor is toasty rather than raw, 3–4 minutes. Whisk in the stock and cook, whisking constantly, until the gravy is smooth and thickened, about 5 minutes. Season with salt and pepper. Thin the gravy with a little more stock if it's too thick. Strain the gravy through a sieve into a gravy boat and serve with the carved roast.

GREEN SAUCE WITH MINT & PARSLEY

Americans love to eat lamb with sweet mint jelly, while the Brits prefer a vinegar mint sauce—this sauce lies somewhere in between. Put 1 cup tightly packed fresh mint leaves and ¼ cup tightly packed parsley leaves in a blender or food processor. Add the zest of 1 lemon, 2 tablespoons fresh lemon juice, 1 garlic clove, and 2 teaspoons superfine sugar, and purée until smooth, about 2 minutes. Transfer to a small bowl and whisk in about ¼ cup really good extra-virgin olive oil. Season with a little salt and pepper, and add more lemon juice, if you like. —— *makes 1 cup*

SISTER FRANCES'S POTATOES

Sister Frances, one of the last Shakers, made these creamy potatoes for us when we visited her community in Sabbathday Lake, Maine, more than a decade ago. They've become a favorite of ours to serve with roasts of all kinds, any time of the year.

Put 8 peeled russet potatoes cut into 1-inch cubes into a heavy deep medium pot. Add 8 tablespoons (1 stick) butter and about 4 cups half-and-half, or enough just to cover the potatoes. Season with salt and pepper. Bring to a gentle simmer over medium heat. Reduce the heat to low and cook until the potatoes are tender and have absorbed most of the half-and-half, about 1 hour. Keep the potatoes submerged as they cook so they don't turn dark. Stir them occasionally with a rubber spatula, being careful to keep the potatoes intact. Season with salt and pepper and garnish with chopped fresh chives. — *serves 8*

PICKLED BEETS WITH HORSERADISH CREAM
serves 8

Beets and eggs are old friends, often pickled together in a jar full of brine. As pretty as those pink-stained eggs are, we prefer to keep the egg flavor unpickled for this salad.

FOR THE BEETS
16 small beets (2–3 pounds), trimmed
3 tablespoons sugar
3 tablespoons cider vinegar
Pepper

FOR THE HORSERADISH CREAM
Large pinch of sugar
2 tablespoons cider vinegar

2 tablespoons Dijon mustard
⅔ cup heavy cream
2–3 tablespoons finely grated
  fresh horseradish
Salt

4 cups watercress or baby arugula
6 hard-boiled eggs, halved
Small handful chopped fresh chives

For the beets, preheat the oven to 400°. Wrap each beet in foil, place on a baking sheet, and roast until tender when pierced with a knife, about 1 hour. Meanwhile, whisk the sugar and vinegar together in a large bowl until the sugar dissolves. Season with a pinch of pepper. When the beets are done, unwrap them to cool. Peel them (the skins will slip right off), cut in half lengthwise, and add to the bowl. Toss the beets and set aside.

For the horseradish cream, dissolve the sugar in the vinegar in a small bowl. Stir in the mustard, then add the cream and horseradish. Season with salt and adjust the seasonings.

Make a pretty bed of watercress on a large platter. Pile the beets in the center. "Butter" the eggs with some of the horseradish cream and arrange the eggs around the beets. Garnish with the chives. Serve the remaining horseradish cream in a bowl.

Overleaf: clockwise from top center, Sister Frances's Potatoes, Pickled Beets with Horseradish Cream, Horseradish Cream, Green Sauce with Mint & Parsley, Roast Leg of Lamb for Easter

LEMON MERINGUE TART
makes one 9-inch tart

Odd as it may seem, we scatter a little minced preserved lemon rind between the sweet-tart lemon curd filling and the sweet-sweet meringue topping to cut through all that delicious sweetness. This tart should be eaten the day it's made.

FOR THE CRUST
1 cup all-purpose flour
Pinch of salt
7 tablespoons cold unsalted butter, cut into small pieces

FOR THE FILLING AND MERINGUE
2 large eggs

4 large eggs, separated
4–6 lemons
2 cups sugar
6 tablespoons unsalted butter, cut into small pieces
1 tablespoon minced preserved lemon rind (page 294), optional
Pinch of cream of tartar

April 24th, 64°
Easter Sunday evening
calm & foggy

For the crust, whisk the flour and salt together in a medium mixing bowl. Work the butter into the flour using a pastry blender, 2 butter knives, or your fingertips until it resembles coarse cornmeal. Gradually sprinkle in 3 tablespoons ice water while stirring with a fork. Press the dough together until it forms a rough ball. Try not to overhandle it; there should be streaks of butter visible throughout. Shape it into a flat disk, wrap in plastic wrap, and refrigerate for at least 1 hour.

Roll out the dough on a lightly floured surface into a 12-inch square or round (to fit your tart pan). Roll the dough around the rolling pin, then unfurl it into a 9-inch fluted tart pan with a removable bottom. Trim off any excess dough. Prick the crust all over with a fork. Cover with plastic wrap and refrigerate for at least 1 hour or overnight.

Preheat the oven to 350°. Line the crust with a sheet of foil that hangs over the edges by at least 2 inches, then fill with pie weights or dried beans. Bake the crust until the edges are pale golden, about 20 minutes. Lift the foil with the weights off the crust and continue baking the crust until it is golden, 5–10 minutes. Make the filling while the crust cools.

For the filling, gently whisk together the 2 whole eggs and 4 yolks in a medium bowl and set aside. Wash the lemons in warm water and pat dry. Finely grate the zest of 4 of the lemons into a medium nonreactive saucepan. Juice enough lemons to make about 1 cup juice. Add the juice to the saucepan and whisk in 1½ cups of the sugar. Set the saucepan over medium-low heat and whisk in the beaten eggs. Cook the mixture, whisking constantly to prevent it from boiling, until it has thickened, 5–8 minutes. Remove the saucepan from the heat and add the butter, a few knobs at a time, whisking until the butter has melted. Strain the lemon curd through a sieve into a medium bowl. Pour the hot curd into the prepared crust and smooth the top with a rubber spatula. Scatter the preserved lemon evenly over the curd, if using. Set the filled crust aside.

continued on page 31

For the meringue, put the 4 egg whites and the cream of tartar in a large mixing bowl and beat with a mixer on medium speed until frothy. Increase the speed to medium-high. Continue beating, gradually adding the remaining ½ cup sugar, 1–2 tablespoons at a time. Increase the speed to high and beat until the whites are glossy and stiff and the sugar is completely dissolved, 5–10 minutes. Cover the lemon curd filling with big spoonfuls of meringue, beginning at the edges and working toward the center. Make sure the meringue covers and attaches itself to the edges of the crust or it will shrink inward as the tart bakes. Bake until the meringue peaks are golden brown, about 15 minutes. Let the tart cool completely on a wire rack before serving.

POACHED CHICKEN WITH TARRAGON & CHIVE MAYONNAISE
serves 4–6

When we are in a hurry, we just doctor up good old Hellmann's or Best Foods mayonnaise.

FOR THE MAYONNAISE
1 large egg yolk
¼ garlic clove, minced
Salt
Juice of 1 lemon
½ cup canola oil
½ cup good, smooth, "buttery" olive oil
½ cup fresh tarragon leaves, chopped

½ cup chopped chives, plus more for garnishing

FOR THE CHICKEN
4 bone-in chicken breast halves
1 onion, peeled and quartered
1 rib celery, halved
1 bay leaf
Salt

For the mayonnaise, whisk together the egg yolk, garlic, a pinch of salt, and about 2 tablespoons of the lemon juice in a medium bowl. Combine the oils in a measuring cup with a spout. Whisking constantly, add the oil to the yolks about 1 teaspoon at a time. The sauce will thicken and emulsify. After you have added about ¼ cup of the oil, continue to whisk and slowly drizzle in the remaining oil. Season with salt and thin with as much of the remaining lemon juice as suits your taste. Stir in the chopped tarragon and chives. Refrigerate until ready to use.

April 25th, 68° still with haze

For the chicken, put the chicken, onions, celery, bay leaf, and a big pinch of salt in a large pot with a lid and cover with water by 1 inch. Bring to a simmer over medium-high heat. Reduce the heat to low. Cover and poach for 15–20 minutes. Remove the chicken from the pot and put on a plate to cool. When the chicken has cooled, remove the skin and bones. (Return the skin and bones to the pot and continue to simmer the stock until it is rich and flavorful; strain the stock and save for another use.)

To serve, cut the chicken into generous-size pieces and arrange on a serving platter. Spoon the mayonnaise on the chicken. Garnish with the chopped chives (and baby arugula, if you like.)

BUTTERY LOBSTER CAPELLINI

For the sake of convenience, your fishmonger can steam the lobsters for you. Specify that you want them undercooked so the meat won't be tough when you make this dish. Save yourself the time and hassle of prying out the meat by using kitchen shears to cut it out of the shells.

Working over a bowl to catch the juices, crack the shells of 2 parboiled 1½-pound lobsters, cut them open with scissors, and remove the meat. Use a sharp knife to cut the meat into small pieces. Melt 6 tablespoons salted butter in a large skillet over medium-low heat. Add 1–2 pinches crushed red pepper flakes, juice of 1–2 lemons, the lobster meat, and reserved juices, and bring to a simmer. Meanwhile cook ¼ pound capellini in a pot of boiling salted water for 1 minute. Drain, reserving ½ cup of the cooking water. Stir the pasta into the skillet with the lobster and cook until just tender, 1–2 minutes. Stir in 4 tablespoons salted butter and lots of chopped fresh chives. Season with salt and pepper. Loosen the pasta with some of the cooking water, if you like. — *serves 4*

April 26th, 75°
clear & breezy

SHAVED ASPARAGUS & ARUGULA SALAD WITH BRUSCHETTA
serves 4–6

This Italian vinaigrette, traditionally tossed with shaved raw vegetables, gets its acidity from the sharp pecorino and its smoothness from good extra-virgin olive oil.

FOR THE VINAIGRETTE
1½ cups finely grated pecorino (about 2 ounces)
½ cup really good extra-virgin olive oil
Salt and pepper

FOR THE SALAD
1 pound (about 12 spears) fat asparagus

8 cups baby arugula, about 4 ounces
4–6 thick slices rustic country bread
1 large clove garlic
Really good extra-virgin olive oil
Salt, preferably fleur de sel

For the vinaigrette, put the cheese into a large bowl. Gradually add ½ cup boiling water, whisking constantly. Drizzle in the olive oil, whisking constantly. Season with salt and pepper.

April 29th, 66°
showery

For the salad, lay the asparagus spears flat on a cutting board to keep them from snapping, and using a vegetable peeler, peel off and discard their skins up to the tips. Trim off the woody ends with a sharp knife. Using the peeler, shave the spears into long thin ribbons and toss them (and any tips that break off) in the vinaigrette. Add the arugula and toss well. Adjust the seasonings.

Toast the slices of bread. While they're still warm, rub one side of each slice with the garlic. Drizzle with some olive oil and sprinkle with salt. Serve the salad with the toasts.

❧ May Recipes ❧

open-faced sandwiches ～ 38

pan-fried chicken thighs with little zucchini ～ 38

galantine of turkey & pork with peas ～ 40

a little bit of meat adds a whole lot of flavor ～ 43

cannellini with smoked ham & rosemary ～ 43

spaghetti with tomato sauce & ricotta ～ 44

spaghetti alla carbonara ～ 45

shrimp risotto ～ 46

spinach tagliatelle & peas in golden chicken broth ～ 46

breast of veal braised with green olives & tomatoes ～ 50

pile it on ～ 51

roasted rhubarb ～ 52

rhubarb syrup ～ 52

amante ～ 52

birthday halibut with beets & asparagus vinaigrette ～ 56

birthday strawberry pavlova ～ 57

silly for strawberries ～ 58

strawberry conserves ～ 60

preserved strawberries & jamón serrano on little toasts ～ 60

strawberry shortcake ～ 62

strawberries romanoff ～ 62

Neither of us attaches much weight to celebrating our birthdays. But ever since we started our studio at Canal House, we've fallen into an unspoken ritual—one we now look forward to each year—and do something special for each other on that day. It always includes a meal, and the plan is never revealed beforehand.

The first birthday comes in May. By then there's a sense of nature's renewal in the air—the weather is warm and everything is in bloom, on its way to green fullness.

One year the treat was dinner in New York City at a favorite restaurant, followed by *The Year of Magical Thinking*, starring Vanessa Redgrave, a Broadway adaptation of the book by Joan Didion. (We had both read the book.) Other years, we've gone on spiritual retreats; walked the sculpture park at Storm King Arts Center in Mountainville, New York; toured the Impressionist collection at the Barnes Foundation in its original home in Merion, Pennsylvania; and had a surprise birthday lunch attended by a wonderful collection of unexpected guests. Another birthday lunch included a visiting sales rep and carried on for four hours, beginning and ending with tall glasses of growers' Champagne. (He later wrote to say it was the most memorable sales call he'd ever made.)

But the birthday celebration that stands out most was the quietest one of them all. It happened on a beautiful day in May, a day with the kind of sunny brightness that makes you glad to be alive. The French doors to the studio were wide open, letting light and warmth flood in. We were feeling the economic pinch and living closer to the bone. Nonetheless, there were some choice things in the refrigerator—slices of Serrano ham, a fat halibut filet, a handful of local asparagus, a pound of salted Irish butter, some eggs from the chickens next door, and a quart of ripe strawberries. A gift had been ordered at the last minute, a book of exquisite photographs of Irish nuns and clergy, the companion book to a gallery show we'd seen the previous fall. We decided to make a simple lunch.

And so we did. We poached the fish, boiled the asparagus, chilled a bottle of Champagne, tossed the strawberries with sugar and a splash of red wine, and sliced open ripe avocados and draped them with the ham. We rolled the orange metal table by the open doors. Early-blooming nasturtiums and unruly fresh thyme, cut from the window boxes on our balcony, were the centerpiece. Still no book, though. We sat down to lunch and sipped the Champagne, clinking to health and many more years to come. Just as we tucked into dessert, the book arrived by special delivery. It was a token of the richness a friendship can bring—but sharing the meal was the real gift.

OPEN-FACED SANDWICHES

Don't let the delicate appearance of these little tea sandwiches fool you. We spread very thin slices of bread with good, flavorful salted butter (preferably Kerrygold Irish butter), then add a layer of whatever strikes our fancy: Major Grey's chutney, or a couple of tinned sardines, or peppery spring radishes. We've even spread cold risotto on the bread—now that ain't half bad! We have them with a cup of tea in the afternoon or with a flute of bubbles at cocktail time.

May 2nd, 71°
clear

Butter 8 slices of thin-sliced white sandwich bread with 4 tablespoons softened salted butter. Lay 2 thin slices of prosciutto over the first two slices of bread. Arrange 2–4 thinly sliced radishes over the next slices, and top the next two with 2 sliced hard-boiled eggs; sprinkle with salt and pepper. Toss 2 handfuls of baby arugula in a bowl with a squeeze of lemon juice, a glug of really good extra-virgin olive oil, and salt and pepper to taste. Top the last 2 slices with the dressed arugula. — *serves 4*

PAN-FRIED CHICKEN THIGHS WITH LITTLE ZUCCHINI
serves 4

We're crazy for pan-fried chicken thighs—thighs are the best part of the chicken. We cook them like we do duck breasts, putting them skin side down in the skillet over moderate heat and resisting the urge to turn them until the fat has rendered and the skin is crisp and golden.

2 tablespoons olive oil	4 tablespoons salted butter
8 chicken thighs	Leaves from 2 big sprigs fresh thyme
Salt and pepper	Juice of ½ lemon
1 pound baby zucchini	1 lemon, cut in wedges

May 3rd, 62°
low ceiling

Put the olive oil into a heavy large skillet over medium heat. Season the chicken thighs with salt and pepper and add them to the skillet skin side down. Without moving them, let them cook until the fat has rendered out and the skin is deep golden brown and crisp, 15–30 minutes. Fiddle with the heat, reducing it to medium-low if the skin begins to burn before it gets evenly golden brown. Turn the thighs over and continue cooking until the meat closest to the bone is cooked through, about 15 minutes.

While the chicken is cooking, cook the zucchini in a medium pot of salted boiling water over high heat until tender, 8–10 minutes. Drain in a colander. Return the empty pot to the stove, add the butter and heat over medium-low heat until it melts. Add the thyme and the lemon juice. Add the drained zucchini to the pot and swirl gently to coat with butter. Serve the thighs and pan juices with the zucchini and lemon wedges.

GALANTINE OF TURKEY & PORK WITH PEAS
makes 2 galantines to serve 6–8

This dish has a big wow factor—everyone who sees it wonders, "How did you get the egg in there?" It's made ahead so it is the perfect thing to serve for a spring Sunday lunch. We also use the galantine mixture (sans the peas and hard-boiled eggs) to make little meatballs to poach in chicken stock or serve in a delicate cream or tomato sauce.

2 tablespoons olive oil
1 onion, finely chopped
1 clove garlic, minced
Salt and pepper
Freshly grated nutmeg
2 large eggs
1 cup whole milk
1½ cups fine fresh bread crumbs
½ cup loosely packed finely chopped
    fresh parsley leaves
2 tablespoons finely minced anchovies

Grated zest of 1 lemon
2 cups fresh or frozen peas or peeled fava
1½ pounds ground turkey
1½ pounds ground pork
6 hard-boiled eggs
4–6 cups chicken stock

FOR THE SAUCE
1 cup homemade or store-bought
    mayonnaise
Juice of 1 lemon
1 tablespoon finely minced anchovies

May 4th, 51°
soft rain

Heat the oil in a large skillet over medium heat. Add onions and garlic and cook, stirring often, until the onions are soft and translucent, about 15 minutes. Season liberally with salt, pepper, and nutmeg. Remove the skillet from the heat and set aside to cool.

Put the eggs and milk into a large bowl and beat together until well mixed. Add the cooled onions, bread crumbs, parsley, anchovies, lemon zest, and peas, and use a rubber spatula to fold everything together. Add the turkey and pork and fold in.

Lay 2 large pieces of double-layered cheesecloth on a work surface. Divide the meat between the pieces of cheesecloth and pat into long rectangles. Place 3 eggs down the center of each rectangle of meat, then wrap the meat around the eggs, shaping into fat sausages. Wrap the cheesecloth tightly around the galantines, twist the ends, and tie with kitchen string. Trim the string and the ends of the cheesecloth.

Pour the chicken stock in a pot just big enough to hold the meat. Put the meat in the pot. Add water until the meat is submerged by 1 inch. Bring to a simmer over medium heat. Reduce heat to low, and cook, partially covered, at the gentlest simmer until the internal temperature reads 160° on a meat thermometer, 1 hour. Remove from heat, allow the meat to cool in the stock, then lift the meat from the stock, wrap well in plastic, and refrigerate.

For the sauce, mix the mayonnaise, lemon juice, and anchovies together in a small bowl. Unwrap the meat and discard the cheesecloth. Slice, arrange on a platter or on individual plates, and spoon the sauce over the meat. Garnish with fresh herbs, if you like.

A LITTLE BIT OF MEAT ADDS A WHOLE LOT OF FLAVOR

We have a love affair with vegetables. We happily cook any and all seasonal veggies that show up in our markets. That said, we are card-carrying carnivores. We love the deep rich flavor of roasted birds, grilled steaks, pan-fried chops, baked hams, and the like. But meat doesn't have to take center stage on our plates; properly directed, a little bit can give a powerful performance. Something porky is always good—bacon, a smoked ham hock, pancetta, prosciutto, guanciale. We are partial to little smoked boneless pork butts that we buy from our butcher—they are lean and fragrant and only weigh about 1 pound. Wrapped in plastic, they will keep in the refrigerator for up to a month. We dice up a slice or two, give it a quick sauté, and add it to scrambled eggs, a pot of beans, collards greens or kale, or a stovetop paella. Just a handful of diced meat can add lots of rich meaty flavor.

CANNELLINI WITH SMOKED HAM & ROSEMARY
serves 6

To quote Diana Kennedy, author of many wonderful cookbooks, on cooking beans: "Don't throw out the soaking water with all the minerals and flavor. Instead, throw out the book that tells you to do so."

3 cups dried cannellini beans, soaked
   for 4 hours or overnight
1 small boneless smoked pork butt,
   about 1 pound
1 clove garlic
2 bay leaves

1 sprig fresh thyme
1 large branch fresh rosemary
¼ cup really good extra-virgin olive oil,
   plus more for drizzling
Salt and pepper

Put the beans and their soaking water into a heavy medium pot. Make sure they are covered by 2 inches or so of water, adding some extra water if necessary. Add the pork butt, garlic, bay leaves, thyme, and rosemary. Bring the beans just to a simmer over medium heat, stirring occasionally. Reduce the heat to low and very gently simmer them until they are swollen and tender, 30–90 minutes (or more), depending on their freshness.

May 5th, 51°
still raining

Remove the pot from the heat. Discard the bay leaves and herb branches. Remove the pork butt and chop or shred the meat into bite-size pieces and add it back to the beans. Add the olive oil and season with salt and pepper. Taste and adjust the seasonings. Serve warm, drizzled with some more really good extra-virgin olive oil.

SPAGHETTI WITH TOMATO SAUCE & RICOTTA
serves 4

Since this very simple dish relies heavily on its ingredients, look for good fresh ricotta and canned San Marzano tomatoes from Italy—they are extra-flavorful—at your local Italian market.

One 28-ounce can chopped tomatoes
1 medium onion, halved
2 cloves garlic
4–6 tablespoons really good
   extra-virgin olive oil

Salt and pepper
1 pound spaghetti
1 cup fresh ricotta
Chopped fresh parsley

May 9th, 66°
scattered clouds

Put the tomatoes into a heavy medium pot, rinse out the container with 2 cups water, and add it to the pot. Add the onions, garlic, olive oil, and salt and pepper to taste. Gently simmer over medium-low heat for about 1 hour. Adjust the seasonings. Add a little more olive oil to round out the flavor, if you like. Discard the onions and garlic.

Cook the pasta in a large pot of salted boiling water until just cooked, 10–12 minutes. Drain, reserving 1 cup of the cooking water. Toss the pasta with the tomato sauce until thoroughly coated. Add the reserved cooking water to loosen the sauce if it is too thick. Divide between 4 plates and top with a big soupspoonful of ricotta and some chopped parsley.

SPAGHETTI ALLA CARBONARA

May 10th, 69°
sunny & lovely

This is our favorite I-forgot-to-go-to-the-store-and-there-is-nothing-in-the-house to eat dinner. If you are like us, even when it is slim pickins, we always have pasta, a couple of eggs, a little piece of parmigiano, and some bacon in the fridge. The starchy pasta water melts the cheese and makes everything creamy.

Cook ½ pound chopped bacon or pancetta in a heavy large skillet over medium heat until crisp and browned, about 10 minutes. Use a slotted spoon to transfer the bacon to a paper towel–lined plate and set aside. Stir together 4 egg yolks, 2 tablespoons softened butter, and plenty of freshly cracked black pepper in a large bowl. Cook 1 pound spaghetti in a large pot of salted boiling water over high heat until just cooked, 10–12 minutes. Drain, reserving 1 cup of the pasta water. Add the hot pasta to the egg yolk mixture and toss until thoroughly coated. Add 1 cup grated parmigiano-reggiano and toss to coat, stirring in some of the reserved cooking water to loosen the sauce and make everything creamy. Scatter the crisp bacon over the top of the pasta and sprinkle with more parmigiano. — *serves 4*

SHRIMP RISOTTO
serves 4

Risotto is traditionally made with short-grain Italian rice grown in Piedmont's Po Valley. There are three main varieties of that rice: arborio, with large plump grains, produces a starchy risotto; carnaroli, smaller grains, produces a looser (wavy) risotto; and vialone nano, with firm grains, cooks up soft with a kernel of chewiness in the center, just the way Italians like it.

1 pound shrimp
4 tablespoons butter
1 tablespoon extra-virgin olive oil
2 small onions, finely chopped
1 rib celery, finely chopped
1 carrot, finely chopped
1 clove garlic, sliced

Handful of parsley stems, chopped
Salt and pepper
One 14-ounce can crushed tomatoes
⅔ cup dry vermouth
Peel of 1 lemon
1 cup arborio, carnaroli, or
    vialone nano rice

May 12th, 73°
puffy clouds

Peel and devein the shrimp, reserving the shells for the broth, and set aside. Melt 1 tablespoon of the butter with the olive oil in a large pot over medium-high heat. Add the shrimp shells, half of the onions, the celery, carrots, garlic, and parsley stems. Season with salt and pepper, and sauté until golden, about 10 minutes. Add the tomatoes, ⅓ cup of the vermouth, and lemon peel, and cook for 5 minutes. Add 4 cups water and cook for 15 minutes. Strain the broth, then return it to the pot. Add the shrimp and place the pot on the stove, off the heat.

Melt 2 tablespoons of the butter in a heavy deep sauté pan over medium-high heat. Add the remaining onions and cook, stirring constantly with a wooden spoon, until soft and translucent, about 3 minutes. Add the rice, stirring until it is coated with butter. Add the remaining ⅓ cup of vermouth.

Add ½ cup of the hot broth, stirring constantly to keep the rice from sticking to the bottom of the pan. Push any rice that crawls up the sides of the pan back down into the liquid. When the rice has absorbed all the broth, add another ½ cup of hot broth. Keep adding broth and stirring. Taste the rice; it is done when it is tender with a firm center. Add the shrimp and the remaining 1 tablespoon of butter and stir until it has melted into the rice.

SPINACH TAGLIATELLE & PEAS IN GOLDEN CHICKEN BROTH

May 13th, 68°
mostly cloudy

Heat 8 cups rich chicken broth in a heavy large pot over medium-high heat. When it comes to a boil, taste and season with salt. Add ½ recipe Spinach Pasta (page 238) cut into tagliatelle (page 236) or ½ pound dried tagliatelle and cook for 1 minute, then add 2 cups fresh or frozen peas and cook for another minute, until the pasta is done. Serve with a sprinkling of grated parmigiano-reggiano, if you like. — *serves 6*

BREAST OF VEAL BRAISED WITH GREEN OLIVES & TOMATOES
serves 4–6

Breast of veal is an often overlooked cut of meat. It looks complicated, with layers of meat interspersed between layers of fat, rib bones, and cartilage. Today's busy cooks tend to grab packages of skinless, boneless chicken breasts—no muss, no fuss—and often steer away from anything that might take longer than 15 minutes to prepare, like breast of veal. We understand the feeling; we too want to get dinner on the table lickety-split! But we know that there is a big payoff from slow-roasting inexpensive cuts until they are flavorful, tender, and juicy. It's actually pretty simple—a little stove-top preparation, then into the oven it goes. That's it.

Sometimes a butcher shop (rather than the grocery store) will sell better and meatier breasts of veal. Don't be intimidated by this complicated cut. After cooking, the fat can be removed, and it's easy to pull the bones and cartilage from the tender meat. We urge you to try it; we know that you're up to the challenge.

1 breast of veal, 5–6 pounds	3 cloves garlic, minced
Salt and pepper	2 medium onions, coarsely chopped
3 tablespoons olive oil	One 28-ounce can plum tomatoes
6 anchovy filets	1 cup green olives, pitted

May 16th, 65°
rain, rain, rain

Preheat the oven to 325°. Rub the veal breast all over with lots of salt and pepper. Heat the olive oil in a heavy large ovenproof pot with a lid over medium-high heat (a heavy roasting pan covered with foil will work too). Put the veal in the pot and brown it well on both sides, about 10 minutes. Remove it from the pot and set aside.

Reduce the heat to medium and add the anchovies and garlic to the pot, stirring to melt the anchovies, about 1 minute. Add the onions, stirring and scraping the bottom of the pot to get all the browned bits up, and cook until softened, about 5 minutes. Add the tomatoes and olives to the pot, crushing the tomatoes with your hand. Put the veal, bone side down, into the pot. Cover and braise in the oven until the veal is very tender, about 2 hours.

Remove the pot from the oven. Transfer the veal to a cutting board. When the meat is cool enough to handle, remove and discard the rib bones, connective tissue, gristle, and any large pieces of fat. Fish out the olives and set aside. Skim off the fat from the top of the sauce. If the sauce looks a little thin, return the pot to the stove and cook over medium-low heat to reduce and thicken slightly. Strain the sauce through a fine-mesh sieve. Return the olives to the sauce and keep it warm over very low heat.

Just before serving, thinly slice the meat on a cutting board, then arrange it on a platter. Spoon the sauce over the meat.

—⟫⟫— PILE IT ON —⟪⟪—

Everyone knows a kid who has to keep each food separate on his or her plate—the peas can never touch the potatoes. We often take the opposite approach. We like to pile it on. That way every bite you take has a little bit of everything. Here's how we do it: First we lay down a foundation of mashed potatoes, pasta, rice, or grits; next we arrange a couple of slices of meat or fish over it; and then generously spoon some pan juices or sauce over the meat. The veg goes on top, seasoned with a sprinkle of flaky salt and pepper. We aren't building a retro-style tower of food, but rather layers of flavors and texture. It's a great way to savor every last drop of sauce.

Overleaf: a big platter of Breast of Veal Braised with Green Olives & Tomatoes; above, breast of veal with string beans piled on mashed potatoes

ROASTED RHUBARB

Rhubarb is one of the first plants to poke its head from the early spring soil. Its tart flavor is refreshingly delicious. We spoon this roasted rhubarb over thick yogurt, ice cream, pound cake, or just enjoy it on its own.

May 18th, 66°
endless rain

Preheat the oven to 350°. Thickly slice 2 pounds rhubarb and put it into a deep ovenproof pot. Add ½ cup sugar and ½ cup red wine. Split open 1 or 2 vanilla beans and add them to the rhubarb. Roast the rhubarb until very tender, about 30 minutes. —— *makes 2–3 cups*

RHUBARB SYRUP
makes 4 cups

Mighty rhubarb, with its heart-shaped leaves and long succulent bright red or green stalks, is known and relied on for its purgative powers—it's a natural spring tonic. If you want to make this before the season, frozen rhubarb works just fine. Hugh Fearnley-Whittingstall turned us on to rhubarb syrup in his cookbook *The River Cottage Year* (Hodder & Stoughton, 2003).

4 pounds fresh rhubarb, cut into pieces, or
  4 pounds frozen rhubarb
1⅓ cups superfine sugar

2 cups (10 blood oranges) fresh blood
  orange or regular orange juice

Put the rhubarb and sugar into a pot and bring to a boil over medium heat. Reduce the heat to low and simmer for 50 minutes. Add the orange juice and cook for 10 minutes. Use a fine sieve to strain the juice into a bowl. Return the juice to the pot, bring to a gentle boil, and cook until it has reduced to a light syrup, about 20 minutes. Measure the syrup and, if necessary, continue to cook over medium heat until it reduces to about 4 cups. Store in a covered container in the refrigerator for up to 1 month.

AMANTE

This drink borrows elements from two great classics: a sugary rim from the sidecar and tequila from the margarita. Deliciously tart rhubarb syrup and sweet orange juice stand in for limes. We prepare our glasses ahead of time, first by wetting the rims with a little rhubarb syrup or orange juice, then rolling the edge of each glass in superfine sugar. We stash the glasses in the freezer so they get frosty.

May 19th, 75°
fog, rain
& thunderstorms

For each drink mix together 3 ounces Rhubarb Syrup and 2 ounces tequila, then pour it into sugar-rimmed glasses filled with lots of ice. Garnish the drink with a slice of orange. Or if you prefer your drink "up", sugar the rim of a stemmed glass, and put it in the freezer until it is frosty, then serve the cocktail in it. —— *makes 1*

BIRTHDAY HALIBUT WITH BEETS & ASPARAGUS VINAIGRETTE
serves 4

We always cook each other a birthday lunch. It's a very special and a much-appreciated treat. The first one comes in May, so we open the doors to the warm spring air, set up a little table overlooking the canal, and pretend we are on the Riviera—*bon anniversaire*!

1 pound small beets

FOR THE HERB MAYONNAISE
2 large egg yolks
½ clove garlic, finely minced
Salt
Juice of 2 lemons
1 cup good, smooth, "buttery" olive oil
1 cup canola oil
2 cups mixed fresh herbs, such as chives, tarragon, chervil, and dill, chopped

FOR THE VINAIGRETTE
1 small clove garlic, finely minced
Salt and pepper
2 teaspoons Dijon mustard
2 tablespoons red wine vinegar
½ cup really good extra-virgin olive oil

1½ pounds center-cut halibut filet
Salt
1 pound asparagus, trimmed and peeled
2 tablespoons chopped fresh chives

May 20th, 72°
morning mist

Preheat the oven to 400°. Wrap each beet in foil and bake until tender, about 1 hour. Unwrap the beets and when cool enough to handle, peel and slice them into wedges.

For the herb mayonnaise, whisk together the yolks, garlic, a pinch of salt, and about 2 tablespoons of the lemon juice in a medium bowl. Combine the oils in a measuring cup with a spout. Whisking constantly, add the oil to the yolks about 1 teaspoon at a time. The sauce will thicken and emulsify. After you have added about ¼ cup of the oil, continue to whisk and slowly drizzle in the remaining oil until you have a thick, glossy mayonnaise. Season with salt and thin with remaining lemon juice to taste. Stir in the chopped herbs. Store in the refrigerator in a covered container for up to 5 days.

For the vinaigrette, whisk together the garlic, salt and pepper, mustard, and vinegar in a small bowl. Whisking constantly, drizzle in the olive oil. Taste and adjust the seasonings.

To poach the halibut, fill a deep medium pan with water and season with salt until it tastes as salty as the sea. Slide the fish into the water and bring to a gentle simmer over medium heat. Poach the fish until just opaque in the center, about 20 minutes. Transfer the fish with a slotted spatula to a warm platter.

While the fish poaches, cook the asparagus in a pan of salted boiling water over medium-high heat until tender, 4–5 minutes. Transfer with a slotted spatula to drain on a clean dishtowel.

Toss the asparagus in the vinaigrette, then transfer them to the platter with the fish. Add the beets to the vinaigrette left in the bowl and toss to coat. Arrange them on the platter. Scatter the chives over the beets. Serve with the herb mayonnaise.

BIRTHDAY STRAWBERRY PAVLOVA
serves 6

With May come strawberries, and this is our version of the perfect birthday cake.

4 large egg whites, at room temperature
Pinch of cream of tartar
1½ cups superfine sugar
1 teaspoon white vinegar

½ teaspoon vanilla extract
4 cups strawberries, hulled
1½ cups heavy cream

Preheat the oven to 275°. Line a cookie sheet with parchment paper and set aside. Put the egg whites and cream of tartar into a large mixing bowl. Using a mixer fitted with whisks, beat the whites on medium speed until they are very foamy. Increase the speed to medium-high and beat until they hold medium-stiff peaks. Continue beating on medium-high speed and gradually add 1 cup of the sugar, 1 tablespoon at a time. Increase the speed to high and beat the whites until they are thick, stiff, and glossy. The total beating time depends on the freshness of the egg whites and the power of your mixer, and we've found that it can take anywhere from 5 minutes to 10 minutes. Fold the vinegar and vanilla into the whites.

Pile the meringue into the center of the parchment paper and gently smooth it out to form a thick 9-inch circle. Put the meringue into the oven and bake for 1 hour.

Turn off the oven and leave the meringue inside to dry out, 2–3 hours. The longer it dries out the chewier, and crunchier it becomes, so leaving it in the turned-off oven as long as overnight is fine too. The meringue will have cracks around the center and sides.

Toss the strawberries and the remaining ½ cup of sugar together in a bowl. Peel off the parchment paper and put the meringue on a cake plate. Whip the cream in a mixing bowl until big soft peaks form. Arrange the berries on the meringue and spoon the whipped cream on top.

Overleaf: the birthday lunch of Halibut with Beets & Asparagus Vinaigrette

A big sign appears in a field at the edge of town. A giant red strawberry is painted on one side, while the other side announces, "Picking from Mother's Day to Father's Day". We've been watching that field for several months and now the green ruffled plants have grown into large mounds filled with bright red berries. Garden strawberries, *Fragaria* spp., are the first berries of the season, arriving here in the Northeast in late spring and lasting only through early summer.

We've grown the tiny, delicate, wildly flavorful woodland strawberries—*Fragaria vesca)*, also known as *fraises des bois*—in our gardens and foraged for them in our spring woods. Either way, they're scarcer than hen's teeth. It's hard to gather even a handful and what we do find, we gobble up as fast as we pick them. We would never dream of eating a berry out of season. So, we wait patiently for the first local harvest and then we go bananas for strawberries. We buy up as many green cartons of the deep red ripe berries that we can carry back to Canal House. Then the feast is on.

CHOOSING ~ We eat local, in-season, ripe strawberries because they taste sweet and juicy, just like a strawberry is supposed to taste. We resist those ubiquitous year-round Driscolls, big pumped-up red berries that are all show and no go. Choose berries that are full and fragrant, unblemished, and red throughout without white or green shoulders (a sign that the berry was picked before fully ripe).

RINSING ~ Ripe summer strawberries are so fragile and full of sweetness that we hate to have to rinse them—they can easily get waterlogged. So when the berries are relatively dirt-free, we gently wipe them with a damp paper towel instead. When they're dirty, we put about a pint at a time in a deep bowl of cold water, push them under, and then quickly lift them out and onto paper towels to drain. When we're feeling flush, we rinse our berries in a bottle of red wine. There's no sacrifice in that.

HULLING ~ It kills us when we see someone slice off the top of a strawberry to get rid of its leaves. Too much of the berry is lopped off; its pretty red "shoulders" are ruined, and part of the white cottony hull is usually still in place. We hull our berries not with a little strawberry hulling tool—that's a gadget that just clutters up the drawer—but with a small paring knife. We simply stick the tip of the knife into the top of the strawberry and cut around the leaves, removing both the leaves and the white cottony hull.

STORING ~ Baskets of strawberries are pretty and convenient for getting berries home, but keeping them packed like that is hard on the fragile fruit. Line a tray with a clean dishcloth or paper towel and spread the unwashed, unhulled fruit out in a single layer so the berries aren't touching. Leave them out at room temperature for up to a day or overnight (refrigerating them diminishes their sugary sweetness) and use them quickly. If you want to store the berries for up to 5 days, drape a clean dishcloth or paper towel over them and store in the refrigerator.

STRAWBERRY CONSERVES
makes 4 half-pints

We always buy extra berries to make small batches of strawberry conserves, the whole-fruit jam that we love. Pectin, the gelatinlike substance naturally present in fruit, helps thicken jams and jellies. But sweet garden strawberries are uniquely low in acid and pectin, so while they are delicious to eat, they're tricky to preserve. So to help set our jam, we add the pithy rind of a lemon—it's full of natural pectin. We never use commercial pectin; it makes the jam set a little too thick and gloppy. We go *au naturel* to get what we like: a conserve of very soft fruit in a barely set syrup.

Because we process just a few jars at a time, the preserve-making doesn't completely take over the kitchen. We simply put up the fruit as we cook through our day, and before we know it, the whole studio is filled with the warm fragrance of cooling strawberry preserves.

4 cups perfect little strawberries, washed and hulled

3 cups superfine sugar
Peel of 1 lemon, including white pith

May 23rd, 70° light showers

Put the strawberries in a heavy wide pot. Use a rubber spatula to fold in 1½ cups of the sugar then bring to a boil over medium-high heat, about 5 minutes. Continue to boil for 3 minutes. Remove the pot from the heat.

Fold in the remaining 1½ cups sugar, return the pot to the heat, and bring to a boil. Boil for 2 minutes, then remove from the heat. Use a slotted spoon to lift the berries from the syrup and spread them out on a plate. Return the pot with the syrup to the heat, add the lemon peel, bring to a boil over medium-high, and boil for 10 minutes. Remove from the heat and let the syrup settle, then use a mesh skimmer to skim off any foam. Allow the syrup to cool, then return the berries to the syrup. Cover and set aside until set, about 6 hours or overnight. Remove the lemon peel. Pack the preserves in sterilized jars and refrigerate.

PRESERVED STRAWBERRIES & JAMÓN SERRANO ON LITTLE TOASTS

For a crunch with your sip in the evening, layer the berries with Serrano ham on little toasts, topped with a drop or two of balsamic vinegar.

May 25th, 81° warm & sunny

Brush both sides of small, thin slices of baguette with some extra-virgin olive oil. Toast them in a preheated 400° oven, turning them once, until golden on both sides. Put a small berry from Strawberry Conserves onto each toast, then pour a few drops of aged balsamic vinegar on each berry. Drape a slice (or half a slice if a whole one is too much) of Serrano ham over the preserves and top with another bit of preserves.

STRAWBERRY SHORTCAKE
serves 6–8

We also use this dough to make little baking powder biscuits—they're the tenderest we've ever eaten. Cut into rounds or squares, they will bake in 15 minutes at 425°.

FOR THE STRAWBERRIES
6 cups small ripe strawberries, hulled
¼ cup sugar

FOR THE BISCUIT
1 cup all-purpose flour
1 cup cake flour
1 tablespoon baking powder

2 teaspoons sugar, plus some for
  sprinkling on top
1 teaspoon salt
1½ cups chilled heavy cream
2 tablespoons melted butter

2 tablespoons salted butter, softened
1 cup heavy cream, whipped to soft peaks

May 27th, 81°
gusty winds

For the strawberries, toss the berries with the sugar and lightly crush with the back of a wooden spoon or the bottom of a bowl. Set aside until the berries release their juices, about 45 minutes.

For the biscuit, preheat the oven to 425°. Whisk together the flours, baking powder, sugar, and salt in a mixing bowl. Add the cream, and gently mix with your hands until the dough holds together. Place dough on a lightly floured surface and knead a few times (don't over-work the dough or it will become tough). Gently flatten the dough with your hands and shape into an 8-inch round about ½ inch thick. Slide the dough onto a cookie sheet. Brush the top and sides with melted butter and sprinkle with a little sugar. Bake for 15 minutes, then reduce the oven temperature to 325° and bake for 10 minutes. While the biscuit is still warm, spread with the softened butter.

Place the biscuit on a cake plate, spoon the strawberries with their syrupy juices over it, and top with whipped cream.

STRAWBERRIES ROMANOFF

Carême, the first celebrity chef, created this for Czar Alexander I (of the House of Romanoff) in 1820.

May 30th, 85°
cloudless sky

Put 4 cups small, ripe, hulled strawberries in a bowl and drizzle with ¼ cup kirsch. Gently crush the berries with the back of a wooden spoon just enough to soften them and release some of their juice. Toss the strawberries with ¼ cup Demerara sugar and a handful of mint leaves, then set aside to macerate, 20–30 minutes.

Using a whisk or a mixer, beat together 1 cup cold heavy cream, ⅓ cup sour cream, and 1 tablespoon granulated sugar in a large bowl until soft peaks form. Spoon layers of strawberries, their syrupy juices, and whipped cream into glasses or bowls. — *serves 4*

❧ June Recipes ❧

how to boil an egg ∾ 70

deviled eggs ∾ 71

"buttered" eggs ∾ 71

open-faced zucchini omelet ∾ 72

canal house year-round caprese salad ∾ 72

poached wild salmon with fresh english peas & morels ∾ 76

wild salmon crudo with arugula salad ∾ 76

smoked salmon with chèvre on crax ∾ 77

rolled flank steak with pesto ∾ 78

rice salad ∾ 81

raviolini with fava beans & parmigiano ∾ 81

roasted chicken in a pot with spring onions ∾ 82

the garden giveth ∾ 84

classic vanilla ice cream ∾ 86

ice creams: cassis, coffee, peppermint crunch, strawberry ∾ 87

apricot & almond upside-down cake ∾ 88

apricot cooler, rummy apricot, apricot sparkler ∾ 91

red currant jelly ∾ 91

mixed berry cobbler ∾ 92

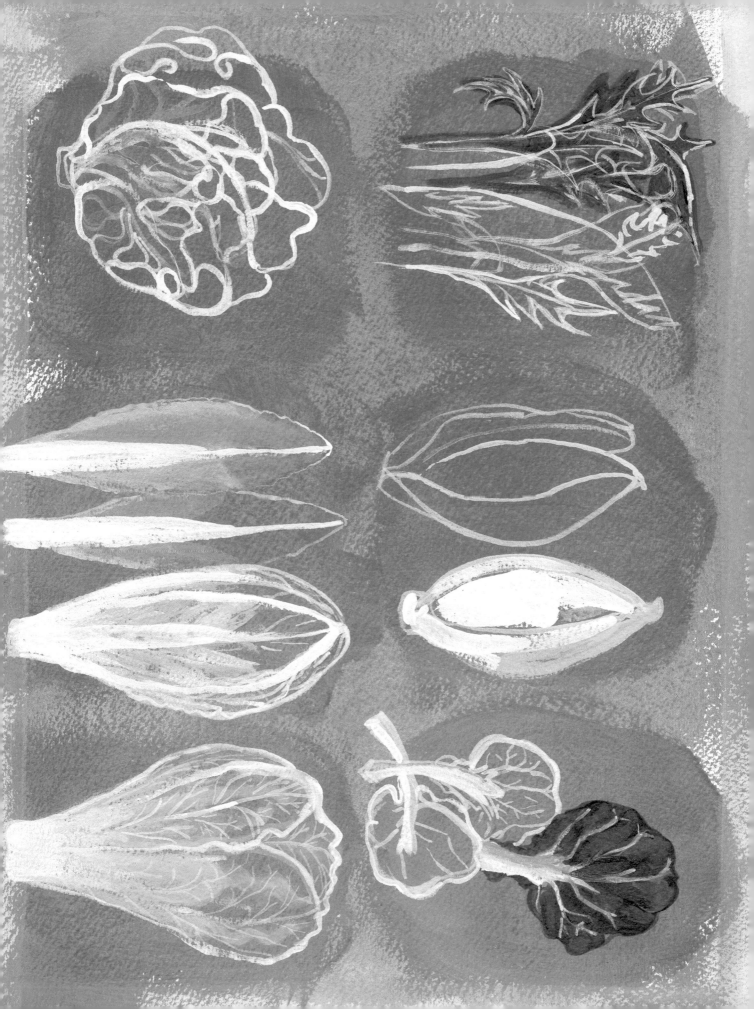

Our studio is an airy room with a soaring ceiling—not grand but just what we need. We are on the second floor of an old redbrick warehouse. A long bank of French doors opens onto a narrow wrought-iron balcony that hangs over the towpath running next to the canal below. In the winter, the doors are shut tight and our old wood stove is at the heart of our daily life.

But as soon as the weather turns warm, the first of us to arrive in the morning opens the doors and lets the outside world in. We hang screen curtains to keep out bugs and birds, and they filter the light and soft air. A ceiling fan whirls overhead, keeping us cool. We'll wait until midsummer to turn on "the air", unless it just gets too hot not to.

Herbs fill the window boxes that hang on the railing and vegetable seedlings go into big black plastic pots on the balcony floor. By June the boxes are overflowing with chives, parsley, thyme, sage, rosemary, tarragon, and strawberries that come back every year. The tomatoes and nasturtiums are climbing up their towers in the pots. Herb-rich, we run back and forth from the kitchen to the balcony, snipping chives and their lovely lavender blossoms. We just love chives, and if we don't watch ourselves, we'll sprinkle them on everything.

In the spring, life returns to the canal. Sometimes we stand on our narrow balcony and lean over the rail as if we're on a ship, to see what's going on below. The ducks are back. Tiny ducklings swim behind their mothers like wind-up toys. Later in the summer they will make a daily pilgrimage from the canal to the river and back, their long waddling parade stopping traffic as they cross the street. We save all our stale bread to throw over the side to feed them. One day a lone swan glides up and down our stretch of the canal, back and forth, and we fear it is looking for its lost mate.

All the sounds of life below float up into the studio. People walk their dogs and stroll with each other, and we catch bits of their conversations, half sentences that waft upward. A couple that knows us says they love to walk beneath our open doors and hear us talking and laughing above them—so it works both ways. Every day a man rides down the towpath. We can hear him coming, singing at the top of his lungs. He sings old Beatles love songs. We run over to catch a glimpse. He's no kid—we can see the top of his gray head of hair—but he must have a young man's romantic heart. We look at each other and smile. Who wouldn't love a man like that? Often kayakers paddle effortlessly by in their brightly colored boats. It looks like such fun. We have a fantasy that we'll buy boats and commute to work that way. We call down to them, "You're the luckiest people in the world." They call back, "No, you are!" And so we are.

HOW TO BOIL AN EGG

Very fresh eggs don't peel well no matter how gently you've boiled them or for how long. The shell clings to the white like a second skin and won't let go without leaving pockmarks. The remedy is to hang on to your very fresh eggs for about a week in the refrigerator before hard-boiling them. The shell will peel off like a glove. But if you are desperate and only have fresh eggs, add about ¼ cup kosher salt to the cooking water; the eggs will be easier to peel. Here's how we hard-boil our eggs so the yolks are pleasantly moist—not crumbly dry—and remain vibrantly yellow with no green-gray ring.

Submerge large eggs straight from the fridge into a pot of gently boiling water. The eggs should be in a single layer and the water should cover the eggs by about 1 inch. Cook for:

> 6 minutes —— the perfect soft-boiled egg
>
> 9 minutes —— the soft yolk hard-boiled egg
>
> 10 minutes —— the perfect hard-boiled egg
>
> 11 minutes —— the firm yolk hard-boiled egg

Drain the eggs in the sink and immediately run cold water into the pot to cool them. When the eggs are cool enough to handle, drain them. Take an egg, tap the shell all over on the counter, then peel the shell off, starting at the fatter end (where the air sac is). Keep any uncracked unpeeled hard-boiled eggs in the refrigerator if you are not going to use them within 4 hours.

DEVILED EGGS
makes 12

For us, summer is big-time egg season. We always keep a dozen hard-boiled eggs in the fridge so we can quickly whip up some of these beauties. Deviled eggs stand on their own but we often embellish the tops with a dab of something savory—like harissa (Tunisian chile-spice sauce), a fat cooked asparagus tip, shards of crisp bacon, chopped ham, prosciutto, a small spoonful of salmon roe, or a thin slice of cornichon.

6 hard-boiled eggs, peeled
½ cup mayonnaise
1 tablespoon sour cream

1 teaspoon Dijon mustard
Salt and pepper

June 3rd, 77°
southerly winds

Cut the hard-boiled eggs in half lengthwise. Pop the yolks out right into a fine sieve set over a bowl. Set the whites aside. Using a rubber spatula, press the yolks through the sieve. Fold in the mayonnaise, sour cream, and mustard. Season with salt and pepper. You can also put everything in a food processor, and pulse several times until the yolks are as smooth as you like.

Use 2 teaspoons to fill each egg white with the filling. Garnish the eggs as you like, even if it's with just a dash of pimentón, a parsley leaf, or a scattering of finely chopped fresh chives.

"BUTTERED" EGGS

Sometimes when we are too busy to make deviled eggs, we do something just as good. We simply "butter" the cut sides of hard-boiled eggs with mayonnaise, arrange the eggs on a plate, and drizzle them with some good olive oil and a generous sprinkle of salt and pepper. We often garnish them with something: chopped Preserved Lemon rind (page 294) or minced chives. Sometimes it's parsley, tarragon, or dill; or bacon, thinly sliced ham, or chutney. These eggs are delicious and one of our favorite things to eat.

Overleaf: A big platter of Deviled and "Buttered" Eggs topped with smoked salmon and scallions, green olives stuffed with anchovies and a dab of anchovy paste, slices of roasted piquillo pepper, chopped baked ham and chives, a dab of harissa and scallions, a sardine filet and a squeeze of lemon, a shard of bacon and a dab of chutney, and hummus and preserved lemon

OPEN-FACED ZUCCHINI OMELET
serves 1

For this quick omelet we don't add milk or water to the eggs. We like the streaks of yellow yolk and the whites throughout—it's pure egg. Allowing the skillet to cool slightly before starting in on the omelet helps keep the eggs from cooking too quickly and getting tough.

2 tablespoons extra-virgin olive oil
6–8 baby zucchini, sliced
½ small serrano chile, thinly sliced
1 clove garlic, thinly sliced

1 or 2 zucchini blossoms, if you have them, sliced in half
2 eggs
Salt and pepper

June 6th, 81°
calm & foggy

Heat 1 tablespoon of the oil in an 8-inch skillet over medium-high heat. Add the zucchini and chiles and cook, stirring occasionally, until well browned, about 3 minutes. Push the zucchini to one side of the skillet, then add the garlic, and cook until fragrant, about 30 seconds. Give everything a stir. Add the zucchini blossoms, if using, and toss until softened. Season with salt and pepper. Remove from the heat and transfer the zucchini mixture to a plate. Allow the skillet to cool slightly before cooking the omelet.

Heat the remaining 1 tablespoon of the oil in the skillet over medium heat. Lightly beat the eggs with a pinch of salt and pepper in a small bowl. Pour the eggs into the hot skillet. Cook, allowing them to set slightly in the skillet. Then tilting the skillet, use a spatula to gently lift the edge of the omelet, allowing the uncooked eggs to run underneath. Repeat on the opposite side. Continue lifting and tilting until the eggs have set on the bottom. Spoon the zucchini mixture over the eggs and season with salt and pepper. Slide the omelet onto a plate and serve hot.

CANAL HOUSE YEAR-ROUND CAPRESE SALAD

Even when it isn't tomato and basil season, little cherry tomatoes always have really good flavor. Good hothouse chives are around all year, so we let them stand in for basil.

June 8th, 86°
hot & sunny

Slice 2 pints cherry tomatoes in half horizontally. Arrange the tomatoes cut side up on a platter. Season with flaky sea salt, a little super fine sugar, and ground black pepper. Put a drop of good balsamic vinegar in each tomato half. Slice about 1 pound fresh mozzarella and arrange on 4 plates. Top with the halved cherry tomatoes and a drizzle of really good extra-virgin olive oil. Season with a little more salt and pepper and scatter a handful of chopped chives over everything. — *serves 4*

POACHED WILD SALMON WITH FRESH ENGLISH PEAS & MORELS
serves 2

Wild king salmon from Alaska's pristine Copper River are caught at the beginning of their spawning migration when the fish are in their prime, rich with omega 3 fats. It's what they need for their epic swim upstream, against the flow of the raging glacier-fed river. If fresh morels are difficult to find, use thickly sliced shiitake mushroom caps.

2 center-cut wild king salmon filets,
  6–8 ounces each
1 cup white wine
Salt
4 tablespoons butter

4 ounces fresh morel mushrooms, cleaned
½ cup shelled fresh English peas
½ cup heavy cream
Pepper
Small bunch fresh chives, finely chopped

June 9th, 90°
thunderstorms

Put the fish skin side down in a deep, wide pan. Add the wine, a generous pinch of salt, and enough cold water to cover the fish by a bit. Cover the pan and bring to a simmer over medium heat. Reduce the heat to medium-low and gently poach the fish until it is just cooked through or barely opaque in the center, 8–12 minutes.

Meanwhile, melt the butter in a medium skillet over medium heat. Add the mushrooms and cook until they begin to soften, about 3 minutes. Add ½ cup of the salmon poaching liquid and the peas, and simmer until the peas begin to soften, 2–3 minutes. Add the cream and gently boil the sauce until slightly thickened, about 2 minutes. Season with salt and pepper.

Using a fish spatula, remove the salmon filets from the poaching liquid, then carefully peel off and discard the skin. Serve the salmon with the peas, morels, and cream spooned on top. Garnish with the chives, and sprigs of fresh pea shoots, if you like.

WILD SALMON CRUDO WITH ARUGULA SALAD
serves 4–8

This raw salmon dish relies on pristine fish, preferably wild, since it's all about the fish (perhaps this is stating the obvious). Use the best quality extra-virgin olive oil you can afford and a good sea salt, like Maldon or fleur de sel. Normally, we don't sweat the specialty ingredients, but in this case, they make a difference.

1 pound center-cut wild salmon filet,
  skin and pinbones removed
2 ounces baby arugula
Juice of 1 lemon, preferably Meyer

3–4 tablespoons extra-virgin olive oil, plus
  more for drizzling
Salt, preferably Maldon, and pepper
4–8 lemon wedges

continued

For the salmon, use a very sharp, long thin knife to cut the salmon across the grain into very thin slices. Evenly divide the sliced salmon between 8 salad plates or 4 dinner plates, arranging the slices in a mosaic pattern. Place pieces of plastic wrap over the salmon, and using a flat meat pounder or a metal measuring cup with a flat bottom, press down on the plastic until the salmon spreads out and covers the whole plate. Repeat with all the plates of salmon. Stack the plates in the refrigerator until the salmon is well chilled.

For the salad, toss the arugula in a large bowl with the lemon juice, olive oil, and salt and pepper to taste, just before serving.

To serve, peel off and discard the plastic wrap from each plate. Drizzle the salmon with some olive oil and sprinkle with salt and pepper. Divide the salad between the plates, scattering it over the salmon, and serve with a wedge of lemon.

SMOKED SALMON WITH CHÈVRE ON CRAX

We are crazy for crackers—Stoned Wheat Thins, Saltines, Ak-Maks, Triscuits, Clubs—their boxes are lined up on the top shelf of our little pantry. They are a crisp platform for all kinds of toppings, perfect for a quick snack or a nibble with a drink at the end of the day. This favorite combo is quick, simple, and delicious.

Smear a little fresh chèvre on crackers, top with slices of smoked salmon, minced fresh chives, and lots of freshly ground black pepper. —— *makes as many as you like*

Overleaf: top, king salmon from Alaska's Copper River; bottom left, Poached Wild Salmon with Fresh English Peas & Morels; bottom right, Wild Salmon Crudo with Arugula Salad

ROLLED FLANK STEAK WITH PESTO
serves 6

We use green olives stuffed with anchovies in this pesto. We first had these delicacies at the bar at Le Caprice in London, during a layover on our way to Rome, and now we always keep them on hand—they're a great salty nibble with a drink. You can always leave out the anchovies, unless you are anchovy-mad like we are. You can grill the steak ahead and serve it cold with a big salad for simple summer-style entertaining. That way you can take a swim or run through the sprinkler before dinner.

FOR THE PESTO
2 loosely packed cups basil leaves
2 loosely packed cups fresh parsley leaves
1 clove garlic, sliced
¼–½ cup pitted green olives
3 anchovy filets

¼ cup really good extra-virgin olive oil
½ cup parmigiano-reggiano

FOR THE STEAK
One 2-pound flank steak
Salt and pepper

*June 16th, 79°
clear still day*

For the pesto, purée the basil, parsley, garlic, green olives, and anchovies with the olive oil in a food processor. Add the parmigiano and pulse a couple of times. Transfer to a small bowl and place a piece of plastic wrap directly on the surface of the pesto to keep it from turning dark.

For the steak, place the flank steak flat on a work surface with the grain of the meat running perpendicular to you. Using a long, thin, very sharp knife, butterfly the meat by slicing through the long side of the steak, opening it up as you go, stopping ½ inch short of cutting the steak in two. Press the meat flat. Season with salt and pepper. Spread the pesto all over the meat, leaving a 1-inch space all around the edge. Roll up the steak, with the grain running the length of the roll (this is the way it "wants" to roll) and tie up with kitchen string every 2 inches. Wrap with plastic wrap and refrigerate until ready to grill.

Grill over a medium-hot fire built on one side of the grill, turning the steak until it has browned on all sides, about 10 minutes. Move the steak over to the side of the grill off the fire, allowing it to cook as it rests, about 10 minutes.

Place the steak on a cutting board and allow to rest for 10 minutes. Remove the strings and slice across the grain into 1- to 2-inch slices.

RICE SALAD
serves 4

While regular cooked long-grain rice turns grainy once it spends some time in the refrigerator, short-grain arborio rice stays tender even when ice-cold. If you do refrigerate the salad, remember to let it come to room temperature before serving to allow the flavors to emerge.

Take a little care to chop the vegetables into even pieces so that everything cooks at the same rate and the salad looks pretty. Feel free to make this salad with whatever you have in the garden or find at the farmers' market.

½ cup arborio rice
Salt
1 clove garlic, finely chopped
¼ cup finely chopped pancetta
Big handful young green beans,
    coarsely chopped
½ cup shelled fresh fava beans, blanched
    and peeled

½ cup shelled peas
Handful sugar snap peas, chopped
2 scallions, finely chopped
½ cup grated parmigiano-reggiano or
    more to taste
¼ cup really good extra-virgin olive oil
Pepper

June 17th, 82°
heavy thunderstorms

Add the rice to a medium pot of salted boiling water over medium-high heat. Add the garlic and pancetta. Cook for about 10 minutes, then add the green beans. Continue cooking, tasting the rice every so often, until the rice is tender, 7–10 minutes. Add the fava beans and peas during the last few minutes of cooking. Drain the rice and vegetables in a strainer, then transfer to a large mixing bowl. Add the sugar snap peas, scallions, and parmigiano to the hot rice and toss everything together. Add the olive oil and season to taste with salt and pepper. Serve right away or refrigerate. Allow the salad to come to room temperature before serving.

RAVIOLINI WITH FAVA BEANS & PARMIGIANO

June 18th, 72°
cloudy

Blanch 1 pound fresh or frozen shelled fava beans in a medium pot of salted boiling water for 1–2 minutes. Drain, then plunge the fava beans into a bowl of cold water. Drain, then peel off and discard their tough outer skins. Put the tender green fava beans into a large bowl. Cook 8 ounces of cheese raviolini in a medium pot of salted boiling water until tender, 3–5 minutes. Drain, reserving a little of the pasta water, and add the raviolini to the bowl with the fava beans. Add ¼ cup really good extra-virgin olive oil, 2–3 tablespoons of the reserved pasta water, 1 cup finely grated parmigiano-reggiano, and ½ cup chopped fresh chives. Season with salt and pepper, and toss everything together. — *serves 4*

ROASTED CHICKEN IN A POT WITH SPRING ONIONS
serves 4–6

We think of this dish as "the best of both worlds" roasted chicken. It has the flavor of a moist roast chicken with the bonus of lots of delicious broth. We serve it with buttered egg noodles, mashed potatoes, or hunks of warm crusty bread to soak up all those wonderful juices.

1 whole chicken, 3–5 pounds
2 tablespoons extra-virgin olive oil
Salt and pepper
12 spring onions, green stems attached

4–6 sprigs fresh parsley
2–3 cloves garlic, crushed
2–4 tablespoons butter

June 20th, 79°
billowing clouds

Preheat the oven to 375°. Put the chicken into a heavy wide pot that holds it easily with the lid on. Drizzle the bird with the olive oil and season the bird with salt and pepper. Tuck the onions, parsley, and garlic into the pot around the chicken. Add the butter and 1–2 cups cold water to the pot.

Cover the pot and roast the chicken for 30 minutes. Remove the pot from the oven and baste the chicken with the brothy juices.

Increase the oven temperature to 450°. Return the pot to the oven, uncovered, and finish roasting the chicken until the skin is golden and the thigh juices run clear when pierced with a sharp knife, about 30 minutes. Let the chicken rest for 10–15 minutes before carving. Adjust the seasonings of the broth with salt and pepper. Serve the chicken and onions in wide bowls with a big ladleful of broth in each bowl.

THE GARDEN GIVETH

We had been waiting for this moment all spring—ever since the days began to grow longer and the ground became warm enough to dig. We had nailed together the frames for the new raised garden beds and nestled them into their trenches, and we had tilled the heavy topsoil, turning in small truckloads of rich black compost. We worried that we had planted a little too early, before the hard frosts were over. But the temperature dropped below freezing only once, and we protected the seedlings by draping the entire garden with long disposable paper tablecloths. For weeks, we watered and weeded, gave support to tendrils, and staked branches before they broke.

Then the moment came when we could cut a head of cauliflower from its roots and unfurl the broad sturdy leaves—which we'd snapped over the head as it grew, blanching it— to reveal its tight white curd. When the English peas had swollen so fully in their pods that they just had to be picked. When we could reach way under the huge green thorny leaves of the zucchini plants and find tiny, pinky-size squash attached to buxom pale orange blossoms. When the turnips filled out and were worth pulling from the ground. And when the chard stood tall and proud.

Just seventy-five days whence we began, we gathered enough from our garden to make lunch. The meal couldn't have been simpler. Nothing could have been more satisfying.

Cauliflower with Brown Butter ☙ We had three fist-size heads. We steamed them until very tender. While that was going on, we made a small skilletful of brown butter with slivers of garlic, then poured that toasted nutty deliciousness over the heads.

Young Turnips ☙ We trimmed and peeled these, then gave them the same luxurious treatment as the cauliflower.

English Peas in Irish Butter ☙ We shelled the fat, starchy sweet English peas and cooked them in a tiny bit of water and lots of salted Irish butter.

Tender Swiss Chard with Cannellini ☙ We sautéed the chard in good extra-virgin olive oil with a pinch of red pepper flakes—first the sliced stalks, then wilting the leaves in the warm oil just at the end. To round out the meal, we added cannellini beans we had on hand. They were meant for each other.

Tiny Zucchini with their Blossoms Fritto Misto ☙ We started off with a quick fritto misto, dipping the small handful of zucchini-laden blossoms in a thin batter and then frying them in good olive oil. Pure heaven.

Salad of Head and Leaf Lettuces ☙ We finished our lunch the way we often do, with tender, floppy greens tossed with an anchovy and lemon vinaigrette.

CLASSIC VANILLA ICE CREAM
makes 1 quart

In late spring we begin to assemble our "summer kitchen", which includes clearing out a shelf in the freezer to make room for the canisters of our ice cream maker. They live there, frozen and at the ready for making a batch of classic vanilla ice cream—or the ultimate summertime flavors when we've got a pile of sweet summer berries or ripe, fragrant peaches. As good as hand-crafted and premium commercial ice creams can be, the taste and texture of just-churned homemade ice cream can't be beat. It never fails as a crowd pleaser for young and old alike. So cool your canisters and get churning!

1½ cups heavy cream
1½ cups whole milk
¾ cup sugar

1 vanilla bean, split lengthwise
6 egg yolks
Pinch of salt

June 21st, 78°
longest day
15 h 02 m

Put the cream, milk, and ½ cup of the sugar into a heavy saucepan. Scrape the seeds from the vanilla bean into the pan, then add the whole bean. Bring the cream and milk to a simmer over medium heat, stirring gently until the sugar dissolves.

Meanwhile, put the egg yolks, salt, and the remaining ¼ cup of sugar into a medium mixing bowl and whisk together until the yolks are thick and pale yellow.

Gradually ladle about 1 cup of the hot cream into the yolks, whisking constantly. Stir the warm yolk mixture into the hot cream in the saucepan. Reduce the heat to low and cook, stirring constantly, until the custard is thick enough to coat the back of the spoon and registers between 175° and 180° on an instant-read thermometer, 10–15 minutes. Stirring the custard constantly as it cooks and thickens prevents it from coming to a boil and curdling.

Strain the custard through a fine-mesh sieve into a medium bowl and add the vanilla bean. Set the bowl into a larger bowl filled with ice, then stir the custard frequently until it has cooled off. Cover the custard and refrigerate it until completely chilled, about 4 hours (though it can keep in the refrigerator for up to 2 days). Discard the vanilla bean.

Churn the custard in an ice cream maker following the manufacturer's instructions. Scoop the ice cream (it will have the consistency of softserve) into a quart container with a lid, cover, and freeze for a couple of hours until it is just firm. If you serve the ice cream after it is frozen solid (it will keep for up to 2 days in the freezer), let it soften slightly before serving.

CASSIS ICE CREAM ∼ Press 1 cup black currant preserves through a sieve into a bowl, then stir in ½ cup crème de cassis. Follow the directions for making Vanilla Ice Cream, stirring the cassis mixture into the chilled custard just before churning the ice cream.

COFFEE ICE CREAM ∼ Follow the directions for making Vanilla Ice Cream, omitting the vanilla bean. Add ¼ cup ground dark-roast coffee or espresso beans to the cream mixture in the first step. (Don't worry, the coffee grounds get strained out in the fourth step.) Add 1 teaspoon vanilla extract to the chilled custard just before churning the ice cream.

PEPPERMINT CRUNCH ICE CREAM ∼ Follow the directions for making Vanilla Ice Cream, omitting the vanilla bean. Stir 2 tablespoons crème de menthe and ¼ teaspoon mint extract into the chilled custard just before churning. Add ¼ cup finely crushed peppermint candies to the ice cream a few minutes before it finishes churning.

STRAWBERRY ICE CREAM ∼ Follow the directions for making Vanilla Ice Cream. While the custard is chilling, toss 2 cups sliced strawberries with 1–2 tablespoons sugar in a small bowl and let macerate for an hour or so. Stir the strawberries and accumulated juices into the ice cream a few minutes before it finishes churning.

Strawberry Ice Cream

APRICOT & ALMOND UPSIDE-DOWN CAKE
makes one 9-inch cake

The apricots on the edges will turn very dark—but don't despair! They will be delicious and create a tortoiseshell pattern when you turn the cake out of the pan.

FOR THE APRICOTS AND SYRUP
2 cups dry white wine
⅔ cup sugar
1 cinnamon stick
Zest of 1 lemon, cut in wide strips
1 tablespoon fresh lemon juice
½ pound dried California apricot halves
    (1¾ cups)

FOR THE CAKE
1 cup almond meal or almond flour

1 cup all-purpose flour
1½ teaspoons baking powder
¾ cup whole milk
4 tablespoons salted butter, cut into pieces
    plus more for buttering the pan
2 teaspoons vanilla bean paste
    or vanilla extract
3 large eggs
1½ cups sugar

*June 23rd, 80°
warm soft rain*

For the apricots and syrup, put the wine, sugar, cinnamon stick, lemon zest, and lemon juice into a medium saucepan. Bring to a gentle boil over medium heat, stirring until the sugar dissolves. Reduce the heat to medium-low, add the apricots to the syrup, cover, and simmer until they are plump, about 15 minutes. Remove from the heat, uncover, and allow the apricots to cool to room temperature in the syrup. Lift the apricots from the syrup. Discard the cinnamon stick and lemon zest, and reserve the apricot syrup for other uses (page 91).

Preheat the oven to 350°. Generously butter a 9-inch springform pan. Line the bottom of the pan with a round of parchment paper, then butter the parchment. Snugly arrange the apricots, cut side up, in a single layer on the parchment. Sprinkle ½ cup of the almond meal evenly over the apricots, and set aside.

Whisk together the flour, baking powder, and remaining ½ cup almond meal in a bowl, and set aside. Heat the milk in a small saucepan over medium heat just to the boiling point. Remove the pan from the heat, and add the butter and vanilla. Cover and set aside.

Using a mixer on medium-high speed, beat the eggs in a mixing bowl until pale yellow and thick, about 3 minutes. Gradually add the sugar, and continue to beat for about 5 minutes. Add the dry ingredients and milk, alternately in thirds, and beat on medium speed until the batter is smooth. Pour the batter over the apricots.

Bake the cake in the middle of the oven until golden and a wooden skewer comes out clean when inserted in the center, about 1 hour. Allow the cake to cool for about 10 minutes, then invert it onto a serving plate, fruit side up. Serve the cake warm or at room temperature.

DELIGHTFUL APRICOT DRINKS

The apricot syrup from the first step of Apricot & Almond Upside-Down Cake (page 88) is liquid gold. We use it to flavor these drinks.

APRICOT COOLER ~ Fill a tall glass with ice cubes. Add enough apricot syrup to reach a third of the way up the glass. Add a splash of cold bubbly water. Add the juice of 1 lemon wedge, and garnish with a twist of lemon. —— *makes 1*

RUMMY APRICOT ~ Fill a small glass with ice cubes. Add 2 ounces light rum and 1 ounce apricot syrup. Give a gentle stir. Add a splash of cold bubbly water, if you like, and garnish with a twist of lemon. —— *makes 1*

APRICOT SPARKLER ~ Add 1 ounce apricot syrup to a Champagne flute, then fill with ice-cold Prosecco. —— *makes 1*

RED CURRANT JELLY
makes about 6 half-pints

Tempted as we are to spoon this luscious old-fashioned jelly onto our morning toast, currants are hard to come by, so we treasure each beautiful jar and serve it as a condiment with grilled and roasted meats. Currants have a high level of pectin, so the jelly sets beautifully.

3 quarts ripe red currants   3–6 cups granulated sugar

Put the currants, stems and all, in a large enameled cast-iron pot. Gently crush the fruit with the back of a wooden spoon. Bring to a low simmer over medium-low heat. Cook until the berries collapse slightly, lose their vibrant color, and begin to release their juice, about 1 hour.

{ June 27th, 82°
a gentle breeze

Transfer fruit and juice to a large jelly bag suspended over a bowl. (You may have to do this in batches). Don't squeeze the bag; it could make the jelly cloudy. When the juice stops dripping after several hours, discard the berries. Each quart of berries should yield about 1 cup juice.

Pour the juice back into the pot, add 1 cup sugar for every 1 cup juice, and bring to a boil over medium heat. Boil for about 10 minutes, skimming off any foam, until the liquid reaches 220° on a candy thermometer.

Pour the jelly into hot, sterilized half-pint jars, leaving ½-inch headspace. Wipe the rims clean, then top with the sterilized lids and screw the bands on. Use tongs to put the jars into a canning pot. Fill the pot with enough water to cover the lids by 2 inches. Bring to a boil and boil for 10 minutes. Use tongs to carefully remove the jars from the water and place jars on a kitchen towel. Allow the jars to cool completely, undisturbed, before you move them. As the jars cool, you will hear a distinct click as a vacuum forms and pulls the lid down. Sometimes a jar will have an imperfect seal; in that case, refrigerate and use it first.

Clockwise from the top: apricots, Red Currant Jelly, apricot syrup

MIXED BERRY COBBLER
serves 6–8

Berry season begins in late spring with the arrival of sweet juicy strawberries; then raspberries and blackberries come on. It's these berries we wait for to make this biscuit cobbler. We don't toss the berries with any sort of starch to thicken the juices because we prefer a clean, pure berry flavor—and plenty of loose juice for the tender biscuits to sop up.

FOR THE BISCUIT TOPPING
½ cup all-purpose flour
½ cup cake flour
2 teaspoons baking powder
1 teaspoon sugar, plus some for
    sprinkling on top
½ teaspoon salt
¾ cup chilled heavy cream
2 tablespoons melted butter

FOR THE BERRIES
3 cups blackberries
3 cups raspberries
¾ cup sugar or more, depending on the
    sweetness of the berries
2 teaspoons vanilla extract

June 29th, 81°
perfect summer day

Preheat the oven to 375°.

For the biscuit topping, whisk together the flours, baking powder, sugar, and salt in a mixing bowl. Add the cream, and gently mix with your hands until the dough holds together. Place the dough on a lightly floured surface and knead a few times (don't overwork the dough or it will become tough). Gently flatten the dough with your hands and shape into a ½–inch-thick rectangle that is slightly smaller than your baking dish. Cut the dough into 9 equal pieces. Brush the top and sides with the butter.

For the berries, combine the berries, sugar, and vanilla in a large bowl. Toss well, then spoon into an 8½ × 11–inch baking dish.

Arrange the biscuits over the berries. Sprinkle a little sugar over the biscuits. Bake until the biscuit topping is golden brown and the berry juices are bubbling and syrupy, 40–45 minutes.

summer

❧ July Recipes ❧

canal house crab louis ∼ 101

string beans vinaigrette with french feta ∼ 101

hoisin-ful spareribs for the fourth of july ∼ 102

old-fashioned layered potato salad ∼ 102

potato salad "buttered" & lemoned ∼ 103

cool cucumber & mint salad with sichuan pepper ∼ 103

thick & chewy brownies ∼ 106

roasted red pepper & tomato gazpacho ∼ 107

chilled corn soup ∼ 108

cold avocado & cucumber soup ∼ 108

tomatoes with tonnato sauce ∼ 111

the fry queen's fried chicken ∼ 112

composed summer salad with lemony aïoli ∼115

sugared berries with crème anglaise ∼ 116

classic tuiles ∼ 116

poached white peaches in lemon verbena syrup ∼ 118

bellini ∼ 121

lemonade ∼ 121

Every Friday night all summer long, our town of Lambertville and the neighboring Bucks County town of New Hope, just across the river, put on a spectacular fireworks display. It's launched from a barge anchored in the river south of the green iron bridge spanning the two communities, and is as good as or better than any you'll see on the Fourth of July.

The show starts off with little teasers—single rockets blasting high into the sky—and builds into a sparkling madness of exploding, whirling, cascading light. The river snuffs out the ones that land. The bridge is packed with pedestrians and lit up by white headlights and red taillights as drivers slowly make their way over the bridge, taking in the show.

So, on Friday evenings during the summer, we've started to invite our families and our friends to come to the studio for a big casual supper. Then at nine-thirty, when the sky is finally dark, we walk down to the river's edge, just a block away.

The fireworks supper gives our summer Friday mornings a new rhythm. One of us stops at a farm stand and grabs a few dozen ears of corn. Then we meet up at a farm market. We may end up with a flat of strawberries, or beady, juicy, pitch-black raspberries for a cobbler or shortcake. We always buy ripe heirloom tomatoes for slicing thick as steaks and serving on platters. While we shop, we tuck into a pint of warm Sun Gold cherry tomatoes, as sweet as candy.

As we work at the studio, we'll spatchcock some chickens and roast them. Or we'll make our "hoisin-ful" sauce, lacquer spareribs with it, and cook the ribs in a slow oven, the sweet bourbon smell filling the studio as the air conditioner cranks. We've fired up the charcoal grill on our breezeway and served whole sides of grilled wild salmon, and spaghetti marinara with homemade meatballs, buttery garlic bread, and a tossed salad.

As the sun sets and the evening cools, we open the French doors to the canal and the river just beyond. We welcome our friends with something sparkling—it only seems fitting—and then we sit down to eat. As dinner ends and twilight turns to dusk, we can see people on the path below, hurrying toward the river—kids, locals with folding chairs and blankets, out-of-towners, and weekenders. It's our cue to join them. We move like a current, everyone on foot, down the middle of the streets and along the sidewalks toward the river.

The show begins. The fireworks burst above us. The river reflects the entire spectacle, and the heart-stopping booms reverberate through the valley. The crowd is delighted! Fifteen minutes later, the fireworks are over, and everyone is clapping and laughing. Everyone is happy.

CANAL HOUSE CRAB LOUIS
serves 4

We fall into a ritual each time we fly out to San Francisco. The plane lands on the West Coast at lunchtime and we're usually starving to death upon arrival. Before we drop our bags or do anything else, we head straight to the city and grab lunch. It always starts off the same way, whether we eat out or at a friend's place. The lunch begins with us quaffing a glass of delicious, crisp, cold California Chablis. Then we tuck into a Crab Louis of sorts: a mound of sweet, pristine Dungeness crabmeat fresh from the Pacific waters, accompanied by pink-hued mayonnaise, and slices of chewy San Francisco sourdough. Nothing says we've arrived like this lunch does. Back on the East Coast, we use fresh jumbo lump meat from blue crabs hauled in from the nearby Maryland coast to make this salad, and we serve it with icy cold Chablis—from *France*.

FOR THE DRESSING
1 cup mayonnaise
2 tablespoons ketchup
½ teaspoon harissa
2 dashes Worcestershire sauce
Juice of ½ lemon, or to taste
6 cornichons, finely chopped
4 scallions, finely chopped

FOR THE SALAD
1 pound Dungeness or other lump
   crabmeat, picked over
Juice of ½ lemon
1 head iceberg lettuce, cored and halved
4 hard-boiled eggs, halved
Handful green olives, pitted
Small handful chopped fresh chives
1 lemon, quartered

For the dressing, stir together the mayonnaise, ketchup, harissa, Worcestershire, lemon juice, cornichons, and scallions in a medium bowl. Adjust the seasonings.

{ July 2nd, 84°
sunny

For the salad, gently toss the crabmeat with the lemon juice, taking care not to break up the lumps. Divide the lettuce leaves between 4 chilled salad plates and carefully spoon a quarter of the crab salad on top of the lettuce on each plate. Spoon some of the dressing over the crab. Garnish each salad with a hard-boiled egg, some olives, a sprinkling of chives, and a wedge of lemon.

STRING BEANS VINAIGRETTE WITH FRENCH FETA

Any variety of feta suits these beans, but we like the creamy mildness of a French feta.

{ July 3rd, 85°
hazy & humid

Mash together 1 chopped clove garlic and some coarse salt and pepper in the bottom of a large bowl. Stir in 1 teaspoon Dijon mustard and 1 tablespoon red wine vinegar, then stir in ¼ cup extra-virgin olive oil. Add 1 pound cooked string beans at room temperature and toss well. Adjust seasonings. Serve the beans on a platter with 6–8 ounces sliced French feta. Garnish everything with a big handful of chopped fresh chives, parsley, and mint. Drizzle with a little more olive oil. — *serves 4*

HOISIN-FUL SPARERIBS FOR THE FOURTH OF JULY
serves 4–6

Even though baby back or county-style ribs look meatier, we prefer pork spareribs for their succulent finger-lickin' goodness. If you don't have the time to babysit these ribs, cook them in the oven, then just finish them off on the grill to add a little smoky perfume.

FOR THE HOISIN-FUL SAUCE
2 cups hoisin sauce
¾ cup bourbon
2 cloves garlic, smashed

FOR THE RIBS
6 pounds pork spareribs
Salt and pepper

July 4th, 91°
hot & sunny

For the hoi-sinful sauce, mix the hoisin sauce, bourbon, and garlic together in a bowl. Set aside and allow the flavors to develop. Fish out the garlic cloves and discard.

For the ribs, remove the membrane on the underside of the ribs by loosening it first with a knife on one edge then by pulling it off diagonally with a pair of pliers. It may come off in pieces, that's fine. (Or ask your butcher to do this for you.) Rub the ribs with lots of salt and pepper, then paint all over with some of the Hoisin-ful Sauce. Cover the ribs and let them marinate in the refrigerator overnight.

Preheat the oven to 275°. Put the ribs on a baking sheet lined with foil and cook until the meat is tender, 2–3 hours. Brush the ribs with sauce every now and then.

To finish the ribs in the oven, continue to cook them for another 30 minutes, brushing the ribs with the sauce every 5 minutes. The ribs will develop a lacquered glaze.

To finish the ribs on the grill, preheat a grill. If using a charcoal grill, build a small charcoal fire to one side. If using a gas grill, fire up the "back burner" to a medium heat. You want heat and smoke but not direct flame which can cause the sugary glaze on the ribs to burn. Put the ribs on the grill away from the fire. Cover with the lid. Stay near the grill to manage any flare-ups. Cook the ribs for 30 minutes, brushing them with sauce every 10 minutes. Let the meat rest for 15 minutes, then cut between the bones into ribs, and serve.

OLD-FASHIONED LAYERED POTATO SALAD

To keep the flavors of this classic potato salad from becoming confused, we assemble it in layers. It still tastes familiar and delicious.

To assemble the salad, layer sliced warm potatoes, salt and pepper, a nice drizzle of really good extra-virgin olive oil, some mayonnaise, finely chopped celery, sliced hard-boiled eggs, chopped scallions or minced red onions, and a little crispy bacon in a large shallow bowl or a platter; repeat the layers. Make it as decadent as you wish. —— *make as much as you want*

POTATO SALAD "BUTTERED" & LEMONED
serves 6

Preserved lemons are a big part of our cooking. Every winter we take advantage of Meyer lemon season, buying them at our local market and receiving them from our friends in California, who pick them from the trees in their backyards and mail us boxes filled with these sweet lemons. We make big jarfuls of preserved lemons (see page 294) to last us throughout the year. During the summer, we use the salty, supple rinds to add a rich, deep lemon flavor to everything from grilled fish to vinaigrettes to potato salads like this one.

2–3 pounds potatoes, any variety will do

Salt

1 cup mayonnaise, or more

2–3 tablespoons sour cream

½ cup really good extra-virgin olive oil

Pepper

Rind from 1 preserved lemon, chopped

Small handful chopped fresh chives or parsley leaves

Peel the potatoes if you use a thick-skinned variety or if you simply prefer peeled potatoes for this dish. Put the potatoes in a large pot of generously salted cold water. Bring to a boil over medium-high heat and cook until they are tender, about 20 minutes. Drain and set aside until they are cool enough to handle.

Mix together the mayonnaise and sour cream in a small bowl. Slice the potatoes and arrange them on a serving platter, "buttering" one side of each potato slice with some of the mayonnaise as you work. Drizzle the potatoes with the olive oil, season them with salt and pepper, and scatter the preserved lemons and chives or parsley on top.

COOL CUCUMBER & MINT SALAD WITH SICHUAN PEPPER

Sichuan pepper doesn't add heat to this cool, crisp salad, but rather a mild lemony flavor, and it produces a tingly, numbing sensation on the tongue—it's a flavor we love. Look for the spice in Asian markets or through mail-order sources.

Toast 1 large pinch Sichuan peppercorns in a small skillet over medium-low heat until fragrant, 1–2 minutes, then crush in a mortar and pestle with a pinch of salt. Set aside. Stir together 1 finely grated clove garlic and 1 finely grated small piece peeled fresh ginger in a medium bowl. Stir in 1 teaspoon sugar, the crushed Sichuan pepper, 3 tablespoons rice wine vinegar, then 3 tablespoons vegetable oil. Season with salt. Add 6–8 mini or 1 large sliced Asian cucumber. Chop 1 large handful fresh mint leaves and 1 small bunch fresh chives and add to the bowl. Toss well. Refrigerate for at least 15 minutes and up to 2 hours before serving. Adjust the seasonings. —— *serves 4–6*

Overleaf: clockwise from top right, Cool Cucumber & Mint Salad with Sichuan Pepper, Hoisin-ful Spareribs for the Fourth of July, Potato Salad "Buttered" & Lemoned, Old-Fashioned Layered Potato Salad, and Thick & Chewy Brownies

THICK & CHEWY BROWNIES
makes 16

Heating the butter and sugar together gives these brownies their distinctive taste and look—rich and fudgy, with a shiny, tissue-thin top crust. The perfect kind of brownie.

12 tablespoons (1½ sticks) butter, plus some for greasing the pan

1 cup all-purpose flour, plus more

2 cups sugar

4 ounces semisweet chocolate, chopped

2 ounces unsweetened chocolate, chopped

1 teaspoon instant espresso powder

¼ teaspoon salt

4 large eggs

2 teaspoons vanilla extract

1 cup chopped walnuts, optional

Preheat the oven to 350°. Grease a 9-inch square baking pan with 1 tablespoon butter, then dust it with flour, tapping out any excess. Melt the butter in a medium saucepan over medium heat. Add the sugar, stirring until it has the consistency of very soft slush and just begins to bubble around the edges, 1–2 minutes. Remove the pan from the heat, add both chocolates, the espresso, and the salt, stirring until the chocolate melts and the mixture is smooth.

Put the eggs in a large mixing bowl and beat with an mixer on medium speed. Gradually add the warm chocolate mixture, about ¼ cup at a time, beating constantly until smooth. Stir in the vanilla. Add the flour and walnuts, if using, stirring until just combined. Pour the batter into the prepared pan. Bake the brownies until a toothpick inserted into the center comes out clean, 45–60 minutes. Let the brownies cool in the pan on a rack, then cut into squares.

ROASTED RED PEPPER & TOMATO GAZPACHO
serves 4

Charring the skins of the peppers adds a subtle smokiness to this cold soup. If you fire up the grill to roast them, throw the tomatoes on too to blister the skins, then peel them.

2 red bell peppers
8–10 ripe plum tomatoes
2 cloves garlic
2 tablespoons sherry or red wine vinegar
¼ teaspoon pimentón piquante (hot)

3 tablespoons really good extra-virgin olive oil, plus more for drizzling
Salt and pepper
2 hard-boiled eggs, chopped
Garlicky croutons

Char the skins of the peppers either on a grill over hot coals, over an open flame on top of the burner plate of a gas stove, or on a sheet pan in a 500° oven. Turn them as they blister and blacken all over. When they have blackened, put them into a plastic bag and close it tightly. Set the peppers aside to "steam" for about 15 minutes. Slip off their skins. Pull off the stems, tear the peppers in half, and remove the cores and seeds. Don't wash the peppers; a few flecks of black left on the peppers will add flavor to the soup.

Drop the tomatoes in a pot of boiling water over high heat and cook for 1 minute. Drain the tomatoes in a colander. When they are cool enough to handle, slip off their skins.

Purée the tomatoes, peppers, and garlic in a food processor or a blender until smooth. Transfer to a large bowl. Add the vinegar, pimentón, olive oil, and salt and pepper to taste. Serve the soup chilled, garnished with eggs, croutons, and a drizzle of olive oil.

July 6th, 88°
big puffy clouds

CHILLED CORN SOUP
serves 4–6

Use sweet white or bi-color corn, picked the day you plan to make this soup, to get the sweetest and milkiest corn flavors.

10 ears sweet corn, shucked
1 large russet potato, peeled and diced
2 bunches scallions, chopped
6 cups whole milk

¼ teaspoon red pepper flakes
Salt and pepper
Sour cream
6–8 fresh chives, snipped

July 7th, 92°
hot & still

Cut the corn kernels off the cobs into a large pot, scraping the cobs to release all the milky juice. Break each cob in two or three pieces. Put all the cobs into the pot along with the potatoes, scallions, and milk. Season with the red pepper flakes and salt and pepper. Bring to a simmer over medium heat. Reduce the heat to low, cover, and simmer for 30 minutes.

Remove and discard the cobs. Purée the soup in a blender or a food processor until very smooth, then strain it through a fine-mesh sieve into a bowl. Season with salt and pepper.

Cover and refrigerate the soup until it is cold. Serve it in chilled soup bowls garnished with a dollop of sour cream and some chives.

COLD AVOCADO & CUCUMBER SOUP

The recipe for this velvety cold soup is a hand-me-down, passed along from a West Coast friend to an East Coast friend, then on to us. The impulse is to share a good thing. And now it's our turn to pass this delicious, simple recipe—a real keeper—on to you.

July 8th, 98°
a scorcher

Working in two batches to avoid overcrowding the blender, put 3 ripe, unblemished, pitted and peeled Hass avocados, 1 cut-up unpeeled cucumber, 2 cloves garlic, 3 tablespoons fresh lemon juice, and 4 cups chicken stock into a blender and purée until smooth. Season with salt. Refrigerate the soup until it is well chilled. Serve it in pretty glasses or chilled bowls garnished with a dollop of sour cream and a dash of hot pepper sauce. We suggest you make this soup the same day you plan to serve it so it retains its pretty pale green color. — *serves 4*

TOMATOES WITH TONNATO SAUCE
serves 4–6

We love this sauce so much we spoon it on everything—boiled potatoes, grilled chicken, steamed summer vegetables hot or cold—but our very favorite is this beautiful ode to tomato season.

FOR THE TONNATO SAUCE
2 large egg yolks
Salt
Juice of ½ lemon
½ cup canola oil
½ cup really good "smooth and buttery" extra-virgin olive oil
1 small can tuna packed in olive oil (about 2 ounces)
3 anchovy filets

1 tablespoon capers
1 clove garlic
Pepper

FOR THE TOMATOES
2 pounds tomatoes of various types and sizes, sliced or halved
Small handful arugula leaves
Salt and pepper
Really good extra-virgin olive oil

For the tonnato sauce, whisk together the egg yolks, a pinch of salt, and half of the lemon juice in a medium bowl. Combine both the oils in a measuring cup with a spout.

{ July 11th, 90° gentle breeze

Whisking constantly, add the oil to the yolks, about 1 teaspoon at a time. The sauce will thicken and emulsify. After you've added about ¼ cup of the oil, you can begin to slowly drizzle in the remaining oil as you continue to whisk, until you have a thick, glossy mayonnaise. Transfer the sauce to a medium bowl.

Purée the tuna, anchovies, capers, and garlic in a food processor until smooth. Add a little olive oil to help the process. Use a rubber spatula to press the puréed tuna through a sieve into the mayonnaise in the bowl. Season to taste with the remaining lemon juice, and salt and pepper. Transfer the sauce to a covered container and refrigerate until ready to use. The tonnato sauce will keep for up to 1 week in the refrigerator.

For the tomatoes, spoon some of the tonnato sauce onto individual plates or a platter and arrange the tomatoes on top. Spoon more sauce over the tomatoes and scatter the arugula leaves on top. Season with salt and pepper and a drizzle of olive oil.

THE FRY QUEEN'S FRIED CHICKEN
serves 4

Our friend and reigning Fry Queen, Julia Lee, cuts her chicken up into pieces that are fairly uniform in size so they can cook evenly—without burning the outside crust before the chicken is done. She brines the chicken pieces first to keep the meat moist and tender, a step we always do when time permits. And the final trick to crispier fried chicken is to drain the pieces on a wire rack.

1 whole chicken	1½ cups flour
1 cup kosher salt, plus more	1 teaspoon baking powder
for seasoning	½ teaspoon pepper
½ cup sugar	Canola oil

July 12th, 81°
perfect summer day

Cut the chicken, separating the thighs, drumsticks, and wings. Cut each breast in half. There will be 10 pieces. Set them aside.

Put the salt, sugar, and 4 cups of cold water in a large bowl and stir until completely dissolved. Put the chicken pieces into the brine and transfer to the refrigerator to let them soak for 2 hours. Drain, rinse, and pat the chicken pieces dry with paper towels.

Whisk together the flour, baking powder, ½ teaspoon salt, and the pepper in a large bowl. Dredge the chicken in the seasoned flour one piece at a time, making sure each piece is well coated. For an extra crunchy coating, double dip the chicken: Dredge the pieces, then dredge them again 10 minutes or so later.

Pour enough oil into a large cast-iron skillet to reach a depth of 2 inches. Heat the oil over medium heat until it registers 350° on a candy thermometer, or dip a wooden chopstick into the hot oil until the tip touches the bottom of the skillet; if bubbles form right away around the tip—lots of bubbles, like Champagne—the oil is ready for frying.

Fry the chicken in the hot oil, larger pieces first, skin side down, working in batches if all the pieces don't fit at the same time. Turn once, and fry until golden and crispy, about 8 minutes per side. Transfer the fried chicken to a wire rack set on top of paper towels to drain. Season to taste with salt while still hot.

COMPOSED SUMMER SALAD WITH LEMONY AÏOLI

serves 4–6

This is the kind of salad that comes together very quickly when you have the vegetables done and ready to go (we often have them cooked and on hand, exactly for this purpose). We keep a small tub of the aïoli in our fridge as well, but for an acceptable substitute, you could doctor store-bought mayonnaise with some finely minced garlic, lots of fresh lemon juice, and some salt and pepper.

FOR THE LEMONY AÏOLI
2 large egg yolks
1 clove garlic, finely minced
Salt
Juice of 1 lemon
½ cup canola oil
½ cup good smooth "buttery" olive oil

FOR THE SALAD
4–6 peeled roasted baby beets, quartered
8–10 ounces cooked string beans
4–8 small peeled boiled potatoes
4–6 hard-boiled eggs, halved
Really good extra-virgin olive oil
Plenty of finely chopped fresh parsley
Salt and pepper

July 14th, 80°
vive la France!

For the lemony aïoli, whisk together the egg yolks, garlic, a pinch of salt, and one-quarter of the lemon juice in a medium bowl. Combine both the oils in a measuring cup with a spout.

Whisking constantly, add the oil to the yolks, about 1 teaspoon at a time. The sauce will thicken and emulsify. After you've added about ¼ cup of the oil, you can begin to slowly drizzle in the remaining oil as you continue to whisk, until you have a thick, glossy aïoli. Season with salt. Thin the aïoli with a little water and more lemon juice to taste. Transfer to a serving bowl. Cover and refrigerate until ready to use.

For the salad, arrange the beets, string beans, potatoes, and hard-boiled eggs on a nice big serving platter. Drizzle everything with some olive oil and sprinkle with the parsley. Season with salt and pepper. Garnish with some nasturtium blossoms, if you like. Serve with the aïoli.

SUGARED BERRIES WITH CRÈME ANGLAISE

We serve this sweetened custard sauce warm in the winter spooned over compotes of dried fruit. In the summer, when berries are sweet and juicy, we serve it chilled like this.

July 21st, 99°
in the shade

Put 2 cups whole milk, 3 tablespoons sugar, and 1 teaspoon vanilla bean paste or 1 vanilla bean, split lengthwise, in a heavy medium saucepan. Heat the milk over medium-low heat, stirring often, until warm and the sugar dissolves. Whisk 4 large egg yolks in a medium bowl until thick and pale yellow. Gradually add half the warm milk to the yolks, whisking constantly. Stir the yolk mixture into the warm milk in the pan and cook, stirring constantly, until it's the consistency of thick heavy cream, about 15 minutes. Strain the custard through a fine-mesh sieve into a medium bowl and add the vanilla bean, if using. Set the bowl into a larger bowl filled with ice, then stir the custard frequently until it has cooled off. Cover the custard and refrigerate until ready to use. It will thicken as it chills. (Discard the vanilla bean.) Toss fresh berries with some sugar and a splash of kirsch or vanilla extract in a bowl and let macerate briefly. Serve the crème anglaise in dessert dishes with the berries. —— *makes 2 cups sauce*

CLASSIC TUILES
makes 2–3 dozen

These delicate curved cookies are named for the terra-cotta roof tiles seen throughout the south of France. It takes a little practice to master lifting them off the parchment paper once they are baked, but don't be discouraged. They are such elegant cookies and fun to make. However, we avoid making them on a humid day. They will not stay crisp.

2 egg whites, at room temperature
Pinch of salt
6 tablespoons sugar
¼ teaspoon vanilla extract
¼ teaspoon almond extract

½ cup sifted cake flour
5 tablespoons very soft (but not melted) unsalted butter
½ cup sliced blanched almonds

July 25th, 81°
no humidity

Preheat the oven to 350°. Line several cookie sheets with parchment paper and set aside. Set out a rolling pin to drape the warm cookies over when they come out of the oven.

Whisk together the egg whites, salt, sugar, and the vanilla and almond extracts in a medium mixing bowl until very frothy. Whisk in the flour in thirds. Whisk in the butter a few tablespoons at a time, until the batter is smooth and opaque.

Drop the batter by the tablespoonful onto the prepared cookie sheets, spaced at least 3 inches apart, and use the back of the spoon in a circular motion to spread the batter out to about a 4-inch round. The batter will look very thin and not necessarily even, but don't worry; the cookies will come out fine. Scatter some almonds over the rounds.

continued on page 118

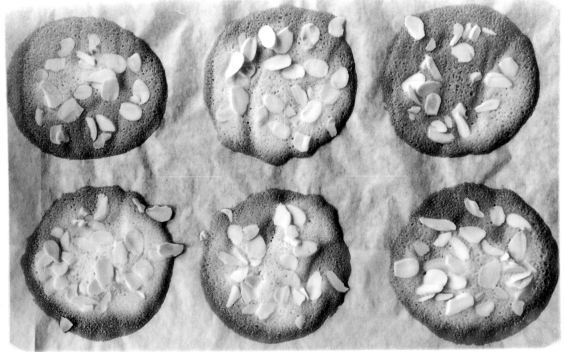

Bake the cookies one sheet at a time until very pale golden brown in the center and deeper brown around the edges, 8–10 minutes. Remove from the oven. Working quickly while the cookies are still hot, use a thin metal spatula to lift each off the parchment paper, then drape it over the rolling pin, gently bending it with your hand to form a curve. Rewarm the cookies in the oven briefly if they have cooled too much and are no longer pliable. Transfer the shaped cookies to wire racks to finish cooling completely.

POACHED WHITE PEACHES IN LEMON VERBENA SYRUP
serves 4–8

Every spring we comb our local nurseries for lemon verbena to plant in tubs on the Canal House balcony and in our gardens. Most summers the plants thrive, growing tall and bushy. We snip off their branches throughout the warm months to make lemon-scented iced tea, simple syrup, crème anglaise, and nice, cool gin and tonics. In the fall, we yank the whole plants out of the dirt and hang them upside down in a dry place. As the leaves lose moisture, they curl and fade to dusty green, but their fragrance remains. We strip off the leaves and put them into clear cellophane bags to give as gifts throughout the cold months, for brewing hot tea, and as a reminder of the taste of summer.

1 cup sugar
1 handful fresh lemon verbena leaves

4 ripe white peaches

July 26th, 86°
beautiful evening

For the lemon verbena syrup, put the sugar and 1 cup water into a heavy medium saucepan. Heat over medium-low heat, gently swirling the pan to help dissolve the sugar. When the syrup comes to a boil, cover the pan to let the steam wash away and dissolve any sugar granules still on the side of the pan, and cook for 2–3 minutes. Remove the pan from the heat. Uncover the pan and add the verbena leaves. Cover and let the syrup steep.

Blanch the peaches in a pot of gently boiling water over medium heat for 15–30 seconds to loosen the skin from the flesh. Lift the peaches out of the water with a slotted spoon. Slip off their skins and put the skins into the syrup in the saucepan. Cover and set aside to let steep for at least 15 minutes. The syrup will turn a pretty pink.

Slice the peaches in half and pull out and discard the pit. Put the peaches cut side down in a deep dish in a single layer. Strain the syrup over them (it's fine if the syrup is still warm; it will bring out more of the fruit's perfume), and add a few of the verbena leaves to the dish. Let the peaches rest in the syrup for at least 30 minutes, turning them once or twice before serving. Covered, they will keep in the refrigerator for up to 2 days.

BELLINI

We've had the privilege of sipping this classic cocktail at Harry's Bar in Venice (where this famous Italian sparkler was born), a moment that lives on fondly in our memories. During white peach season in the Northeast, we stock up on Prosecco, and make batches of white peach purée to recreate that delicious experience. It works every time.

Purée 4 peach halves from Poached White Peaches in Lemon Verbena Syrup (page 118) in a blender until smooth. Thin the peach purée with about ½ cup lemon verbena syrup (page 118). Refrigerate the purée until well chilled. For each drink, pour about ¼ cup cold white peach purée into a chilled champagne flute. Top it off with chilled Prosecco, stirring as you pour. —— *makes about 6*

July 27th, 86°
a fine calm day

LEMONADE

The lemon-infused simple syrup that sweetens this refreshing summertime classic can be stored in the refrigerator indefinitely—so make a jarful of it to have at the ready for making lemonade, or lemon soda: Add some to a tall glass filled with ice cubes, then top it off with cold sparkling water.

Put 1 cup sugar and ½ cup water into a heavy medium saucepan. Heat over medium-low heat, gently swirling the pan to help dissolve the sugar. When the syrup comes to a boil, cover the pan to let the steam wash away and dissolve any sugar granules still on the side of the pan, and cook for 2–3 minutes. Peel the thin yellow zest from 1 washed lemon (preferably a Meyer lemon) and add it to the hot syrup. Let the syrup steep and cool to room temperature. Juice enough lemons to measure 2 cups fresh juice (10–12 lemons, preferably Meyer lemons). Put the lemon juice into a tall pitcher. Strain the cooled syrup into the pitcher and add 4 cups cold spring water. Serve the lemonade in tall glasses filled with ice cubes. Garnish each glass with big sprigs of fresh mint or lemon verbena. —— *makes 6 cups*

July 28th, 93°
muggy

❧ August Recipes ❧

tomatoes all dressed up for summer ∼ 127

the splendid summer tomato sandwich ∼ 127

tomato "rollmops" ∼ 127

cold white corn soup with lobster & avocado ∼ 128

hot spaghetti tossed with raw tomato sauce ∼ 128

tomatoes take a warm oil bath ∼ 130

sliced tomatoes with arugula ∼ 130

roast beef sandwich with avocado & tomato ∼ 130

whole beef tenderloin, peppered & grilled ∼ 134

two steaks feed four ∼ 134

compound butters: fresh herb butter, lemon butter,
fresh horseradish butter, pimentón butter ∼ 135

caponata ∼ 136

grilled salmon ∼ 139

chilled potato & celery soup ∼ 140

cold carrot soup ∼ 140

fritto misto ∼ 143

sautéed zucchini with scallions & fresh mozzarella ∼ 144

olive oil–poached zucchini & raw tomatoes ∼ 144

tisane of fresh or dried lemon verbena ∼ 146

simple syrup ∼ 147

melon water ∼ 147

strong coffee granita ∼ 148

pink lemon granita ∼ 148

It was time to pick the last tomato. It had grown so beautifully, and for eighty-five days, but now we were playing against the odds. Something might get it—a worm, a bug, or a fungus. Or a storm might blow up suddenly and knock it off its impossibly slender vine.

We both have big gardens at our homes. But we spend so much time at Canal House that we plant up the window boxes with herbs and strawberries and fill the narrow balcony with pots for growing tomatoes up trellises. This satisfies our agrarian urges. A friend, an avid gardener herself, knows of our planting passion. She arrived on a late spring day carrying four trembling, heirloom ox heart tomato plants that she'd found at a Pennsylvania country garden sale. We planted them up against a trellis amidst the parsley and chives—it seemed like they'd be good potmates.

They grew, reaching up to catch the rays of sun that flood our southwest-facing balcony all afternoon. The growing conditions weren't ideal; the plants only produced six tomatoes, and one of those was out of our reach. Looking up at our balcony from the towpath below, you could see—and almost, but not quite, pluck—a tomato that hung from a vine that had escaped its staking and flopped down through the wrought-iron balusters. It reminded us of the Aesop's fable "The Fox and the Grapes". Passersby tried to grab it; they jumped, or balanced on the pedals of their bikes to gain a little more height, and we even saw a young mother hoist her child up on her shoulders, but the tomato was always elusive. It hung there until the birds had their fill of it.

As for the other five tomatoes, they were mammoth, deep red, heart-shaped fruit. We had shown proper respect for such works of art, ceremoniously picking them as they ripened, and now we were down to the last one. It was perfectly ripe, so we picked it. We passed it back and forth to each other. To hold that warm living fruit in the palm of our hands we could almost feel it beat. It must have weighed close to a pound.

Then we peeled it. We ran a paring knife over the outside of the tomato to loosen the skin from the flesh, and peeled the skin off in thin sheets, in clean, smooth motions, leaving all the luscious meaty fruit. We ate it simply—no need to gussy up a natural beauty—with a drizzle of really good extra-virgin olive oil, a sprinkle of flaky Maldon salt, freshly ground Tellicherry pepper, a spoonful of mayonnaise, and a sprinkle of fresh chives.

TOMATOES ALL DRESSED UP FOR SUMMER
serves 4–6

The private pleasure of eating a tomato sandwich over the sink with the juices dripping through our fingers and down our chins is one of our constant summer rituals. These tomatoes are so sensual that they should probably be eaten behind closed doors.

8–12 slices crusty bread
1 clove garlic, peeled
½ cup really good extra-virgin olive oil
Salt
4–6 tomatoes, cored and thickly sliced

½ cup mayonnaise
Pepper
Small handful fresh chives, chopped
Small handful fresh parsley leaves, chopped

Toast the bread. While the toast is still warm, rub each slice with garlic, rubbing more or less firmly depending on how much flavor you're after. Drizzle the toast with some of the olive oil and sprinkle with salt.

Slather the tomato slices with mayonnaise and arrange them on a serving platter. Drizzle the remaining oil over them, season well with salt and pepper, and scatter the fresh herbs on top. You can make open-faced tomato sandwiches or just serve the toasts on the side.

August 1st, 97°
hot gusty winds

THE SPLENDID SUMMER TOMATO SANDWICH

Choose a dead-ripe meaty tomato (such as a big beefsteak), preferably just picked and still warm from a sunny garden. Using a very sharp thin-bladed knife, peel the skin from the flesh, then slice the tomato horizontally into thick rounds and arrange them on a large plate. Sprinkle with a good flaky salt, a tiny pinch of sugar, and coarsely ground black pepper. Toast 2 slices of good white bread. Spread butter on the warm toast, then slather with mayonnaise. Pile the tomatoes on one slice, then top with the other. It is a very good idea to wear a bathing suit when eating this sandwich. —— *makes 1*

August 3rd, 85°
welcome rain

TOMATO "ROLLMOPS"

Halve ripe plum tomatoes lengthwise and remove the seeds, leaving just the meaty shells. Drizzle really good extra-virgin olive oil into the shells, give a few grinds of pepper, and place ½ anchovy filet and 1 basil leaf into each one. Stack the filled tomatoes in a container with a lid and add enough olive oil to cover the tomatoes completely. Refrigerate and use in salads, on toasts, or with pasta. They will keep for a week. We prize the deliciously flavored oil and use it with everything. —— *makes as many as you like*

August 4th, 81°
more rain

COLD WHITE CORN SOUP WITH LOBSTER & AVOCADO
serves 4

In midsummer, corncobs are so large and full that you may need to use fewer ears of corn. Most fish stores will be happy to spare you the hassle and steam the lobster for you.

8 ears white corn, shucked
6 cups whole milk
½ teaspoon red pepper flakes
Salt and pepper
2 Hass avocados, pitted, peeled, and cubed

Meat from 1 cooked lobster,
    cut into large pieces
1 thin-skinned lime, quartered
Chopped scallions

August 5th, 86°
scattered showers

Cut the corn kernels off the cobs into a large pot, scraping the cobs well to release all the milky juice. Break each cob in two or three pieces and add to the pot along with the milk. Add the red pepper flakes and season with salt and pepper. Bring to a simmer over medium heat. Adjust the heat to maintain a very low simmer, cover, and cook for 30 minutes.

Using tongs, remove and discard the cobs. Purée the soup in a food processor, then strain it through a fine-mesh sieve into a large container with a lid. Season with salt and pepper, then refrigerate the soup until cold.

Pour the soup into individual chilled bowls. Garnish, dividing the avocado and lobster between the bowls. Serve with a squeeze of lime and lots of chopped scallions.

HOT SPAGHETTI TOSSED WITH RAW TOMATO SAUCE
serves 4–6

Use the juiciest, sweetest summer tomatoes you can find for this light, fresh sauce. (Maybe you have a garden full of them? It's everyone's dream.)

1½–2 pounds ripe tomatoes, halved
1–2 cloves garlic, finely minced
½ cup *passato di pomodoro,* or strained
    tomatoes

4–6 tablespoons really good extra-virgin
    olive oil, plus more for drizzling
Salt and pepper
1 pound spaghetti
Freshly grated parmigiano-reggiano

August 9th, 82°
afternoon storm

Grate the fleshy sides of the tomatoes on the large holes of a box grater into a big bowl. Discard the skins. Add the garlic, *passato,* and olive oil, and season with salt and pepper.

Cook the spaghetti in a large pot of salted boiling water over high heat until just cooked through, about 12 minutes. Drain. Toss the pasta with the sauce. Drizzle with olive oil and season with salt and pepper. Serve with lots of freshly grated parmigiano-reggiano, and basil leaves, if you like.

TOMATOES TAKE A WARM OIL BATH

These tomatoes, just barely warmed through in a fragrant bath of olive oil, are about as sensuous as it gets. We use really big, ripe, fleshy tomatoes and treat each one like a piece of meat, carving off thick slabs and serving them with a spoonful of olive oil before moving on to slicing the next. We like to infuse the oil with the flavor of fresh basil. Rosemary or thyme are good too. Though these tomatoes can be prepared on top of the stove, we often make them in a paella pan outside over an open fire so they catch a little smoke.

August 10th, 85°
hot soupy day

Pour good extra-virgin olive oil in a deep, wide, heatproof pan to a depth of about 1 inch. Add several whole branches fresh basil and 3–5 crushed garlic cloves. Gently warm the oil over low heat until it is fragrant but not too hot. Add large ripe whole tomatoes stem side down in the pan. Don't crowd the tomatoes. Baste them in the oil for a few minutes. Remove the pan from the heat. Slice the tomatoes into thick slabs, serving them as you carve. Spoon some oil over each slice and season with salt. Serve with good crusty bread to sop up more of the fragrant oil from the pan. —— *makes as many as you like*

SLICED TOMATOES WITH ARUGULA

Peppery wild arugula and sweet summer tomatoes are a perfect pairing. So we dress this salad simply. Why mess with Mother Nature's perfection?

August 11th, 79°
cool & breezy

Slice as many dead-ripe tomatoes as you can eat and arrange on a platter. Scatter a handful wild arugula over the tomatoes, then drizzle with plenty of really good extra-virgin olive oil. Sprinkle with flaky sea salt, such as Maldon, and freshly cracked black pepper. —— *serves as many as you like*

ROAST BEEF SANDWICH WITH AVOCADO & TOMATO

We also make this sandwich with leftover grilled steak, or even cold roast chicken. The horseradish mayonnaise adds a little heat and zing.

August 12th, 80°
picnic weather

Stir together a dollop of mayonnaise with a small spoonful freshly grated or prepared horseradish, a squeeze of fresh lemon juice, and plenty of freshly cracked black pepper in a small bowl. Taste and adjust the seasonings. Cut a ciabatta roll in half and butter both halves with the horseradish mayonnaise. Lay a few slices roast beef over the bottom half, then top with a few slices ripe, buttery avocado, and a thick, juicy slice of ripe tomato. Season everything with coarse salt and pepper. —— *serves 1*

WHOLE BEEF TENDERLOIN, PEPPERED & GRILLED
serves 12

For those of us who enjoy a good piece of chewy, on-the-bone, grilled steak, a filet seems kind of wimpy—the meat is so lean and mild. But it's these very qualities and its supreme tenderness that make it the perfect choice for grilling whole and serving either warm or cold.

FOR THE BEEF
1 whole beef tenderloin, 6–7 pounds
¼ cup coarsely ground black pepper
Salt

FOR THE SALAD
6–8 anchovy filets, finely chopped
Salt and pepper

Juice of 1 lemon
4–6 tablespoons really good
  extra-virgin olive oil
1 bunch arugula, torn in pieces
1 small head Bibb lettuce, torn in pieces
Handful fresh parsley leaves, chopped
Handful celery leaves, chopped
Handful fresh tarragon leaves, chopped

*August 15th, 87°
hot & sunny*

For the beef, using a sharp knife, trim off any fat from the tenderloin. Slide the blade under the long sinewy silver skin, trimming it off. Fold under about 6 inches of the thin end of the meat. This should be about as thick as the rest of the filet so it will cook evenly. Tie into a neat package with kitchen string. Rub with the pepper, pressing it into the meat, and season with salt.

Prepare a medium-hot hardwood charcoal fire or heat a gas grill. Grill the filet over the hottest part of the grill, turning it as a good brown crust develops. When the meat is browned all over, move it to a cooler spot on the grill to finish cooking, turning occasionally, until the internal temperature reaches 120° for rare and 130° for medium-rare. The grilling time will vary depending on your grill and the heat. Start checking the internal temperature after 20 minutes. Take the meat off the grill and let it rest for 15 minutes. Serve warm or let it cool, then wrap and refrigerate it for up to 3 days before serving it cold and sliced.

For the salad, mash together the anchovies with pinches of salt and pepper in the bottom of a salad bowl. Whisk in the lemon juice, then the olive oil. Pile the greens and herbs into the bowl and toss when you are ready to serve with the grilled filet.

TWO STEAKS FEED FOUR

Prepare a hot charcoal or gas grill. Meanwhile, take 2 ribeye steaks on the bone, 2–3 inches thick, and tie each into a nice neat package with kitchen string, so the meat cooks evenly and doesn't pull away from the bone. Generously season both sides of the steaks with salt and pepper.

continued

Grill the steaks over the hottest section of coals until a good browned crust has developed on the first side, about 8 minutes. To ensure a good crust, resist the urge to move or fiddle with the steaks while they are cooking, but if flare-ups threaten to burn the meat, you've got to move it to a cooler spot on the grill. Turn the steaks and grill the second side for 5 minutes.

Move the steaks to a cooler spot on the grill to finish cooking them, turning occasionally, until the internal temperatures reach 120° for rare, 130° for medium-rare, and 140° for medium, 5–15 minutes depending on the thickness of the steaks and the desired doneness. Pull the steaks off the grill and let them rest for 10–15 minutes. Cut the steak from the bone and slice the meat. Serve both the bones and the meat—you will be fighting over the bones! — *serves 4*

COMPOUND BUTTERS
makes 1 cup

We use salted Irish butter because it makes everything taste better. You can make the compound butter ahead of time, cover it up, and keep it in the fridge for 3–4 days, or freeze it and use it within a month.

FRESH HERB BUTTER

Beat ½ pound (2 sticks) softened salted butter in a medium bowl with a wooden spoon until smooth and creamy. Add ½ cup chopped fresh herbs (use one or a combination of your favorite herbs), 1 small finely chopped shallot or scallion, and 1 small minced garlic clove, if you like. Season with salt and pepper.

LEMON BUTTER

Beat ½ pound (2 sticks) softened salted butter in a medium bowl with a wooden spoon until smooth and creamy. Wash and dry 2 lemons, then finely grate the zest over the butter. Squeeze in the juice of ½ lemon and season with salt and pepper. Stir well to incorporate the lemon juice into the butter.

FRESH HORSERADISH BUTTER

Beat ½ pound (2 sticks) softened salted butter in a medium bowl with a wooden spoon until smooth and creamy. Add 2–3 tablespoons finely grated peeled fresh horseradish root (or 2 tablespoons drained prepared horseradish) and season generously with cracked black pepper and salt.

PIMENTÓN BUTTER

Beat ½ pound (2 sticks) softened salted butter in a medium bowl with a wooden spoon until smooth and creamy. Add 1 tablespoon pimentón, and season with salt and pepper.

Overleaf: left, Whole Beef Tenderloin, Peppered & Grilled; right, Two Steaks Feed Four with Fresh Herb Butter

CAPONATA
makes about 8 cups

We like to make this classic Sicilian eggplant antipasto on the chunky side to play up the eggplant's soft, silky texture. This caponata has big flavors and a delicious balance of sweet and sour. We make a generous batch, keep it in the fridge at the ready, and find ourselves serving it not only as an antipasto alongside sliced salumi, bruschetta, or hard-boiled eggs, but also spooned over grilled or poached fish and chicken, stirred hot or cold into pasta, and fried chicken (page 112). It keeps for up to 1 week, and the flavor improves each day.

2 large eggplants, cut into 1-inch cubes
¼ cup kosher salt
½ cup white wine vinegar
1 tablespoon sugar
¼ cup dried currants or raisins
¾ cup olive oil
3 ribs celery, cut into large dice
1 medium onion, chopped

4 anchovy filets, chopped
One 28-ounce can whole peeled plum tomatoes, quartered, and their juices
1 cup large green olives, preferably Sicilian, pitted and halved
2 tablespoons capers
1 bay leaf
Pepper

August 16th, 93° heat lightning

Toss the eggplant with the salt in a colander and let the bitter liquid drain out for about 1 hour. Meanwhile, combine the vinegar and sugar in a small bowl. Add the currants and set aside to plump.

Pat the eggplant dry with paper towels. Heat ½ cup of the oil in a heavy wide pot over medium-high heat. Working in batches, fry eggplant until browned all over, about 10 minutes. Transfer the eggplant with a slotted spatula to a bowl.

Add the remaining ¼ cup of oil, the celery, and onions to the pot. Cook over medium heat until just soft, about 10 minutes. Stir in the anchovies. Add the tomatoes with juices, the olives, capers, and bay leaf. Return the eggplant to the pot. Stir in the currants and vinegar. Simmer, stirring gently and often, until the juices thicken a bit, 10–15 minutes. Season with pepper. Refrigerate for at least 1 day and up to 1 week. Remove the bay leaf before serving.

GRILLED SALMON
serves 4–8

One of our favorite things to cook is this grilled salmon. Grilling fish can be a challenge because its fragile flesh doesn't tolerate too much handling. Our trick here is to lay a whole side of salmon on the grill skin side down. Then we don't touch it until we take it off the grill. The smoke will turn the flesh a pale golden color.

1 side salmon, scaled, and
  pin bones removed
Extra-virgin olive oil

Salt and pepper
Fresh parsley
2–3 lemons, halved

Preheat the grill. If using a charcoal grill, build the fire to one side of the grill. If using a gas grill, fire up the "back burner".

August 17th, 77°
clear starry night

Rub the salmon flesh with olive oil and season it well with salt and pepper. Lay the fish skin side down on a rimless cookie sheet. Slide the fish off the cookie sheet onto the grill away from the direct flame. Cover the grill with the lid and grill the salmon over medium-hot heat until the fish is just cooked through, about 30 minutes (or less depending on the size of salmon). To test if the fish is cooked through, slip the point of a paring knife into the center of the thickest part of the fish. Remove the knife and quickly (carefully) press it to your lower lip. If it is very warm, the fish is cooked. Slide the cookie sheet under the salmon between the flesh and skin, leaving the skin stuck to the grill. Use another cookie sheet or a very large spatula to scoot the fish onto the cookie sheet.

Slide the fish onto a fish platter, drizzle with a little more olive oil, and season with salt and pepper. Serve garnished with parsley and squeeze lemon juice over the salmon.

CHILLED POTATO & CELERY SOUP
serves 4–6

This may just be the coolest and most unusual summer soup we know. The celery adds a clean green flavor and the potato adds body and creaminess.

2 heads celery, including hearts and leaves, chopped (2 pounds; reserve a small handful of celery leaves for garnish, if you like)

1 large russet potato, peeled and chopped

1 large leek, sliced

6 cups chicken stock

Salt and pepper

Freshly whipped cream

2 tablespoons chopped fresh chives

August 23rd, 82°
tornado watch

Put the celery, potatoes, leeks, and chicken stock in a heavy large pot and bring to a boil, then reduce the heat to medium-low and cook until the vegetables are very soft, about 20 minutes. Season with salt and pepper.

Allow the soup to cool slightly. Working in small batches, purée the soup in a blender or food processor until very smooth, then pour through a fine-mesh sieve into a clean bowl. Refrigerate the soup until it is well chilled. Serve the soup garnished with a dollop of whipped cream and a sprinkling of chopped chives or finely chopped celery leaves.

COLD CARROT SOUP
serves 6

You want to be able to taste nutmeg's sweet earthy flavor here, so don't be afraid to season this soup like you mean it! The carrots and potatoes can take it.

2 pounds carrots, peeled and chopped

1 large russet potato, peeled and chopped

1 large onion, chopped

6 cups chicken stock

¼–½ whole nutmeg, finely grated

Pinch of ground cinnamon

Juice of ½ Meyer lemon

Salt and pepper

Sour cream

2 tablespoons chopped fresh chives

August 24th, 91°
marble-sized hail

Put the carrots, potatoes, onions, and chicken stock in a heavy large pot and bring to a boil over medium-high heat. Reduce heat to medium-low and cook until the vegetables are very soft, 30–40 minutes.

Working in small batches, purée the soup in a blender or food processor until silky smooth. Transfer to a bowl. Stir in the nutmeg, cinnamon, and lemon juice, and season with salt and pepper. Taste and adjust the seasonings, adding a pinch of sugar, if you like. Refrigerate the soup until chilled. Serve garnished with a spoonful of sour cream and a sprinkling of chopped chives.

FRITTO MISTO
enough batter to serve 6

A fritto misto is a mix of ingredients—from tiny fish to zucchini blossoms—that has been deep-fried. Our thin all-purpose batter is good for dredging everything from delicate parsley or sage leaves to sturdier lemon slices, mushrooms, or zucchini batons. The batter should be about the consistency of heavy cream. If it is too thick (flours differ), add a little more wine.

1 cup all-purpose flour
½ teaspoon salt
1 cup white wine

Whatever you want to fry (see below)
Canola, peanut, or corn oil
Salt

For the batter, whisk the flour and salt together in a medium bowl. Gradually add the wine, whisking until the batter is smooth. Give it a quick whisk again just before you're ready to use it.

{ August 25th, 75°
strong winds

Prepare whatever you are going to fry by cutting it into pieces of uniform shapes and sizes so that things cook at the same rate. Make sure everything is dry, as water/moisture will cause the oil to splatter.

Pour oil in a heavy skillet or wok to a depth of about 2 inches. Heat the oil to a temperature of 350° on a candy thermometer.

Dip the pieces into the batter, shake off any excess, and carefully lower into the oil. (Be careful not to burn your fingers or splatter the oil!) Fry in small batches, turning frequently for even browning. Remove the fritto misto when it is golden or a pale brown. (You'll get the hang of it as you go along.) Use a slotted spatula to lift the fritto misto out of the oil and drain on paper towels. Skim out any frying debris from the oil between batches.

Season the fritto misto with salt while it is still hot. Serve as you fry and be sure to keep some for yourself. It's the cook's job to maintain quality control!

— FOODS WE LIKE TO DIP & FRY —

Zucchini batons or blossoms, fresh sage leaves, fresh parsley sprigs, asparagus, shiitake mushroom caps, Japanese eggplant slices, lemon slices (one of our favorites), scallions, small whole okra, peeled shrimp, small pieces of fresh fish . . . you get the idea, it's whatever you want to fry!

SAUTÉED ZUCCHINI WITH SCALLIONS & FRESH MOZZARELLA
serves 2

We grow *zucchino lungo fiorentino*, an Italian fluted variety, and as soon as the first zucchini are big enough to pick, we make this dish. The still-warm vegetables slightly melt the little cubes of mozzarella.

2 tablespoons extra-virgin olive oil,
 plus more for drizzling
6 small zucchini, sliced
6 scallions, chopped

Salt and pepper
3 ounces fresh mozzarella, cut into
 small cubes
1 lemon

*August 26th, 86°
pouring rain*

Heat the olive oil in a medium skillet over medium heat. Add the zucchini and cook until they begin to brown, about 5 minutes. Using 2 forks, flip the zucchini over to brown on both sides. Add the scallions and salt and pepper to taste, and cook until the zucchini is golden and tender, 2–3 minutes. Remove from the heat and transfer the zucchini to a platter. Scatter the mozzarella on top of the hot zucchini. Squeeze the lemon over everything, and drizzle with more olive oil.

OLIVE OIL–POACHED ZUCCHINI & RAW TOMATOES
serves 4–6

Zucchini and tomatoes are quintessential summer vegetables. We have a thing for making salads with cooked and raw veggies—this is one of our favorites.

1–2 pounds small zucchini, cut into
 thick batons
2 cloves garlic, crushed
1 small dried red chile or a pinch of
 red pepper flakes

1–1½ cups really good extra-virgin olive oil
3 large ripe tomatoes
1–2 handfuls fresh basil leaves
Salt and pepper

*August 27th, 75°
windy & heavy rain*

Put the zucchini, garlic, and chile in a heavy medium saucepan, and add enough oil to cover the zucchini. Cover and poach over medium-low heat until the zucchini are tender, about 15 minutes.

While the zucchini are poaching, peel the tomatoes with a thin-bladed knife. Core and cut into generous chunks. Put in a large mixing bowl.

Use a slotted spoon to add the zucchini to the bowl. Pour in about ½ cup of the warm poaching oil. Tear the basil leaves into the bowl and season with salt and pepper. Shake the bowl to mix everything a bit. Serve at room temperature.

TISANE OF FRESH OR DRIED LEMON VERBENA

We make this infusion when fresh herbs are going gangbusters in our gardens. But we also dry the leaves to use all winter long. Clip branches of lemon verbena, tie the stems together, and slip them into a paper bag. Crimp the bag around the stem ends and tie the bag closed. Hang it in a dark, dry place for a week or so. Strip the leaves off and store them in a closed tin.

August 29th, 81°
river is flooding

Bring 4 cups spring water to a boil in a medium pot or a kettle over high heat. Put 2 large handfuls fresh lemon verbena leaves (or 2 large loose "pinches" of dried leaves) into a warmed teapot (we use a glass teapot so that we can see the pretty herbs). Pour the boiling water over the herbs, cover, and steep for 5–10 minutes. Strain and serve, or allow the tisane to cool and serve in ice-filled glasses garnished with sprigs of fresh mint. —— *serves 2–4*

SIMPLE SYRUP
makes 2 cups

We use this syrup plain, to sweeten iced tea; then we infuse it with spices, herbs, or citrus zest for drizzling over pound cake to moisten and flavor the crumb, spooning over fresh berries or sliced stone fruit, and adding to fruit purées when making sorbet. As long as you remember the formula—2 parts sugar to 1 part water—you can make as much or as little as you like.

Put 2 cups sugar and 1 cup water into a heavy saucepan. Heat over medium-low heat, gently swirling the pan to help dissolve the sugar. When the syrup comes to a boil, cover the pan to let the steam wash away and dissolve any sugar granules still on the side of the pan, and cook for 2–3 minutes. Let the syrup cool to room temperature. Store in an airtight container in the refrigerator for up to 6 months.

VARIATIONS: Add one of the following flavors to the hot syrup just after it has finished cooking. Once the syrup has cooled, strain it before storing:

2 branches fresh mint, tarragon, basil, rosemary, thyme, or lemon verbena

4 whole star anise

2 teaspoons fennel seeds

1 split vanilla bean

Strips of zest of 1 lemon, orange, lime, or grapefruit

MELON WATER

Consider the melon: a big juicy orb of sweet, perfumed rainwater. Cookbook author Niloufer Ichaporia King turned us on to yellow watermelon (but any variety or combination of melons will do). Make sure that you work over a bowl to catch every drop.

Crack open a ripe melon. Scrape or pick out the seeds and cut off the rind. Put the chunks of melon and any accumulated juices into a blender and purée until smooth. Strain the purée through a sieve into a pitcher, pushing the juice through with a rubber spatula. Discard the pulp. Add some Simple Syrup (see above) to sweeten it, if you like.

*August 30th, 90°
hazy, hot & humid*

Serve the melon water in a glass over ice with a big squeeze of lime, a big sprig of mint, and a shot of white rum (though the drink is perfectly delicious without the rum).

STRONG COFFEE GRANITA
makes about 1 quart

During the hot summer months, we like to end our meals with this simple refreshing sweet—dessert and espresso in a single glass. A dollop of whipped cream spooned over the "grainy" coffee ice crystals adds an unexpected lusciousness to its refreshing taste. The granita will stay fresh-tasting in a covered plastic container in the freezer for up to 1 week.

1 cup sugar
2 cups very strong hot coffee

Sweetened whipped cream

August 31st, 102°
a real scorcher

Stir the sugar into the coffee until it has dissolved, then set it aside to cool. Pour the cooled coffee into a pan (about 9 × 13 inches) or a wide container that will fit on a shelf in the freezer. Slide the pan into the freezer. The liquid will become slushy around the edges within an hour or so. Scrape the granita with the tines of a fork where it is beginning to freeze. Continue stirring, scraping, and breaking up any lumps every 30 minutes, until the granita has frozen icy crystals throughout. Serve in chilled glasses with a big spoonful of whipped cream on top.

PINK LEMON GRANITA
makes 3–4 cups

One day while making a batch of lemon granita, we noticed we had a lone blood orange on hand, so we decided to add its rosy juice to the mix—pink lemon juice! Since blood oranges are only available in the winter, we substitute pink grapefruit juice when blood oranges aren't around. The granita will stay fresh-tasting in a covered plastic container in the freezer for up to 1 week.

Finely grated zest of 2 lemons
1 cup fresh lemon juice (6–8 lemons)
Juice of 1 blood orange or
   1 red grapefruit

½ cup sugar
Sweetened whipped cream

Put the lemon zest, citrus juices, sugar, and ¼ cup water into a medium bowl and stir until the sugar dissolves completely. Pour the sweetened juice into a pan (about 9 × 13 inches) or a wide container that will fit on a shelf in the freezer. Slide the pan into the freezer. The liquid will become slushy-frozen in 1–2 hours. Scrape the granita with the tines of a fork, making frozen icy crystals throughout. Return the granita to the freezer to finish freezing, about 1 hour. Give the granita a final scrape, breaking up any icy chunks with a fork. Serve small portions in chilled glasses with a big spoonful of whipped cream on top.

❧ September Recipes ❧

simple puff pastry ❧ 155

tomato tart ❧ 156

roast chicken ❧ 158

chicken en gelée sandwiches ❧ 158

roast chicken smothered with chanterelles ❧ 158

golden chanterelles—the forest's treasure ❧ 160

soft scrambled eggs & chanterelles ❧ 160

chanterelle salad ❧ 162

fricassée of chanterelles ❧ 162

corn, string bean & potato succotash salad ❧ 164

green lentil & smoked ham hock salad ❧ 165

cranberry beans in olive oil ❧ 166

cold leg of lamb with cannellini & lemon mayonnaise ❧ 166

duck breasts with apples & caraway ❧ 168

confit of duck legs with potatoes sarladaise ❧ 172

duck soup with cabbage, ham & chinese rice noodles ❧ 173

apple tart ❧ 174

W e're mad for chanterelles. In midsummer and early fall after there's been a good rainy spell, we forage for the golden beauties in the woods nearby. It's their meaty texture and their fragrance of moss and apricot that gets us. The thrill of finding them—their pale orange shapes often obscured by the damp leaves and needles on the dark forest floor—must be a primeval one. It delights us to the core every time.

Finding chanterelles (*Cantharellus cibarius*) is never a sure thing, so we begin looking for them in our secret spots early in the season, in mid-July. We take a morning walk up the dirt road when the air is still cool. When we reach a part along the way where the forest is dark and moist, where the sunlight is blocked by the dense foliage and there is no green undergrowth, we head in. Our eyes adjust to the darkness as we wander around. In the carpet of brown leaves we look for that distinctive pale golden color, poking under the decaying leaves with a stick that one of us grabbed along the way. We sometimes find immature chanterelles, little orange buds—reassurance that there will be mushrooms before long. We make a mental note to return to that spot later in the season.

One year, we had a particularly rainy summer, hot and muggy. The only good thing that comes from a summer like that is the promise of finding wild mushrooms. Driving back from the market one morning in early September, we pulled off the road, walked into the woods, and climbed up a steep bank to check out one of our primo mushroom spots. There before us lay the mother lode, a carpet of golden chanterelles. We ran back to the car, grabbed our shopping bags, and gathered more than twenty pounds of mushrooms each that day.

We invited friends for a week of mushroom feasts. We sautéed them in olive oil and butter with a little garlic, then piled them over roast chicken or crusty toast, or folded them into omelets. We stewed them with some late-season tomatoes from the garden and spooned the ragù over soft polenta. We made a fricassée and stirred it into long strands of wide pappardelle. And for a delicate salad, we steamed the mushrooms and tossed them in a vinaigrette with lots of chopped parsley. When chanterelle season is in full swing, we eat like queens.

SIMPLE PUFF PASTRY
makes one 10 × 12-inch sheet

Traditional puff pastry—the classic French dough for leaflike, flaky napoleons, turnovers, and cheese straws—requires an involved process of rolling, folding, and turning a sheet of dough with a cold block of butter to create upward of 730 thin, uniformly even layers. In this simplified recipe, also known as "rough puff" because it's more rustic and the layers may rise unevenly when baked, the butter is worked into the flour as for a traditional pie dough. The dough is then rolled, folded, and turned several times, giving it flakiness when baked. It is a wonderful substitute for classic puff pastry, is easy to make, and inspires great confidence, even in a novice baker. Use salted Irish butter or another European-style butter with a high fat content for the best results.

8 tablespoons (1 stick) cold salted butter, preferably Irish or European-style high fat butter, cut in ¼-inch-thick slices

1 cup all-purpose flour

September 5th, 77° southerly breezes

Measure out the ingredients for making the dough: the slices of butter; ice water; a 1-cup measuring cup for dry ingredients with the flour (1). Mound the flour on a clean work surface (marble is ideal because it's cool and smooth). Scatter the butter slices over the flour (2) and sprinkle some of the flour over them to coat them (3). Using your fingers, work the butter into the flour, squeezing the flour into each slice of butter (4) until the mixture is crumbly and full of thin, soft chips of floury butter. Gather the flour mixture into a mound again.

Sprinkle 6 tablespoons ice water over the flour and butter (5), using a dough scraper to pull back any water that dribbles away from the mound. Lightly work the flour-butter mixture together, folding the edges toward the center with the dough scraper until it begins to hold together but is still a shaggy mass with large streaks of butter. Gather the dough together, shaping it into a 1-inch-thick square block (6). Wrap the dough in plastic wrap and refrigerate for 30 minutes.

Dust the dough with flour and roll it out on a floured surface with a floured rolling pin to make a ½-inch-thick rectangle (about 4 × 8 inches) (7); there will be pieces of butter visible. Starting with a short end of the dough, fold the dough into thirds, like a business letter (8). Repeat the rolling and folding steps once more. Wrap the dough in plastic wrap; refrigerate for 30 minutes.

Dust the dough with flour and put it seam side down on the floured work surface. With the rolling pin perpendicular to the seam, roll out the dough into a ½-inch-thick rectangle (about 4 × 8 inches), squaring the edges with your hands. Fold it into thirds again. Turn the dough seam side down. Repeat the rolling, folding, and turning process 2–3 more times, rolling the dough out to a ½-inch thickness each time and dusting it with flour as necessary. The dough should be supple and smooth. Fold it into thirds (9). Wrap in plastic wrap. Refrigerate for at least 1 hour and up to 2 days before using.

TOMATO TART
serves 4–6

We usually make this simple tart with large ripe tomatoes in season, tucking some halved supersweet cherry tomatoes in between the slabs. But we've found that using even those hothouse varieties—a little more acidic and certainly less juicy—can be quite delicious too. Eat this tart warm or at room temperature, but definitely the same day you make it, as the crisp, delicate crust becomes limp if it sits too long.

There are commercial brands of puff pastry available in the frozen foods section of the grocery store, and although they make life easier, they are not all the same. The best have real butter; avoid those without a trace of the good stuff—they'll taste like flaky cardboard. For the best pastry of all, we encourage you to make your own. It's really not that tough.

1 recipe Simple Puff Pastry (page 155) or
  1 sheet store-bought puff pastry
Flour
2–3 tomatoes, cored and sliced
2–3 branches fresh thyme

Really good extra-virgin olive oil
Pepper
Salt, preferably Maldon or other crunchy
  sea salt

September 6th, 83°
clear, dry & sunny

Preheat the oven to 375°. Line a large baking sheet with a piece of parchment paper and set aside. Roll the Simple Puff Pastry out on a lightly floured surface into a ¼-inch thick rectangle the shape of the baking sheet. Transfer the pastry to the baking sheet. Or, if using store-bought puff pastry (which is already rolled out), lay it out on the baking sheet. Using the tip of a paring knife, lightly score a border about ½ inch from the edge of the pastry. Prick the dough inside the border all over with the tines of a fork to prevent it from puffing up too much during baking.

Arrange the tomatoes on the pastry in a single layer (crowding or overlapping the tomatoes will make the puff pastry soggy). Strip the branches of thyme, scattering the leaves over the tomatoes. Drizzle the tart with some olive oil and season with pepper.

Bake the tart until the pastry is crisp and deeply browned on the bottom and around the edges, 30–40 minutes. Season with salt.

ROAST CHICKEN
serves 4–6

To ensure flavorful, juicier meat, we dry-brine the chicken, generously seasoning it with salt and then letting it rest before roasting. To keep the skin taut and crisp, we cook the bird in two phases: first at a high temperature, and then, after a brief time out of the oven, at a lower one. Slightly fussy, but we think it's worthwhile.

1 whole chicken, 3–5 pounds, rinsed and
    patted dry

1 tablespoon kosher salt
3 tablespoons butter, melted

September 7th, 73°
cool & rainy

Put the chicken breast side up on a large plate. Pat the salt onto the breasts, legs, and thighs. Refrigerate, uncovered, for at least 8 hours or up to 2 days.

Position the oven rack in the top third of the oven. Preheat the oven to 500°. Pat the chicken dry with paper towels (don't rinse the bird). Put it breast side up on a roasting rack set in a heavy roasting pan or in a large cast-iron skillet. Tie the legs together with kitchen string. Tuck the wings under the back. Brush the chicken all over with some of the melted butter. Add 1 cup water to the pan. Roast the chicken until the skin is golden and taut, 20–30 minutes, brushing it with butter halfway through. Remove the bird from the oven. Brush it with butter; let it rest for 15–20 minutes.

Reduce the oven temperature to 350°. Return the chicken to the oven and finish roasting it until the skin is deep golden brown and the thigh juices run clear when pierced, about 30 minutes. Carve the chicken and serve with the drippings. Serve it with buttered peas, if you like.

CHICKEN EN GELÉE SANDWICHES ⟿ Make these with any cold leftover roast chicken and the jellied pan juices. To make plenty of sandwiches with plenty of delicious gelée, refrigerate the whole bird in the pan after it's roasted and cooled. Slather a slice of good white bread with mayonnaise and cold jellied pan juices. Put 1–2 leaves Bibb lettuce and cold roast chicken slices on top. Spread more mayonnaise and gelée on top. Season with lots of salt and pepper.

ROAST CHICKEN SMOTHERED WITH CHANTERELLES

September 8th, 73°
foggy, misty day

Melt 6 tablespoons butter in a large skillet over medium-high heat. Add 1–2 thinly sliced garlic cloves and 2 pounds halved or quartered cleaned fresh chanterelles. Season with salt and pepper. Sauté the mushrooms until they have released their juices and are tender, 5–10 minutes. Remove the skillet from the heat. Stir in 1 large handful chopped fresh parsley leaves. Adjust seasonings. Cut 1 Roast Chicken (above) into pieces and arrange on a serving platter. Pile the mushrooms on top. Pour any pan juices over the mushrooms. — *serves 4–6*

❧ GOLDEN CHANTERELLES—THE FOREST'S TREASURES ❧

CLEANING ❧ Like most mushrooms, chanterelles need a little cleaning up first. Dirt and bits of dried leaves cling to the stems and wavy caps, yet washing ruins their texture and makes them waterlogged. When they are particularly dirty, a quick plunge into cold water will do. Otherwise, all you really need is a soft damp cloth or paper towel to gently wipe them off. Then use a pastry brush to dislodge any remaining dirt from the gills or crevices.

TRIMMING ❧ Chanterelles have a thick stem that widens at the top into the cap—the two parts are not as distinct from each other as they are in other mushroom varieties—and both parts are equally meaty and delicious. If the base of the stem is dried out or woody, trim it off with a paring knife.

STORING ❧ Chanterelles keep well in the refrigerator (up to a week or two), unwashed and stored in a closed paper bag so they can breathe; never in plastic—they'll turn slimy. Sautéed chanterelles freeze well.

SOFT SCRAMBLED EGGS & CHANTERELLES
serves 4–6

When we've had a moist summer and the chanterelles are plentiful in the nearby woods, we face picking a surplus of mushrooms. Poor us! When this happens, we sauté them as in the first step below, then store them in the freezer to use when chanterelle season is long over.

8 tablespoons (1 stick) butter
1 tablespoon extra-virgin olive oil
2 cloves garlic, very thinly sliced
1 pound fresh chanterelles, cleaned and trimmed, and halved or quartered

Salt and pepper
Large handful fresh parsley leaves, chopped
6 eggs
3 tablespoons heavy cream

September 12th, 69°
cool & damp

Melt 4 tablespoons of the butter and the olive oil together in a large skillet over medium-high heat. Add the garlic and mushrooms. Season with salt and pepper. Sauté the mushrooms, stirring occasionally, until they have released their juices and are tender, 10–15 minutes. Add the parsley.

Melt the remaining 4 tablespoons butter in a medium nonstick skillet over medium-high heat. Lightly beat the eggs and cream together in a medium bowl. Season with salt and pepper. Pour the eggs into the bubbling butter. After a few seconds, pull the eggs into the center of the skillet with a spatula. The uncooked eggs will rush out to the edges. Wait until the uncooked eggs begin to set again, then pull them into the center, making big soft curds. Continue doing this until all the eggs are softly set, about 2 minutes. Serve the eggs and mushrooms together.

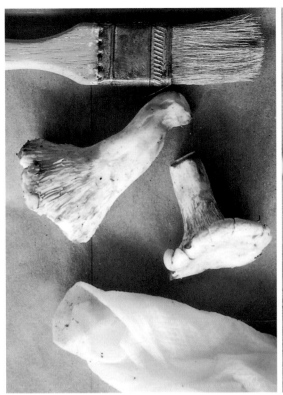
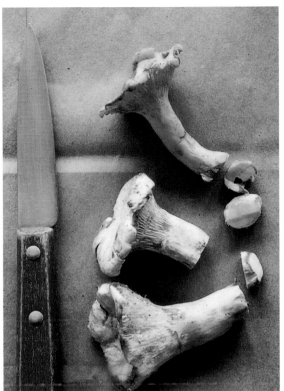

CHANTERELLE SALAD
serves 2–4

Chanterelles are meaty mushrooms that can stand up to a good browning sauté, but for this salad we prefer to steam the mushrooms, which makes their texture tender and delicate.

1 pound fresh chanterelles, cleaned and trimmed, and halved or quartered
1 small clove garlic, minced
1 shallot, finely chopped

Salt and pepper
2 tablespoons white wine vinegar
2 tablespoons extra-virgin olive oil
Handful fresh parsley leaves, chopped

September 13th, 75° scattered clouds

Put the mushrooms into the basket of a steamer, cover, and set it over a pot of boiling water over high heat. Steam the mushrooms until they are tender, 5–10 minutes. Remove the mushrooms from the heat and set aside to cool.

Put the garlic, shallots, and a good pinch of salt and pepper into a medium bowl. Add the vinegar. Stir in the olive oil, then the parsley. Add the mushrooms and toss gently. Adjust the seasonings. Let the salad marinate for about 30 minutes before serving.

FRICASSÉE OF CHANTERELLES
serves 4

This fricassée is delicious served over supple pappardelle. Or pile the mushrooms on thick crisp slices of toasted country bread. We even spoon them into baked potatoes—earth in earth!

6 tablespoons butter
1 medium onion, finely chopped
1–2 cloves garlic, finely minced
Grated fresh nutmeg
Salt and pepper
2 tablespoons Marsala or white wine

1 pound fresh chanterelles, cleaned and trimmed, and halved
Small handful fresh oregano leaves
½ cup heavy cream
½ pound pappardelle

September 14th, 71° blustery

Melt 3 tablespoons of the butter in a large skillet over medium heat. Add the onions and garlic, and season with nutmeg and salt and pepper. Cook, stirring occasionally, until the onions are soft, about 10 minutes. Add the Marsala and cook for a few minutes. Add the remaining 3 tablespoons butter. When it has melted, add the mushrooms and oregano. Taking care not to break up the mushrooms, stir everything together and cook for about 5 minutes. Add the cream and cook until slightly thickened, about 2 minutes.

Cook the pasta in a large pot of salted boiling water until just tender. Drain the pasta in a colander. Add the pasta to the mushrooms and fold everything together. Season to taste.

CORN, STRING BEAN & POTATO SUCCOTASH SALAD
serves 4–6

We'll often make this salad with leftover cooked corn. And if we have some summer squash or fresh shell beans like limas or cranberry beans on hand, we'll cook them up and add them. You needn't worry if you have a little more of one ingredient or a little less of another—this salad isn't finicky. From time to time we'll toss in (at the end) some pitted oil-cured olives and small chunks of salty cheese like feta or ricotta salata. Add those, and you've got a pretty tasty meal.

4 thin-skinned waxy potatoes
4 ears corn, shucked
½ pound string beans, trimmed
1 shallot, 2 scallions, or ½ a small onion,
   finely chopped

Handful fresh parsley leaves, chopped
⅓ cup really good extra-virgin olive oil
Salt and pepper

continued

Put the potatoes in a large pot filled with salted cold water and bring to a boil over medium-high heat. While the potatoes are cooking, add the corn to the pot and cook for 3–5 minutes. Pull the corn from the boiling water and let it cool. Next add the string beans to the pot and cook until tender, about 5 minutes. Scoop the string beans out of the boiling water with a large slotted spoon or a pair of tongs and put them into a bowl of cold water to cool them down quickly. Drain the potatoes when they are tender, about 20 minutes depending on their size.

September 16th, 78°
sunny warm day

Cut the corn off the cob into a large bowl. Cut the potatoes into slices or chunks and add them to the bowl. Drain the beans and add them to the bowl. Add the shallots, parsley, and olive oil. Season with salt and lots of pepper. Toss and adjust seasonings. Add more oil if the salad needs it.

GREEN LENTIL & SMOKED HAM HOCK SALAD
serves 6–8

Lentils don't need to soak before cooking. Check on them as they cook and pull them off the heat when they are just tender. They can quickly overcook and become mushy.

1 smoked ham hock, 1–1½ pounds

1 leek, white part only, halved lengthwise and cleaned

3 cloves garlic

1 bay leaf

2 cups green lentils (about 1 pound), rinsed

1 cup really good extra-virgin olive oil

Salt and pepper

2 teaspoons Dijon mustard

4–5 tablespoons red wine vinegar

1 bunch scallions, thinly sliced

Large handful fresh parsley leaves, chopped

Put the ham hock, leeks, 2 cloves of the garlic, and the bay leaf in a medium pot with 10 cups cold water. Gently simmer over medium-low heat until the ham is tender, 1–1½ hours.

September 19th, 68°
hint of fall

Add the lentils to the pot with the ham hock and gently simmer over medium heat until the lentils are tender, about 25 minutes. Drain the lentils in a colander. Retrieve the ham hock and set aside to cool. Discard the leeks, garlic, and bay leaf. Spread the lentils out in a wide dish to cool, drizzle with ½ cup of the olive oil, and season with salt and pepper. When the ham hock is cool enough to handle, tear the meat into bite-size pieces, discarding the fat, gristle, and bones.

Using the back of a wooden spoon, mash together the remaining garlic clove and some salt and pepper in a small bowl. Stir in the mustard and vinegar, then the remaining ½ cup olive oil. Add the vinaigrette to the lentils, and the ham and scallions, and toss well. Adjust the seasonings. Drizzle with more olive oil, if you like. Garnish the salad with parsley.

CRANBERRY BEANS IN OLIVE OIL

September 20th, 72°
golden afternoon

Shell 2–3 pounds fresh cranberry beans; you should have about 3 cups shelled beans. Put the beans into a heavy medium pot and cover with cold water by 1 inch. Add 1 halved medium onion and 1 large branch fresh sage leaves. Bring the beans just to a simmer over medium heat. When they come to a simmer, add a generous pinch of salt and 2 tablespoons really good extra-virgin olive oil. Reduce the heat to low and very gently simmer the beans until they are tender, 45–60 minutes. Remove the pot from the heat. Season the beans with a little more salt, if you like. Use a slotted spoon to serve the beans. Serve them in wide soup bowls, drizzled with plenty of olive oil and seasoned with cracked black pepper. —— *serves 4*

COLD LEG OF LAMB WITH CANNELLINI & LEMON MAYONNAISE
serves 4

As with a roast turkey, or a smoked ham, you can pretty much count on having leftovers from a Roast Leg of Lamb (page 26), which, happily, means there's the makings for hashes, rissoles, the best sandwich in the world, or a simple cold lunch like this—a whole second meal unto itself.

FOR THE MAYONNAISE
1 large egg yolk
¼ clove garlic, finely minced
Salt
Juice of 1 lemon
½ cup "buttery" extra-virgin olive oil
½ cup canola oil
FOR THE LAMB AND BEANS
1 small shallot, minced

Juice of ½ lemon
Salt and pepper
3–4 tablespoons "buttery" extra-virgin olive oil, plus more for drizzling
2 cups cooked cannellini beans
Small handful chopped fresh parsley
Cold leftover roast leg of lamb, sliced
Cornichons

September 21st, 79°
first day of fall

For the mayonnaise, whisk together the egg yolk, garlic, pinch of salt, and half the lemon juice in a medium bowl. Combine the oils in a measuring cup with a spout. Whisking constantly, add the oil to the yolk about 1 teaspoon at a time. The sauce will thicken and emulsify. After you have added about ¼ cup of the oil, continue to whisk and slowly drizzle in the remaining oil. Season with salt and thin with as much of the remaining lemon juice as suits your taste.

For the lamb and beans, make a vinaigrette by whisking together the shallots, lemon juice, some salt and pepper, and the olive oil in a large bowl. Add the cannellini beans and parsley and gently toss until well combined. Adjust the seasonings. Arrange the slices of lamb on 4 plates. Divide the beans between the plates and drizzle with some olive oil. Garnish with some cornichons. Pass the mayonnaise at the table.

DUCK BREASTS WITH APPLES & CARAWAY
serves 4

In this recipe, we treat the apples like pan-roasted potatoes. If you buy duck breasts on their own, they'll probably be larger than those you'd get from a whole duck that you cut up yourself. Keep that in mind as you cook them; they may need a little more time in the pan.

2 boneless duck breasts, trimmed
Salt and pepper
1 tablespoon duck, goose fat, or olive oil
½ teaspoon caraway seeds, lightly crushed

2 apples, such as honeycrisp, peeled, cored, and cut into thick wedges
1 teaspoon sugar
2 sprigs fresh rosemary, for garnish

September 26th, 64°
fog & rain

Prick the skin of the duck breasts all over, then season with salt and pepper. Heat the duck fat in a heavy large skillet over medium heat. Sprinkle the caraway seeds over the bottom of the skillet. Place the duck breasts skin side down in the middle of the skillet. Arrange the apples in a single layer around the duck. Sprinkle the apples with the sugar. Cook the breasts without moving them until the skin is deep golden brown and crisp, 18–20 minutes. Use a fork to turn the apples as they cook so they brown on all sides. Turn the breasts over and cook for about 5 minutes.

Transfer the duck breasts to a plate and let them rest for 5–10 minutes. While the duck breasts rest, continue to gently cook the apples until they are tender and golden brown all over. To serve, slice the duck breasts and arrange on a platter with the apples. Garnish with rosemary.

Clockwise from top left: a duck cut into parts, consisting of 2 breasts, skin, 2 legs with thighs, liver, 2 wing drumlets

CONFIT OF DUCK LEGS WITH POTATOES SARLADAISE
serves 2

The ancient technique of cooking and preserving duck in its own fat is one we take great pleasure in doing ourselves. And the duck legs are exquisite eating—silky-tender and full-flavored. Having the residual duck fat on hand for frying up things like these potatoes is a bonus; or to our minds, it's the art of simple delicious cooking at its most practical.

FOR THE DUCK CONFIT
2 whole duck legs
2 teaspoons coarse salt
2–3 cups rendered duck fat
2 bay leaves
1 sprig fresh thyme

FOR THE POTATOES
3 medium waxy potatoes, peeled
¼ cup rendered duck fat
Coarse salt
Handful fresh parsley leaves, chopped
1 clove garlic, finely chopped
Pepper

September 23rd, 69°
cool & crisp

For the duck confit, put the duck legs skin side up in a glass or ceramic dish in a single layer. Season the legs all over with the salt. Cover and refrigerate for 1–2 days.

Preheat the oven to 250°. Heat the duck fat in a deep heavy pot over low heat until just warm. Remove the pot from the heat. Pat the seasoned duck legs dry with paper towels and slip them into the warm fat. The legs should be completely submerged. Add the bay leaves and thyme. Transfer the pot to the oven and gently cook the legs, uncovered, until they are very tender, 2½–3 hours.

Transfer the legs, herbs, and fat to a deep bowl or crock, making sure the legs are completely submerged in the fat. Cover and refrigerate the confit of duck for at least 2 days and up to 3 months. The flavor improves with time.

Gently pry the duck legs out of the fat (the fat can be reused to make more confit of duck). Scoop out 2 tablespoons of the fat and heat it in a medium heavy skillet over medium heat. Add the duck legs to the skillet skin side down. Cook them like this, without moving them, until the skin is deep golden brown and crisp, about 20 minutes. Reduce the heat to medium-low if the skin begins to burn. Turn the legs over and cook for 2–3 minutes.

For the potatoes, slice the potatoes into rounds about ⅛ inch thick. Rinse, drain well, and pat dry with paper towels. Heat the duck fat in a medium cast-iron skillet over medium-high heat. Add the potatoes, season with salt, and gently toss until evenly coated. Cook the potatoes, turning them occasionally, until deep golden brown and crisp around the edges and tender in the center, 10–12 minutes. Remove the skillet from heat. Scatter the parsley and garlic over the potatoes. Season with salt and pepper. Serve with the duck legs.

DUCK SOUP WITH CABBAGE, HAM & CHINESE RICE NOODLES
serves 4

We make this soup when we've taken a whole duck and carved out the breasts to make dishes like Duck Breasts with Apples & Caraway (page 168) and turned the legs into Confit of Duck Legs (opposite page) and are left with the raw carcass. Then the whole bird gets used, for goodness' sake.

FOR THE BROTH

1 raw carcass of a duck, including the back, wings, giblets, and any extra skin

1 medium onion, quartered

1 carrot, peeled and coarsely chopped

1 rib celery, coarsely chopped

FOR THE SOUP

Pinch of Sichuan peppercorns

8 cups duck broth

6 large dried shiitake mushrooms, rinsed

1 large hand fresh ginger, halved lengthwise

3 whole star anise

½ cup Chinese rice wine

Salt

¼ head Napa cabbage

8 ounces Chinese flat, wide rice noodles

½ bunch scallions, thinly sliced

½ cup thinly sliced cooked ham

Handful fresh cilantro leaves

For the broth, put the duck carcass parts, onions, carrots, celery, and 12 cups cold water into a heavy large pot. Bring to a boil over high heat, skimming any foam that rises to the surface, then reduce the heat to medium-low. Simmer the broth, uncovered, for 4 hours. Strain the broth into a large bowl, discarding the solids. Allow the broth to cool to room temperature. Cover and refrigerate until it is cold (the broth will keep for up to 2 days in the fridge). Skim off and discard the layer of white fat on the surface of the cold broth.

September 24th, 65°
chilly morning

For the soup, toast the Sichuan peppercorns in a small skillet over medium-low heat until fragrant, 1–2 minutes. Put them in a large pot, along with the duck broth, and bring to a simmer over medium-high heat. Add the mushrooms, ginger, and star anise. Reduce the heat to medium and simmer for 30 minutes. Using a slotted spoon, fish out and discard the mushrooms, ginger, and star anise. Stir in the rice wine and season with salt.

Separate the sturdy ribs of the cabbage from the frilly leaves. Thinly slice the ribs and leaves, keeping them separate. Add the ribs to the broth and simmer until tender, 1–2 minutes.

Meanwhile, cook the noodles in a large pot of boiling water over medium-high heat until just tender, about 4 minutes. Drain in a colander and rinse under cold running water until cool.

Divide the noodles, sliced cabbage leaves, and scallions between 4 large, deep soup bowls, then ladle the broth into the bowls. Garnish the soup with the ham and cilantro.

Overleaf: left, Confit of Duck Legs with Potatoes Sarladaise; right, Duck Soup with Cabbage, Ham & Chinese Rice Noodles

APPLE TART
serves 6–8

In September hard fruits replace soft fruits in our markets. We even see local apples as early as August, but September marks their true arrival. Local Golden Delicious is our apple of choice. It's a little low on acid, but we love its sweet perfume in this tart.

FOR THE PASTRY DOUGH
1½ cups pastry flour
¼ teaspoon salt
¼ teaspoon granulated sugar
4 tablespoons cold unsalted butter, diced
4 tablespoons cold salted butter, diced
2 tablespoons cold vegetable shortening

FOR THE APPLE FILLING
3 tablespoons Demerara or brown sugar
1 teaspoon ground cinnamon
6 apples of your favorite variety, peeled, cored, and thickly sliced
¼ cup heavy cream

September 29th, 70° warm & sunny

For the pastry dough, whisk the flour, salt, and sugar in a mixing bowl. Cut in both butters and the shortening with a pastry blender or a fork until crumbly. It should resemble coarse cornmeal. Sprinkle in 3 tablespoons ice water and toss together lightly until the dough comes together (add a little more ice water if you need to). Shape the dough into a flat rectangle (don't overhandle). Wrap the dough in plastic wrap, and chill for at least 1 hour.

Preheat the oven to 375°. Roll out the dough into a large rectangle on a lightly floured surface. It should be about ⅛ inch thick and fit into a 9 × 13-inch baking sheet. Roll the dough loosely around the rolling pin, then unfurl it into the baking sheet. Lightly press the dough into the pan, leaving ½ inch of dough hanging over the edge. Trim any excess off with a sharp knife. Tuck the dough under itself to make a nice edge.

For the apple filling, mix 2 tablespoons of the sugar and the cinnamon together in a small bowl. Put the apples into a large mixing bowl, sprinkle with the cinnamon sugar, then add the cream and toss everything together. Arrange the apples in an even layer on the pastry. Bake until the apples are soft, 45–55 minutes. Remove from the oven and sprinkle the apples with the remaining 1 tablespoon of Demerara sugar.

APPLE TALK

Our friend Karen Bates of famed Philo Apple Farm in Northern California taught us that. . .

Early apples tend to break down very easily—great for applesauce and very tender juicy pies, but the apples lose their shape. Midseason apples generally cook up fairly tender and hold their shape with more integrity, so the choice is mostly about flavor. Late season apples can border on being a little too firm with much less juiciness. So make your applesauce early in the season and keep your late apples as long as you can—they store beautifully all winter long.

autumn

❧ October Recipes ❧

warm beet soup ∾ 183

chicken roasted over potatoes & lemon ∾ 184

chicken soup with ditalini ∾ 186

marinated chicken salad with radicchio & iceberg ∾ 186

rigatoni with passato & parmigiano-reggiano ∾ 188

sausage & clam stew ∾ 188

roasted pumpkin soup ∾ 189

chicken broth with spinach & little meatballs ∾ 193

grilled quail with braised chestnuts & kabocha squash ∾ 194

roasted kabocha squash ∾ 196

kabocha squash, yukon gold potatoes & cipolline ∾ 196

pork stewed in guajillo chile mole ∾ 198

cornbread ∾ 201

deconstructed carbonara ∾ 201

vin santo–roasted pears ∾ 203

gianduia ∾ 203

gianduia & caramel tart ∾ 204

Just inside the door to our studio, there's a thick wooden post that shoots straight up for twenty-five feet to a ridge beam and the exposed rafters. It has two plain coat hooks on which we hang our kitchen aprons. Each day when we arrive at the studio, the first thing we do is put on our aprons—whether we're cooking or not. Wearing an apron feels good. It readies us for the day. It protects us. (And it does a nice job of cinching our waists and flattening our tummies!) It gives us something to wipe our hands on and use to pick up hot dishes and pots and cradle a few eggs or apples as we carry them from one place to another. The apron's deep front pockets give us a comfortable spot to tuck our hands or lose a pair of reading glasses or a cell phone. We take Henry the studio dog out for a walk along the towpath wearing our aprons. We run errands wearing our aprons. We wear our aprons all day long.

Over the years, the apron collection on the hooks has grown. There are a couple of chocolate brown ones that we've had since we started our studio. They're soft and worn, like an old pair of jeans. They hang behind newer ones in rich colors—Dutch blue, paprika, mustard gold, kicky pink. But whatever their color, our aprons are all the same: They drape like a dress and function like a workhorse. They're hand-cut and sewn from elegant, durable linen, calf length with a roomy bib and long, wide straps. A friend of ours makes them, and she built her thriving linens company on the artisanal model—one piece at a time. You know this woman must know how to cook.

We order new aprons from Franca a few times a year, which always involves a nice back-and-forth about linen colors, cloth weight and availability, the weather, embroidery and thread color, our businesses, and cooking and eating. The exchange is often followed up with a card in the mail, meticulously handwritten, with neatly stapled swatches of linen and threads in different colors taped on just like they were a baby's first lock of hair. Soon afterward the new aprons arrive. We tear open the box. Pressed, folded, and held in place just so with straight pins, they're so beautiful and perfect we're afraid to put them on. We'll get them dirty! But we can't resist, and before long the aprons' creases are completely relaxed, the pockets are ringing, and the fronts are spattered with sauce. Just as they were meant to be.

WARM BEET SOUP
serves 4–6

Beets are one of the first root vegetables we plant in our gardens each year and one of the last we pull from the cold dirt in the fall, usually after a frost. We steam or sauté their stems and greens, then season them with a good olive oil and lots of salt and pepper. Or we bathe them simply in melted salted butter with a splash of fresh lemon juice or balsamic vinegar, or serve them with a generous spoonful of garlicky aïoli. The beets themselves, roasted or boiled, can be served just like the tops. But beets are also one of our favorites for making soup, cold or hot—in this case a warm velvety soup of outrageous color, and sweet, earthy flavor. We hope it puts the roses back in your cheeks (it always does in ours).

Garnish this soup with a lot of snipped fresh chives and a dollop of sour cream. A small handful of finely diced roasted beets is a tasty finishing touch too.

2 pounds beets (4–6 medium beets)
1 large onion, chopped
1 large russet potato, peeled and diced
1 carrot, peeled and chopped
6 cups beef broth

2 tablespoons freshly grated or store-bought prepared horseradish
Juice of ½ lemon, preferably Meyer
Salt and pepper
Small bunch fresh chives, chopped

October 3rd, 57°
cloudy & cool

Preheat the oven to 400°. Wrap each beet in foil and bake until tender when pierced, about 1 hour. Unwrap the beets and when they are cool enough to handle, peel off and discard the skin. Coarsely chop the beets and set aside.

Put the onions, potatoes, carrots, and broth into a heavy large pot and bring to a boil over medium-high heat. Reduce the heat to medium-low and cook until the vegetables are very tender, about 30 minutes. Add the chopped beets and horseradish to the pot. Set the soup aside to cool slightly.

Working in small batches, purée the soup in a blender or food processor until very smooth. Thin the soup with a little more broth or water if it's too thick. Stir in the lemon juice and season with salt and pepper. Before serving, return the soup to the pot and warm it up over medium-low heat. Garnish with plenty of chives.

CHICKEN ROASTED OVER POTATOES & LEMON
serves 4–6

Our two little apartment-size stoves at Canal House do not come with a rotisserie oven feature. So when we want to "rotisserie" a chicken, we put the bird directly on the oven rack and slide a pan of sliced crusty bread, root vegetables, or potatoes and lemons onto the rack below to catch the flavorful juices.

When we roast a bird this way, we like to spatchcock it—that is, split it so it lies flat, like an open book. It makes the chicken easier to handle and carve, and it cooks quicker, too.

FOR THE CHICKEN
1 chicken, 3–4 pounds
1 tablespoon extra-virgin olive oil
¼–½ teaspoon pimentón
Salt and pepper

FOR THE POTATOES
6 medium waxy potatoes, such as Yukon
    gold, sliced into ¼-inch-thick rounds
1 lemon, sliced into thin rounds
Leaves from 8–10 sprigs of fresh thyme
¼ cup extra-virgin olive oil
Salt and pepper

*October 4th, 66°
blustery*

Place one oven rack in the upper third and another oven rack in the middle of the oven. Preheat the oven to 475°.

For the chicken, use kitchen shears to cut out the backbone (save it for making stock, if you like). Rinse the chicken and pat it dry with paper towels. Spread the bird out skin side up so it lays flat. Tuck the wing tips neatly behind the wings or snip them off. Rub the olive oil all over the chicken and season it with the pimentón and salt and pepper. Set the bird aside.

For the potatoes, put the potatoes, lemon, thyme, and olive oil in a large bowl. Season with salt and pepper and gently mix everything together. Cover the bottom of a shallow roasting pan with the potatoes and lemon, drizzling any of the remaining olive oil from the bowl on top.

Place the chicken in the oven breast side up directly on the upper rack in the oven. Put the pan of potatoes on the lower rack beneath the bird to catch the drippings. Roast the chicken and potatoes for 30 minutes. Reduce the oven temperature to 400° and continue roasting the chicken until the skin is golden brown and the thigh juices run clear when pricked, about 20 minutes. The potatoes should be browned and tender by the time the chicken is finished roasting. Leave them in the oven longer if they need more time.

Lift the chicken off the rack and place it in the pan with the potatoes and lemons. Let it rest out of the oven for 10–15 minutes before carving. Serve the chicken with the potatoes and lemons.

CHICKEN SOUP WITH DITALINI

The beauty of serving a roast chicken is there is usually enough leftover meat clinging to the bones (you don't need much) to make a simple soup like this one for another meal on another day. If you are a boneless, skinless chicken-breast lover, use that instead—no muss, no fuss!

October 6th, 61°
early morning rain

Cook 1 cup ditalini or other short-shaped pasta in a small pot of salted boiling water until just tender; drain. Bring 6 cups chicken broth along with 1 wide strip lemon zest to a simmer in a medium pot over medium heat. Add a few handfuls torn pieces of cooked chicken and about 2 cups cooked greens, such as kale, Swiss chard, and/or spinach. Season with salt and pepper. Simmer the soup for a few minutes. Divide the pasta and soup between 2–4 soup bowls. Discard the lemon zest. Drizzle some really good extra-virgin olive oil into each bowl. — *serves 2–4*

MARINATED CHICKEN SALAD WITH RADICCHIO & ICEBERG
serves 4–6

These two salads—with their lively flavors of bright vinegar, salty capers and anchovies, sweet raisins, and bitter radicchio—can each stand alone, but together they make a lovely match.

For the chicken salad
4 poached chicken breasts, at room temperature, skin and bones discarded
½ cup really good extra-virgin olive oil
Juice of 1 lemon
2 tablespoons white wine vinegar
¼ cup golden raisins
2 tablespoons capers
Large pinch of red pepper flakes
1 teaspoon sugar
Salt and pepper

For the radicchio and iceberg salad
3 anchovy filets, coarsely chopped
1 small clove garlic
Salt and pepper
1 teaspoon Dijon mustard
1 tablespoon fresh lemon juice
3–4 tablespoons really good extra-virgin olive oil
1 head radicchio, cored and leaves torn
1 small head iceberg lettuce, cored and coarsely chopped

October 7th, 66°
warm fall day

For the chicken salad, slice or tear the chicken into nice-size pieces and put them into a glass or ceramic dish. Add the olive oil, lemon juice, vinegar, raisins, capers, red pepper flakes, and sugar. Season with salt and pepper and gently mix everything together. Cover and marinate the chicken salad in the refrigerator overnight. Bring to room temperature before serving.

For the radicchio and iceberg salad, mash together with a fork the anchovies, garlic, and salt and pepper to taste in the bottom of a salad bowl. Stir in the mustard and lemon juice. Stir in the olive oil. Adjust the seasonings. Add the radicchio and iceberg lettuce to the bowl just before serving, and toss with the vinaigrette. Serve the two salads together.

RIGATONI WITH PASSATO & PARMIGIANO-REGGIANO
serves 4–6

3–4 cups *passato di pomodoro* (strained
    tomatoes)
1 medium onion, halved
4–6 tablespoons butter

1–2 tablespoons extra-virgin olive oil
Salt and pepper
1 pound rigatoni
Grated parmigiano-reggiano

October 10th, 68°
azure blue sky
Put the strained tomatoes and a splash of water into a medium saucepan. Add the onions, butter, and olive oil, and season with salt and pepper. Simmer over medium-low heat, stirring occasionally, until the onions soften and the sauce thickens a bit, about 30 minutes.

Taste the sauce. Depending on the acidity of the tomatoes you've used, you may want to soften the sauce; the more butter you use, the softer and rounder the flavors. On occasion, we've even added a pinch or two of sugar to balance the acidity. Remove and discard the onions from the sauce before using. Keep the sauce warm over low heat.

Cook the pasta in a large pot of salted boiling water over high heat until just tender, 12–15 minutes. Drain, reserving some of the pasta cooking water, and return the pasta to the pot. Pour the sauce over the pasta and gently stir to combine, adding some of the pasta cooking water to thin and loosen the sauce, if necessary. Serve the pasta sprinkled with plenty of grated cheese.

SAUSAGE & CLAM STEW
serves 4–8

We were doing a little spring cleaning one fall day at the studio and came across our forgotten copper *cataplana* high up on a shelf. There was nothing else to do but cook a quick Portuguese-inspired stew of clams and sausages spiced up with Aleppo pepper. We rolled up our sleeves and sopped up the broth with good crusty bread. A wide pot with a lid will work for this stew too, but this beautiful vessel is an inspiration.

4 tablespoons extra-virgin olive oil
1½ pounds Italian sausage (any variety),
    sliced into thick rounds
1 small onion, chopped

2–3 cloves garlic, finely chopped
4 pounds small clams, such as cockles or
    littlenecks, scrubbed
2–3 pinches of Aleppo pepper or pimentón

October 11th, 60°
crisp & cool
Heat 2 tablespoons of the olive oil in a large *cataplana* or heavy pot with a lid over medium-high heat. Add the sausages and cook, stirring occasionally, until browned all over, about 10 minutes.

continued

Add the onions and garlic and cook until softened, about 5 minutes. Add the clams and Aleppo pepper, then drizzle with the remaining 2 tablespoons of olive oil.

Clamp the lid shut or cover the pot and cook, shaking the pan over the heat occasionally, until the clams open, 10–12 minutes. Discard any clams that don't open. Serve in wide soup bowls with warm, crusty bread for sopping up the flavorful broth.

ROASTED PUMPKIN SOUP
serves 6–8

Use a heavy, thick-fleshed pumpkin variety like the orange Cinderella (Rouge Vif d'Etampes), the beige cheese, or the blue Jarrahdale for this soup. Their thick sturdy walls won't collapse as the pumpkin roasts in the oven.

1 Cinderella, cheese, or blue Jarrahdale
   pumpkin, 5–8 pounds
4–8 tablespoons butter, softened
1 teaspoon ground fennel seeds
2 generous pinches of piment d'Espelette
   (Basque red chile powder)

Salt and pepper
2 cloves garlic, thinly sliced
1 cup fresh white bread crumbs
2–3 cups grated Gruyère cheese
2 bay leaves
4–6 cups chicken stock

Preheat the oven to 350°. Cut out a wide lid around the stem of the pumpkin, scrape off and discard any seeds, and set the lid aside. Using a metal spoon, scoop out and discard the seeds and strings from the inside.

October 12th, 62°
soup weather

Put the pumpkin in a roasting pan. Rub the flesh inside the pumpkin with the butter, then with the ground fennel, piment d'Espelette, and salt and pepper to taste. Add the garlic, bread crumbs, cheese, and bay leaves. Pour enough stock into the pumpkin to come within about 3 inches of the rim. Fit the lid back on the pumpkin.

Roast the pumpkin for 1 hour. Remove the lid and place it flesh side up beside the pumpkin. Continue roasting the pumpkin until the flesh inside is soft when pierced with a paring knife, taking care not to puncture the skin, 30–90 minutes depending on the size of the pumpkin.

Carefully transfer the pumpkin to a serving platter. Remove and discard the bay leaves. Replace the lid for effect, if you like. Serve the pumpkin soup at the table, scraping big spoonfuls of the flesh from the bottom and sides into the broth, then ladling the soup into bowls.

Overleaf: left, Sausage & Clam Stew; right, Roasted Pumpkin Soup

CHICKEN BROTH WITH SPINACH & LITTLE MEATBALLS
serves 8–10

The recipe for these meatballs is one of our all-purpose meatball favorites. The meatballs can be rolled larger or smaller, depending on what they're to be used for. We like bigger ones to go with our spaghetti or buttered noodles, and walnut-size ones to serve with cocktails or put in soup. The ricotta keeps them tender and moist and their flavor is delicate, unlike those that have bread or crackers as a binder.

FOR THE MEATBALLS
½ pound ground pork
½ pound ground veal
2 ounces prosciutto, finely chopped
½ cup fresh whole-milk ricotta
½ cup grated pecorino
1 egg, lightly beaten
Handful fresh parsley leaves, finely chopped
Handful fresh mint leaves, finely chopped

¼ whole nutmeg, finely grated
1 teaspoon salt
½ teaspoon pepper

FOR THE SOUP
10–12 cups chicken broth
1 pound baby spinach leaves
Salt and pepper
Really good extra-virgin olive oil

For the meatballs, gently mix together the pork, veal, prosciutto, ricotta, pecorino, egg, parsley, mint, nutmeg, salt, and pepper in a large mixing bowl until it is well combined; do not overwork. Using a spoon, scoop out a small amount of the meat mixture into your hands and roll it into a ball. Make all the meatballs the same size, about 1 inch, so they will cook evenly. Arrange them in a single layer on a sheet pan or tray as you work. You should end up with about 80 meatballs. The meatballs can be made a few hours ahead and stored in the refrigerator, covered with plastic wrap, until you are ready to cook them.

October 14th, 69°
warm with a light rain

For the soup, bring the chicken broth to a gentle simmer in a large pot over medium heat. Working in batches, cook the meatballs in the simmering broth until they float to the surface and are cooked through, 3–4 minutes. (The meatballs will need to cook for about 1½ minutes after they've floated to the surface.) Transfer the cooked meatballs to a wide dish, add a ladleful of hot broth, and cover with plastic wrap to keep them warm as you work.

Strain the broth through a fine-mesh sieve into a medium bowl, then return it to the pot. Bring the broth to a simmer over medium heat. Add the spinach and cook until it collapses and wilts, about 2 minutes. Season the soup with salt and pepper to taste. Divide the meatballs between the soup bowls, then ladle some of the soup into each bowl. Drizzle with olive oil and serve.

GRILLED QUAIL WITH BRAISED CHESTNUTS & KABOCHA SQUASH
serves 4

You can start off eating quail with a fork and knife, but by the time you get to the last meaty bits, you really should abandon utensils and use your fingers. At some tables this may not fly, but it's how we do it at ours.

2 tablespoons butter

3 cups peeled kabocha squash cubes,
   approximately the same size
   as the chestnuts

Salt and pepper

3 tablespoons extra-virgin olive oil

4 ounces pancetta, diced

1 medium onion, chopped

1 cup red wine

1 cup rich poultry broth

1½ cups peeled whole chestnuts, preferably
   from a jar

2 sprigs fresh thyme

4 quail

¼ teaspoon ground cinnamon

Melt the butter in a deep large pan over medium heat. Add the squash, season with salt and pepper, and stir well with a wooden spoon. Add ¼ cup water and bring to a simmer. Reduce the heat to medium-low, cover the pan, and cook until the squash is tender and glazed, about 20 minutes. Add a splash or two of water if the squash begins to dry out. Transfer the squash to a wide bowl.

Return the pan to medium-high heat and add 2 tablespoons of the olive oil. Add the pancetta and cook until it just begins to brown, about 5 minutes. Add the onions and cook, stirring occasionally, until soft, 5–10 minutes.

Increase the heat to high. Add the wine to the pan and cook until reduced by about half, scraping up any browned bits stuck to the bottom of the pan. Add the broth, chestnuts, and thyme and bring to a boil. Reduce the heat to medium-low and simmer until the sauce is slightly thickened, about 20 minutes. Season with salt and pepper.

Meanwhile, rinse the quail inside and out and pat them dry with paper towels. Rub the birds with the remaining 1 tablespoon of olive oil, then generously season them with salt and pepper, and with the cinnamon. Grill the quail over a hot charcoal fire or in a grill pan over high heat, turning them when they are well browned and a little charred in places and just cooked through, 5–15 minutes.

Return the squash to the pan with the chestnuts and cook until just warmed through, about 5 minutes. Serve with the quail.

ROASTED KABOCHA SQUASH

October 18th, 65°
amazing clouds

Some nights, a big wedge of roasted squash is all we need for dinner. Who needs meat?

Preheat the oven to 400°. Cut a 3-pound kabocha squash in half across its width. Scoop out and discard the seeds. Arrange the squash flesh side up in a roasting pan and drizzle with 4 tablespoons extra-virgin olive oil. Season with salt and pepper. Roast the squash until tender, 1–1½ hours. To serve, cut the squash into wedges and season with the chopped rind of ½ preserved lemon and a small handful of fresh oregano leaves. — *serves 2–4*

KABOCHA SQUASH, YUKON GOLD POTATOES & CIPOLLINE
serves 4

It was a beautiful late October day and we were in need of some pumpkins for Halloween. We hopped in the car and headed across the river into Bucks County, Pennsylvania, to visit a local farm that grows an increasingly impressive variety of pumpkins and squash each year. Outside, the pumpkins were lined up along the stone wall of the old barn. We chose a couple of hefty orange beauties to carve into jack-o'-lanterns, then went inside to pay. To our surprise, the little market tucked into the corner of the barn was packed with the farm's autumn harvest—baskets, bins, and cans brimming with squashes, onions, potatoes, herbs, fresh shell beans, and even last-of-the-season tomatoes. We gathered up what we were hungry for, drove back to Canal House, and made ourselves this fine vegetarian plate lunch, full of rich flavors and *prana*.

One 3-pound kabocha squash
Extra-virgin olive oil
Salt and pepper
1 pound cipolline onions, unpeeled

1 pound Yukon gold potatoes
4 ripe plum tomatoes, halved lengthwise
4–6 tablespoons butter, preferably salted Irish butter

October 19th, 69°
trees are ablaze

Preheat the oven to 375°. Cut the squash in half and scoop out the seeds. Quarter the halves and arrange them in a roasting pan in a single layer, flesh side up. Rub the flesh with plenty of olive oil and season with salt and pepper. Roast the squash until the flesh is tender, about 1 hour.

Boil the onions in a medium pot of salted water over medium-high heat until tender, 10–15 minutes. Drain, then slip off their skins. Cut the onions in half horizontally. Heat 2 tablespoons of the oil in a large skillet over medium heat. Add the onions cut side down. Season with salt and pepper and cook, without turning them, until golden brown, about 5 minutes. Meanwhile, boil the potatoes in a medium pot of salted water over medium-high heat until tender, 15–20 minutes.

Divide the squash, potatoes, cipolline, and tomatoes between 4 plates. Gently crush the potatoes and put a knob of butter on top. Season everything with olive oil and salt and pepper.

PORK STEWED IN GUAJILLO CHILE MOLE
serves 6–8

The leathery skin of a guajillo chile, the mildly hot dried Mexican pepper that flavors this stew, needs to soak until it's soft enough to purée. Serve this stew with Cornbread (page 201).

12 whole guajillo chiles, wiped
    with a damp paper towel
5 cups hot chicken stock
⅔ cup blanched almonds
1 tablespoon ground cumin
1 tablespoon dried oregano
2 teaspoons ground cinnamon
10 black peppercorns
Salt

1 cup raisins
3 cloves garlic
4 tablespoons vegetable oil
6 pounds boneless pork butt or Boston
    butt, cut into 1-inch cubes
3 medium onions, sliced
Pepper
½ bunch scallions, chopped
Large handful cilantro leaves, chopped

October 20th, 53°
hard frost

Tear off the stems of the dried chiles and shake out the seeds. Heat a large cast-iron or other heavy skillet over medium heat. Toast the chiles in the skillet, pressing them down with tongs and turning once or twice, until they are fragrant and turn a slightly darker shade, 30–60 seconds. Transfer the chiles to a medium bowl. Pour 2 cups of the hot chicken stock over the chiles and set them aside to soak until soft and pliable, about 30 minutes.

Toast the almonds in the skillet over medium heat, stirring frequently, until pale golden brown, 6–8 minutes. Transfer to a plate to cool completely. Add the cumin, oregano, cinnamon, and peppercorns to the skillet and toast the spices over medium heat, stirring, until fragrant, about 30 seconds. Transfer to a small bowl to cool. Finely grind the almonds with 1 teaspoon of salt in a food processor or blender. Add the chiles and their soaking liquid, along with the toasted spices, raisins, and garlic. Purée to a smooth paste.

Heat 2 tablespoons of the oil in the skillet over medium heat. Add the spice paste and fry, stirring to keep it from burning, until it becomes a shade darker and is very fragrant, about 5 minutes. Remove the skillet from the heat and set aside.

Heat the remaining 2 tablespoons of oil in a heavy large pot over medium heat. Working in batches, brown the pork all over, about 5 minutes. Transfer the meat to a bowl as it browns. Add the onions to the pot and cook, stirring often, until soft, about 5 minutes.

Return the pork and any accumulated juices to the pot. Stir in the spice paste. Add 2 cups of the stock and season with salt and pepper. Bring to a simmer. Cover the pot and simmer the stew over medium-low heat, stirring occasionally, until the pork is tender, 2–3 hours. Add a little more stock to the pot if the stew begins to dry out. Serve the stew garnished with scallions and cilantro.

CORNBREAD

We're definitely Northerners when it comes to cornbread—we like ours a little sweet. Serve this with Pork Stewed in Guajillo Chile Mole (page 198), if you like.

Put a 9-inch cast-iron skillet in the oven, then preheat the oven to 425°. Whisk together 1 cup yellow cornmeal, 1 cup all-purpose flour, 1–2 tablespoons sugar, 1 tablespoon baking powder, and ½ teaspoon salt in a medium mixing bowl. Stir in 1 cup buttermilk and 2 lightly beaten eggs. Remove the hot skillet from the oven. Add 4 tablespoons butter to the skillet, swirling it around until it melts and coats the bottom and sides of the skillet. Pour all but 1 tablespoon of the melted butter into the batter and stir to combine. Pour the batter into the hot skillet and slide the skillet back into the oven. Bake the cornbread until the top is golden brown and a wooden skewer inserted into the center comes out clean, about 25 minutes. Serve warm. — *serves 6–8*

DECONSTRUCTED CARBONARA
serves 2

When we are short on time and need only a few small sheets of pasta, we use packaged fresh. Don't think we're slackers not to make our own—the packaged is just right for a quick dish like this one.

1 cup diced pancetta	4 eggs
2 tablespoons butter	4 sheets fresh pasta (about 4 inches long)
Salt	Pepper
Splash of vinegar	Shaved pecorino

Cook the pancetta in a medium skillet over medium heat, stirring occasionally, until browned and crisp, 8–10 minutes. Add the butter to the skillet and keep warm over the lowest heat.

October 25th, 66°
sweater weather

Bring a medium saucepan of salted water to a boil over high heat. Add the vinegar and reduce the heat to medium-low to maintain a gentle simmer. Crack the eggs into 4 small cups. Give the water a good circular stir, then tip 1 egg at a time into the center of the swirling water. Simmer the eggs until the whites are white and the yolks remain soft, about 3 minutes. Transfer the eggs with a slotted spoon to a clean dishcloth to drain.

Cook the sheets of pasta in a medium pot of salted boiling water over medium-high heat until just tender, 2–3 minutes. Using a slotted spatula, divide the pasta between 2 warm plates, letting most of the water drain off before spreading the sheets out on the plates. Put 2 poached eggs on top of the pasta on each plate, then spoon the pancetta and butter over the top of each. Season with a little salt and lots of pepper. Serve with shaved pecorino.

VIN SANTO–ROASTED PEARS

We roast Anjou, Comice, or Bartlett pears for this simple dessert in any number of Italian *passiti*, or sweet dessert wines—vin santo from Tuscany, Recioto di Soave from the Veneto, or any of the nonsparkling *moscati*. The prices and delicate flavors of these wines vary; choose one that suits your budget and taste.

Preheat the oven to 375°. Put ¼ cup sugar, juice of ½ lemon, and 1 cup vin santo or other sweet dessert wine into a medium baking dish and stir until the sugar dissolves. Split 1 vanilla bean lengthwise, scrape the seeds into the dish, and add the pod. Halve 4 ripe semifirm pears lengthwise and peel them. Use a measuring spoon or a melon baller to scoop out the core. Arrange the pears in the dish in a single layer cut side down. Spoon the wine over the pears. Scatter 2 tablespoons soft butter in pieces around the pears. Roast the pears, basting them once or twice, until they are tender and the juices are syrupy, about 1 hour. Let the pears cool before serving them. — *serves 4–8*

{ October 26th, 41°
our first fire

GIANDUIA
makes about 2 cups

We slather this creamy chocolate and toasted hazelnut spread—our purer, more flavorful version of Nutella, the commercial brand available throughout the world—on warm toast for breakfast. It's part of what makes our Gianduia & Caramel Tart (page 204) so delicious. (We've found that it also tastes sinfully good with Oreo cookies, but let's just keep that our little secret.)

1 generous cup (5 ounces) skinned hazelnuts	8 ounces semisweet chocolate
Large pinch of sugar	½ cup heavy cream
	4 tablespoons salted butter, cut into pieces

Preheat the oven to 350°. Spread the hazelnuts out on small baking sheet or in an ovenproof skillet and toast them in the oven until they are a deep toasty brown, about 15 minutes. Remove them from the oven and set aside to cool completely. Grind the hazelnuts with the sugar in batches in a food processor to a fairly smooth, buttery paste.

{ October 27th, 48°
rain & wind

Melt the chocolate in a heatproof medium bowl set over a pot of simmering water over medium-low heat, stirring often. Remove the bowl from the heat and whisk in the cream and butter. Stir in the ground hazelnuts. The gianduia will thicken and become soft and peanut butter–like as it cools. It will keep at room temperature in a covered container for up to 2 weeks.

GIANDUIA & CARAMEL TART
makes one 4 × 13-inch tart

We're suckers for the classic combination of caramel and chocolate. Here we've matched up gianduia, the chocolate-hazelnut spread, with caramel to make a new classic at Canal House, layering the two flavors in this intensely delicious tart. A little goes a long way, so cut the tart into thin slices and serve with a big spoonful of unsweetened softly whipped heavy cream, if you like—and definitely an espresso.

FOR THE CRUST
1 cup all-purpose flour
Pinch of salt
6 tablespoons cold unsalted butter, cut into small pieces
1 tablespoon vegetable shortening

FOR THE FILLING
1 cup sugar
2 tablespoons light corn syrup
4 tablespoons unsalted butter
¼ cup heavy cream
1 tablespoon sour cream
1 cup Gianduia (page 203)

October 29th, 52° the leaves are gone

For the crust, whisk together the flour and salt in a medium mixing bowl. Work the butter and shortening into the flour using a pastry blender or 2 knives until it resembles coarse cornmeal. Gradually sprinkle in 3 tablespoons ice water while stirring with a fork. Press the dough together until it forms a rough ball. Don't overhandle it; there should be streaks of butter visible throughout. Shape it into a flat disk, wrap in plastic wrap, and refrigerate for at least 1 hour.

Roll out the dough on a lightly floured surface into a 7 × 16-inch rectangle about ¼ inch thick. Roll the dough loosely around the rolling pin, then unfurl it into a 4 × 13-inch fluted tart pan with a removable bottom. Trim off any excess dough. Prick the crust all over with a fork. Cover with plastic wrap and refrigerate for at least 1 hour or overnight.

Preheat the oven to 350°. Line the crust with a sheet of foil that hangs over the edges by at least 2 inches, then fill with pie weights or dried beans. Bake the crust until the edges are pale golden, about 20 minutes. Lift the foil and weights off the crust and continue baking until the crust is golden brown, 15–20 minutes. Let the crust cool completely on a wire rack.

For the filling, put the sugar, corn syrup, and ¼ cup water in a heavy medium saucepan. Boil over medium-high heat, swirling the pan over the heat frequently, until the syrup turns a dark amber caramel, about 15 minutes. Carefully whisk in the butter, cream, and sour cream (the caramel will hiss and bubble up, so stand back). Remove the pan from the heat and whisk until smooth. Pour the hot caramel into the prepared crust and let it cool for about 1 hour. It will thicken and set.

Melt the Gianduia in a heatproof bowl set over a pot of simmering water over low heat. Pour the Gianduia evenly over the set caramel filling, smoothing out the top with a metal spatula. Let the tart set for at least 4 hours before serving.

Top, Gianduia slathered on toast; bottom, Gianduia & Caramel Tart

❧ November Recipes ❧

bratwurst with sautéed caraway cabbage ∾ 210

bratwurst with fingerling potatoes ∾ 210

golden bread crumbs with pancetta & prunes ∾ 213

cauliflower with bread crumbs, pancetta & prunes ∾ 213

skirt steak with buttered spinach & french fries ∾ 214

lamb shoulder chops with rosemary potatoes ∾ 216

roast turkey ∾ 220

turkey gravy ∾ 220

turkey stock ∾ 221

cranberry-port gelée ∾ 221

brian's mashed potato trick ∾ 221

chestnut & pearl onion stuffing ∾ 222

agee's pecan pies ∾ 223

kabocha squash pie ∾ 226

pumpkin chiffon pie ∾ 227

day-after-thanksgiving turkey sandwich ∾ 228

turkey & potato soup ∾ 228

escarole salad with lemon & parmigiano ∾ 228

apple galette ∾ 230

November begins the holiday season. Those long golden afternoons of October have disappeared along with the sun that now sinks behind the hills by four o'clock. It's officially cold, and a whole new round of rituals begin.

We order wood for our Franklin stove, politely but firmly requesting good dry wood with some weight. The last cord was too green and wouldn't burn, and the time before that, the wood was so light and dry it burned up like kindling. This time it's just right. Every morning, the first one to work builds the fire and it adds sweet cheer to the place. We are thrilled with our cozy studio.

All summer we drank glass after glass of water. "Hydration!" we reminded each other. Now we brew pots of dark, delicious Pu-erh from Yunnan, China, for our well-being, so mugs of tea start the day. Our five o'clock cocktails have morphed from white wine or gin to bourbon, scotch, or a glass of something red. We are happily hunkering down.

In early November, Thanksgiving discussions begin. We signed up for our turkeys back in October, from a local farm that raises the most beautiful birds. Their chickens are the Marilyn Monroes of the avian world—big, plump, and full-breasted, with smooth creamy skin. Their pasture-raised turkeys are just as handsome and delicious. After work the Monday before the holiday, we go to pick up our birds from the farm. We drive across winding country roads, and by the time we peel into the gravel farmyard it's after dark. It's first come, first choice, and we are last, so both of us stagger home with 26-pound birds.

Last year, we decided to have a turkey dinner a day ahead of the holiday. We invited the Canal House cast of characters—friends, colleagues, and neighbors. We dubbed it "Thanksgiving With No Tears" since the whole affair would be free of tricky family dynamics. Everyone was to bring their essential Thanksgiving dish, food that resonated in his or her memory. The meal was a hodgepodge. We roasted one of the giant turkeys, stuffed with chestnut and cipolline dressing, and made lots of giblet gravy. We served everything set right down the center of the long dinner table, family style: Brussels sprouts with bacon, mashed potatoes, sweet potato casserole with miniature marshmallows, creamed onions, green beans with slivered almonds, pineapple bread pudding, two kinds of cranberry sauce and more. Perhaps there even was a Jell-O salad with nuts! We did however, drink beautifully. Someone brought elegant Italian whites that made up for all our culinary indiscretions.

The whole evening was fun, funny, happy—the vibe was so spontaneous, and not a single tear was shed. It would be hard to re-create. But why not try? Maybe it will become our ultimate November ritual.

BRATWURST WITH SAUTÉED CARAWAY CABBAGE
serves 2

The cabbage, flavored with caraway and vinegar, and the rich bratwurst complement each other perfectly. This simple meal can be on the table in 20 minutes.

FOR THE CABBAGE
2 tablespoons olive oil
½ red cabbage, cored and sliced
Large pinch of caraway seeds, crushed
   in a mortar
Salt and pepper

5 tablespoons red wine vinegar
Pinch of sugar
FOR THE BRATWURST
1 tablespoon olive oil
4 bratwurst sausages, pricked

November 3rd, 34°
biting cold wind

For the cabbage, heat the olive oil in a large pan over medium heat. Add the cabbage and caraway seeds, season with salt and pepper, and cook, stirring, until slightly wilted, about 5 minutes. Add the vinegar, sugar, and a splash of water, and cook, stirring occasionally, until just tender, 10–12 minutes. Taste and adjust the seasonings.

Meanwhile, for the bratwurst, drizzle the olive oil in a medium skillet, and put the bratwurst in. Add ¼ cup water and cook over medium-high heat until the water has evaporated and the bratwurst are browned on one side, 12–14 minutes. Flip over the bratwurst and cook on the other side until browned, about 3 minutes. Serve the dish with Dijon mustard, if you like.

BRATWURST WITH FINGERLING POTATOES

Bratwurst is a German-style sausage made of veal or beef and pork, and is traditionally pan-fried or grilled. We sometimes add beer instead of water to the pan to add a little more flavor.

November 5th, 33°
an icy rain

Put 1 pound fingerling potatoes in a large pot of salted cold water and bring to a simmer over medium-high heat. Cook until tender, 10–15 minutes. Drain. After they are cool enough to handle, cut the potatoes in half lengthwise. Heat 2 tablespoons olive oil in a heavy large skillet over medium heat. Add the potatoes in one layer cut side down, season with salt and pepper, and cook, undisturbed, until they have developed a nice crust, 5–8 minutes. Meanwhile, drizzle 1 tablespoon olive oil in a medium skillet, then put in 4 bratwurst and ¼ cup water or beer. Cook over medium-high heat until the water is evaporated and the bratwurst are browned on one side, 12–14 minutes. Flip over the bratwurst and cook on the other side until browned, about 3 minutes. To serve, sprinkle the potatoes with chopped fresh parsley leaves. Serve the dish with Dijon mustard and cornichons, if you like. —— *serves 2*

GOLDEN BREAD CRUMBS WITH PANCETTA & PRUNES

We love these bread crumbs so much that we make a big batch of them to sprinkle over cooked vegetables, toss into pastas, and add to green salads to give them a little crunch.

November 10th, 41°
cold & sunny

Melt 4 tablespoons butter in a heavy large skillet over medium heat. Add about 2 cups finely diced pancetta and cook, stirring often, until lightly browned, about 15 minutes. Stir in 8 cups fresh bread crumbs, and toast, stirring frequently, until deep golden brown, about 15 minutes. Remove the skillet from the heat. Stir in 2 pinches of red pepper flakes and 1 cup finely diced pitted prunes, using the back of the spoon to break up the prunes and evenly mix them throughout the crumbs. Season with salt and pepper. Allow to cool completely and store in an airtight container in the refrigerator. Warm in a skillet over medium heat before using. —— *makes about 6 cups*

CAULIFLOWER WITH BREAD CRUMBS, PANCETTA & PRUNES
serves 4–6

We went off to The Omega Institute near Rheinbeck, New York, to hear the wise words of American Buddhist Pema Chödrön. The prediction was for an untimely snowstorm—8 inches of the white stuff. It was a great adventure (that's what we were hoping for). Before we left, we fortified ourselves with a vegetarian lunch of roasted cauliflower smothered in butter-toasted bread crumbs with pancetta and Marsala-softened prunes.

¼ cup finely diced pitted prunes
1–2 tablespoons Marsala
5 tablespoons butter
½ cup finely diced pancetta (3 ounces)
2 cups fresh plain bread crumbs

Small pinch of red pepper flakes
Salt and pepper
1 head cauliflower, core removed
  and head left intact

November 12th, 45°
cloudy then sunny

Soften the prunes in the Marsala. Melt 1 tablespoon of the butter in a heavy large skillet over medium heat. Add the pancetta and cook, stirring frequently, until lightly browned, about 10 minutes. Stir in the bread crumbs and cook, stirring frequently, until they are a deep golden brown, about 15 minutes.

Remove the skillet from the heat. Stir in the red pepper flakes and prunes, using the back of the spoon to break up the prunes and evenly mix them throughout the crumbs. Season with salt and pepper.

Cook the cauliflower in a large pot of salted boiling water over medium heat until tender, about 10 minutes. Drain in a colander, then place on a platter, like a flower. Melt the remaining 4 tablespoons of butter in a small saucepan, then drizzle over the cauliflower. Spoon the bread crumbs over and around the cauliflower.

SKIRT STEAK WITH BUTTERED SPINACH & FRENCH FRIES
serves 4

When we are in a pinch we pull out the frozen French fries. When they are double fried (as all classic French fries are), they taste mighty close to homemade fries. The trick to skirt steak—a flavorful but not so tender cut—is to slice it across the grain. Then it is one of the most delectable pieces of beef around.

For the French fries
Canola oil
2-pound bag frozen French fries

For the spinach
8 tablespoons butter
1 pound fresh spinach

Salt and pepper

For the steak
1¼ pounds skirt steak, cut in half crosswise
Salt and pepper

November 15th, 48°
dark overcast day

For the French fries, add enough oil to a heavy medium pot to reach a depth of 3 inches. Heat over medium-high heat until the oil reaches a temperature of 350°on a candy thermometer. Or, if a wooden chopstick dipped into the bottom of the oil sends bubbles up right away, the oil is ready for frying. Working in batches, carefully slip the frozen French fries into the hot oil. Fry until pale golden, about 2 minutes. As you fry, adjust the heat to maintain the temperature. (The second frying will make them crisp, so don't worry.) Transfer the fries with a slotted spatula to a wire rack set over paper towels to drain.

For the spinach, melt the butter in a large pot over medium heat. Add the spinach by handfuls, turning with tongs to coat with butter. As it wilts, add more handfuls of spinach and keep tossing with each addition. Once all the spinach is in, cover, reduce heat to medium-low, and cook, tossing or stirring occasionally, until the spinach is very silky, 10–12 minutes. Remove from the heat. Season with salt and pepper and cover to keep warm.

For the steak, heat a large grill pan over medium-high heat. Season the steaks well on both sides with salt and pepper. When the pan is hot, cook the steaks until well browned, 2–3 minutes per side. Remove from the heat and allow them to rest on a cutting board.

As the steaks rest, reheat the oil to 350° and fry the potatoes again, working in batches, until deep golden, 2–3 minutes. Transfer the fries to the wire rack to drain. Season with salt.

Thinly slice the steaks across the grain, and serve with buttered spinach and hot French fries.

LAMB SHOULDER CHOPS WITH ROSEMARY POTATOES
serves 4

Thin, inexpensive lamb shoulder "blade" chops are a great cut of meat. Blade chops stay flat in the pan so they'll brown all over. Conversely, lamb shoulder "arm" chops, which have a cross-section of the round arm bone, tend to curl as they cook, making for uneven browning. For the potatoes, use waxy ones, like Yukon golds, that don't fall apart when they're cooked. We peel the potatoes, then pan-roast them to create a crisp golden crust. Avoid the temptation to fiddle with the potatoes as they cook. Just let them do their thing and they'll be delicious.

5 medium Yukon gold potatoes, peeled
 and quartered
2 pounds lamb shoulder chops
Salt and pepper

2 tablespoons extra-virgin olive oil
2 cloves garlic, peeled and smashed
3 large sprigs fresh rosemary

November 16th, 53°
light rain

Put the potatoes in a large pot of salted cold water and bring to a boil over medium-high heat. Reduce the heat to medium and cook the potatoes until they are barely tender, 5–10 minutes. Drain and set aside.

Season the lamb chops well with salt and pepper. Heat a heavy large skillet over medium-high heat. When it's hot, add the olive oil, then put the lamb chops in the skillet. Cook in batches, if necessary, to brown the chops (crowding the skillet will braise them instead). Cook until well browned, about 5 minutes, then flip and cook for about 3 minutes for medium-rare. Transfer the chops to a plate and keep warm in a very low oven, if you like.

Add the garlic and rosemary to the sizzling oil in the skillet, reduce the heat a bit if the garlic is browning too quickly, and cook until fragrant, about 1 minute. Add the potatoes in one layer, season with salt and pepper, and cook undisturbed until they have developed a nice crust, about 5 minutes. Continue to cook, turning only occasionally, until the potatoes are tender and golden brown on all sides, 10–15 minutes. Serve the chops with the potatoes, garnished with more fresh rosemary, if you like.

ROAST TURKEY
serves 12

We've cooked turkeys every which way: in a brown grocery bag (turns out to be highly unsanitary); draped with butter-drenched cheesecloth; deep-fried; even deboned and shaped into a melon (oh là là!). We've wrestled with a hot twenty-five pounder, breast side down, then breast side up, and on and on. But we think we've found the answer to achieving the perfect Thanksgiving turkey—the easy dry salt brine.

November 24th, 32°
early morning flurries

Rinse a 14–16-pound fresh turkey (not injected or pre-brined) and pat dry with paper towels. Rub or pat 3 tablespoons kosher salt onto the breasts, legs, and thighs. Tightly wrap the turkey completely in plastic wrap or slip it into a very large resealable plastic bag, pressing out the air before sealing it. Set the turkey in a pan breast side up and refrigerate it for 3 days. Turn the turkey every day, massaging the salt into the skin through the plastic.

Unwrap the turkey and pat it dry with paper towels (don't rinse the bird). Return the turkey to the pan breast side up and refrigerate it, uncovered, for at least 8 hours or overnight.

Remove the turkey from the refrigerator and let it come to room temperature for at least 1 hour. Preheat the oven to 325°.

If you've decided to serve your turkey stuffed, spoon the stuffing into the cavity of the bird. (Put any extra stuffing into a buttered baking dish, cover, and put it in the oven to bake with the turkey for the last hour.) Tie the legs together with kitchen string. Tuck the wings under the back. Rub the turkey all over with 3–4 tablespoons softened butter. Place the turkey breast side up on a roasting rack set into a large roasting pan. Add 2 cups water to the pan. Roast the turkey until it is golden brown and a thermometer inserted into the thigh registers 165°, about 3 hours for an unstuffed bird or 3–4 hours for a stuffed one.

Transfer the turkey to a platter, loosely cover it with foil, and let it rest for about 20 minutes before carving. Serve the turkey and stuffing, if using, with gravy.

TURKEY GRAVY

FOR THE BROWNED FLOUR ⌁ We use browned flour, cooked until it is the color of a wooden spoon, to add rich deep flavor while it thickens our gravy.

Add 1–2 cups flour to a medium cast-iron skillet over medium-low heat. Cook, stirring frequently with a wooden spoon, until the flour begins to turn a warm beige color; then stir frequently until the flour turns golden brown, about 1 hour. Store in an airtight container. —— *makes 1–2 cups*

continued

FOR THE TURKEY STOCK ⌁ While the turkey roasts, make the turkey stock by gently simmering the neck, giblets, and heart (save the liver for another use) in a large pot with 10 cups salted water, 1 quartered onion, 1 peeled and chopped carrot, and 1 chopped celery rib over medium heat. After 3–4 hours, and by the time the turkey is out of the oven, you will have a flavorful broth for making gravy. If there's not enough, simply add chicken stock to make 8 cups. The turkey neck has lots of good meat on it; chop it, along with the giblets, and add it to the gravy, if you like. —— *makes 8 cups*

FOR THE GRAVY ⌁ When the turkey comes out of the oven, transfer it from the roasting pan to a cutting board or a large platter. Put the roasting pan on the stove top straddling two burners. Bring the pan drippings to a simmer over medium heat, stirring and scraping the bottom of the pan with a whisk or wooden spoon to loosen any browned bits stuck to the bottom. Sprinkle ¾ cup browned flour into the simmering pan drippings and whisk until smooth and thickened, about 1 minute. While whisking constantly, pour in 8 cups turkey stock. Simmer over medium heat, whisking occasionally, until the gravy is thick and smooth, 10–15 minutes. Season with salt and pepper. Serve hot in a gravy boat. —— *makes 6–8 cups*

CRANBERRY-PORT GELÉE

Use a good port, red wine, or even a Madeira if that's what you have on hand. Cranberries have so much natural pectin that this sauce will set up even if you don't refrigerate it.

Put 1 cup port, 1 cup sugar, 1 tablespoon juniper berries, and 10 black peppercorns into a heavy saucepan and bring to a boil over medium-high heat. Add 1 bag (12 ounces) fresh cranberries and return to a boil. Reduce the heat to low and simmer until the cranberries burst and are very soft, about 10 minutes. Strain the sauce into a bowl through a fine-mesh sieve, pushing the solids through with a rubber spatula. Transfer to a pretty serving bowl. Cover and refrigerate. —— *makes about 2 cups*

BRIAN'S MASHED POTATO TRICK

Our friend Brian Beadle is kind of a finicky eater—he's a meat and potatoes man. You could say he is sort of a "spuds specialist". His mashed potato recipe is fairly standard, but his trick is to slip tiny pats of cold butter down into and throughout the hot potatoes when they are in their serving dish. The butter melts into hidden pools buried deep in the mashed potatoes, to be discovered with each delicious forkful.

Overleaf: left, Roast Turkey; right, clockwise from top left: Cranberry-Port Gelée, Turkey Gravy, Chestnut & Pearl Onion Stuffing, Brian's Mashed Potato Trick

CHESTNUT & PEARL ONION STUFFING
serves 12

We're cooks who have endless patience for "process". But when a recipe calls for 5 cups of peeled chestnuts, we know we're in for some serious labor: scoring their skins with x's, roasting them, peeling them while they are still hot, then removing the fuzzy inner skins. Life is too short. We cut ourselves some slack and reach for jars of those nice already peeled French chestnuts—they're delicious.

8 tablespoons butter

2 pounds pearl onions, peeled

¼ pound pancetta, finely diced

Two 14.8-ounce jars peeled whole
  chestnuts (5 cups)

1 cup Madeira

Salt and pepper

5 cups coarse fresh bread crumbs

2–3 large sprigs fresh sage,
  leaves finely chopped

2 large handfuls fresh parsley,
  leaves finely chopped

1–1½ cups chicken stock

Melt 4 tablespoons of the butter in a very large skillet over medium heat. Add the onions and pancetta, and cook, stirring often, until the onions are tender and lightly browned, about 30 minutes. Add the chestnuts and wine and cook for about 30 minutes, covering the pan if it begins to look dry. Transfer to a large bowl, season with salt and pepper, and set aside.

Melt the remaining 4 tablespoons of butter in the same unwashed skillet over medium-high heat. Add the bread crumbs and cook, stirring from time to time, until lightly golden, 10–15 minutes. Transfer the bread crumbs to the bowl with the chestnuts. Add the sage and parsley and mix everything together. Use the back of a wooden spoon to break most of the chestnuts into large pieces. Taste and adjust the seasonings.

Stir some chicken stock into the stuffing, mixing in just enough to moisten it without making it soggy or dense.

Spoon the stuffing into the turkey and roast it. Or, put the stuffing in a large buttered baking dish and bake in a preheated 325° oven, covered, for 45 minutes.

AGEE'S PECAN PIES
makes two 8-inch pies

Afra Lineberry, Agee to her family, opened The Jerre Anne Bake Shoppe in St. Joe, Missouri, in 1930. It was the last stop on the trolley line. Conductors would leave their cars running while they ran into Agee's for a cup of coffee and a piece of pie. "It seems like I just always knew how to make a good pie crust. It may take a little practice for some, but the only time to get excited about a pie crust is when you're eating it," Agee used to say. The little shop grew to be a smashing success, and by 1990, with Geraldine Lawhon (Agee's niece) running the place, it was selling 625 pies at Thanksgiving alone. Sadly, The Jerre Anne closed its doors in 2008. When you eat Agee's pie, send your thanks heavenward.

These pies should be baked in 8-inch pie pans. We use the aluminum variety found in any grocery store—technically speaking they measure 8¾ inches. They are thin delicate pies with just the right amount of filling.

FOR THE PIE CRUST
1½ cups all-purpose flour, plus some for rolling for rolling dough
½ teaspoon salt
8 tablespoons cold unsalted butter, cut into small pieces
2 tablespoons cold vegetable shortening

FOR THE PECAN FILLING
1½ cups light corn syrup
5 tablespoons butter, melted
1 cup light brown sugar (not packed)
Pinch of salt
½ teaspoon vanilla extract
4 eggs, beaten
3 cups pecan halves (not pieces)

For the pie crust, whisk together the flour and salt in a bowl. Blend in the butter and shortening with a pasty blender or a fork until crumbly. It should resemble fine pieces of grain. Sprinkle with 4–5 tablespoons ice water and toss lightly. Divide the dough evenly and form into 2 disks. Don't overhandle. Wrap dough in plastic wrap and chill for at least 1 hour.

Roll out one ball of dough on a lightly floured surface into an ⅛-inch-thick round. Roll dough loosely around the rolling pin then unfurl it into an 8-inch pie pan. Lightly press dough into the pan. Trim the excess dough from the edge with a sharp knife. Use your thumb and forefinger to crimp the edges. Repeat with the remaining dough and the second pie pan.

Preheat the oven to 350°. For the pecan filling, mix together the corn syrup, melted butter, and brown sugar in a large bowl until the sugar has dissolved. Add the salt, vanilla, and eggs, mixing well after each addition.

Arrange 1½ cups of the pecans right side up in each unbaked pie shell, then gently pour in the filling. The pecans will float to the top. Bake until a knife inserted in the middle comes out clean, 40–45 minutes. Cool to room temperature.

KABOCHA SQUASH PIE
makes one 9-inch pie

We prefer the sweet flavorful flesh of the kabocha squash over any other pie pumpkin.
The chestnutlike texture of this pie makes it especially toothsome.

FOR THE PIE CRUST

1 cup all-purpose flour, plus some for
rolling out the dough

1 tablespoon sugar

Small pinch salt

6 tablespoons cold unsalted butter, cut
into small pieces

1 tablespoon cold vegetable shortening

FOR THE FILLING

3 pounds kabocha squash, to measure
about 2½ cups when baked

¾ cup packed light brown sugar

2 tablespoons molasses or sorghum

3 egg yolks

½ cup heavy cream

1 teaspoon ground ginger

1 teaspoon ground cinnamon

1 teaspoon ground mace

Pinch of salt

1 tablespoon granulated sugar

1 teaspoon ground cinnamon

Freshly whipped cream

For the pie crust, whisk together the flour, sugar, and salt in a mixing bowl. Work the butter
and shortening into the flour using a pastry blender or 2 knives, until it resembles coarse cornmeal. Sprinkle in 3 tablespoons ice water and toss together lightly until the dough comes
together. Shape the dough into a flat disk; don't overhandle. Wrap the dough in plastic
wrap, and chill for at least 1 hour.

For the filling, preheat the oven to 400°. Cut the squash in half horizontally. Scoop out and
discard the seeds. Place the squash cut side down on a baking pan and add a splash of water to
the pan. Bake the squash until tender when pierced with a knife, about 1 hour. Remove from the
oven, set aside, and allow to cool. Reduce the oven temperature to 375°.

When the squash is cool enough to handle, scoop out enough flesh to measure 2½ cups. Discard
the skins. Put the flesh into a large bowl. Add the brown sugar, molasses, egg yolks, cream, ginger,
cinnamon, mace, and salt, and mix together until the filling is smooth.

Roll out the dough into a 12-inch round on a lightly floured surface. Roll the dough loosely
around the rolling pin, then unfurl it into a 9-inch pie pan. Lightly press it into the pan. Leave
1 inch of dough hanging over the edge. Trim any excess off with a sharp knife. Tuck the dough
under itself, then use your thumb and forefinger to crimp the edge.

Pour the filling into the unbaked pie crust and smooth the top with a rubber spatula. Bake for
1 hour. Mix the granulated sugar and cinnamon together in a a small bowl. Sprinkle the top of
the pie with the cinnamon sugar. Serve with dollops of the whipped cream.

PUMPKIN CHIFFON PIE
makes one 9-inch pie

Even people who aren't big pumpkin pie fans will like this genteel version. Light, delicate, and sweet, it is a recipe from a kinder, gentler time. Its very name—chiffon—evokes a sheer and floaty fabric, a long way from today's sturdy Spandex. Even after a hearty holiday meal, we find there's always room for a small slice of this lovely pie.

FOR THE CRUST
2 cups crumbled ginger snaps
¼ cup sugar
1 teaspoon ground cinnamon
6 tablespoons butter, melted

FOR THE FILLING
1 tablespoon powdered gelatin
3 eggs, separated

¾ cup sugar
1¼ cups fresh cooked or canned pumpkin
½ cup whole milk
½ teaspoon ground cinnamon
¼ whole nutmeg, grated, or
   ½ teaspoon ground nutmeg
¼ teaspoon salt
Freshly whipped cream

For the crust, preheat the oven to 350°. Put the crumbled cookies into a large resealable plastic bag and seal, pressing out the air. Roll back and forth over the bag with a rolling pin until the cookies are ground into fine crumbs. (Or alternately, finely grind the ginger snaps in a food processor.) Transfer the crumbs to a large mixing bowl and stir in the sugar and cinnamon. Drizzle the melted butter over the crumbs and stir to combine. Pat the mixture evenly into a 9-inch pie pan and bake for 5 minutes. Remove from the oven and set aside to cool.

For the filling, soak the gelatin in ¼ cup cold water. Put the egg yolks, ¼ cup of the sugar, the pumpkin, milk, cinnamon, nutmeg, and salt in a saucepan and cook over medium heat, stirring until thickened, about 10 minutes. Stir in the softened gelatin, then transfer to a large mixing bowl and allow to cool.

Beat the reserved egg whites in a large mixing bowl on medium speed until foamy. Continue beating, gradually adding the remaining ½ cup sugar until egg whites are thick, glossy, and hold soft peaks. Fold the whites into the filling, taking care not to deflate the whites. Pour into the baked pie crust and smooth the filling with a spatula. Chill until set, about 2 hours. Serve with dollops of the whipped cream.

Overleaf: left, Kabocha Squash Pie; right, Pumpkin Chiffon Pie

DAY-AFTER-THANKSGIVING TURKEY SANDWICH

November 25th, 37°
clear as a bell

The very best part of Thanksgiving is the day-after leftover turkey sandwich. We like ours on good white bread slathered with mayonnaise, a spoonful of turkey drippings or gravy, and Cranberry-Port Gelée (page 221); with a leaf or two of crisp lettuce and a pile of thinly sliced turkey breast meat seasoned with lots of salt and pepper. A cold glass of milk is our beverage of choice, although there may be a splash of last night's Champagne left in the refrigerator door (with a small silver spoon hanging in the neck of the bottle to preserve precious bubbles). Better stick with milk. — *makes 1*

TURKEY & POTATO SOUP
serves 4

We came up with this soup years ago simply by using two things we always have plenty of at Thanksgiving: turkey stock and leftover mashed potatoes. Now we even make this when we don't have leftover potatoes. This soup is quite delicate and soothing after all the Thanksgiving gluttony.

2 large russet potatoes, peeled and sliced
¼ cup whole milk
3 tablespoons unsalted butter

3–4 cups hot Turkey Stock (page 221)
Salt and pepper
2 tablespoons chopped fresh chives

November 26th, 31°
hoarfrost

Put the potatoes in a pot of salted cold water. Bring to a boil over medium-high heat and cook until very soft, 20–30 minutes. Drain off almost all the water, then mash the potatoes with a potato masher until very smooth, adding the milk and butter as you go.

Stir in enough of the hot turkey stock to make a smooth, velvety soup. Season with salt and pepper. Serve the soup hot with a sprinkling of chopped chives.

ESCAROLE SALAD WITH LEMON & PARMIGIANO

Use the best olive oil you can find to make this salad. You can make nice, thin shavings of cheese using a swivel-blade vegetable peeler.

Mash together ½ clove garlic and a pinch of salt with the back of a wooden spoon in a salad bowl. Stir in the diced rind of ¼ preserved lemon (page 294) and the juice of ½ lemon. Whisk in 4–6 tablespoons really good extra-virgin olive oil, adding more to taste. Toss 4–6 cups dry, trimmed escarole leaves with the vinaigrette. Serve the salad garnished with plenty of thin shavings of parmigiano-reggiano and some cracked black pepper. — *serves 4*

APPLE GALETTE
serves 8

Baking the galette on a pizza stone ensures a very crisp bottom crust. But a baking pan or cookie sheet will work just fine too. Patch any little tears in the crust with extra pieces of dough and smooth them with a wet finger so the juices won't leak out of the galette. Don't fret when you are folding over the dough; if the edges are a little rough, they will only add to the rustic character of this delicious dessert.

FOR THE CRUST
1½ cups all-purpose flour
Pinch of salt
8 tablespoons cold unsalted butter, cut into small pieces
2 tablespoons vegetable shortening

FOR THE APPLE FILLING
8 apples, such as Honeycrisp or Jonagold
½ cup sugar
1 teaspoon ground cinnamon
3 tablespoons salted butter
½ vanilla bean, halved lengthwise
2 tablespoons heavy cream

November 29th, 36° stormy night

For the crust, whisk together the flour and salt in a mixing bowl. Work the butter and shortening into the flour using a pastry blender or 2 knives until it resembles coarse cornmeal. Sprinkle in 5 tablespoons ice water and toss together lightly until the dough comes together (add a little more ice water if needed). Shape the dough into a flat disk; don't overhandle. Wrap the dough in plastic wrap and chill for at least 1 hour.

For the apple filling, peel and core the apples, then cut them into thick wedges. Put the apples in a large bowl and toss with the sugar and cinnamon. Melt the butter in a large skillet over medium heat, add the vanilla bean, then arrange the apple wedges in a single layer and cook, turning occasionally with a fork, until the apples are tender, about 45 minutes. Scrape the seeds from the vanilla pod into the skillet and spoon the pan juices over the apples. Remove the skillet from the heat.

Preheat the oven to 375°. Roll out the dough on a lightly floured surface into a 14-inch round. Roll the dough around the rolling pin and unfurl on a cold pizza stone or a large baking sheet.

Starting in the middle of the dough, arrange the apples in a tight circular pattern to about 3 inches from the edge. Spoon the pan juices over the apples. Fold the edge of the dough over the apples, pleating the dough as you go. Brush the dough with the heavy cream.

Bake until the crust is golden, about 45 minutes. Remove from the oven and allow to cool for 10 minutes before slicing.

December Recipes

fresh pasta ~ 236

spinach pasta ~ 238

balsamella ~ 240

simple tomato sauce ~ 240

ragù bolognese ~ 241

spinach tagliatelle bolognese ~ 241

pappardelle bolognese ~ 241

green lasagne with tomato sauce & fresh ricotta ~ 244

lasagne bolognese ~ 244

pappardelle & mushrooms ~ 245

cannelloni ~ 248

spinach tagliatelle with tomato sauce & ricotta ~ 250

butternut squash & candied bacon on fresh pasta ~ 250

milk punch ~ 252

cheese straws ~ 252

pickled shrimp & celery ~ 254

lobster stew ~ 255

roast prime rib of beef ~ 256

little yorkshire puddings ~ 256

roast goose with ten legs ~ 258

apples cooked with cumin ~ 258

marmalade cake ~ 261

ginger spice cake with dried cherries ~ 262

Sisters Margherita and Valeria Simili taught the celebrated cuisine of the Emilia-Romagna at their small Bologna cooking school, *Corsi di Cucina Sorelle Simili*, from 1986 to 2001. They wore crisp white cotton blouses, strings of pearls, glasses on thin gold chains, straight skirts and linen pants, and soft leather sandals. And, they wore aprons. Everything about them was classic. With handsome faces full of character, they weren't today's Food Channel femme fatales—they were better; they were the real thing. In fact, they are our heroes, wonderful cooks who taught and encouraged home cooking.

So we take their lead and do as they, and so many other good Italian cooks, do—we make homemade pasta for the holiday season. The festivities take precedence, and we set aside our day-to-day work to do some big-deal cooking. We clear the books and papers from our worktables and wipe those tables clean. Then we put on our aprons. We are ready to roll.

We give ourselves over to the process; nothing is hurried. Our floury hands keep us from answering our phones, texts, or emails. We put on music and roll sheet after sheet of smooth spinach and egg pasta. We make our version of the Simili sisters' magnificent recipe for lasagne Bolognese—layers of silky spinach pasta, rich Bolognese sauce, creamy balsamella, and grated parmigiano-reggiano. It is a dish for Christmas. We also make one of our families' recipes, cannelloni, involving squares of the sheerest egg pasta rolled around a chicken forcemeat, then covered in velvety balsamella and a bright tomato sauce. We serve two per person to begin the dinner and the first bites never fail to quiet the entire table—the cannelloni are so delicate, yet each mouthful is completely satisfying.

While we work, we tell each other stories of our families. One such story is about an Italian uncle who made wine in his basement, and on Christmas Eve after dinner he would take over the family's small kitchen. He'd play Italian opera records on their old Victrola, and while Enrico Caruso sang his heart out, Uncle Fred would pour himself a small tumbler of his own "Dago red" and begin. His specialty was Christmas ravioli, learned from watching his mother, as all Italians do. The kids would sit on chairs pushed up against the wall to watch the spectacle. Uncle Fred would roll out that pasta by hand until it eventually covered the top of the kitchen table and draped over the sides. Then he'd run a fluted ravioli cutter over the sheet, dividing it into a grid of scalloped squares, and dollop meat filling (which he'd made the night before) onto each one. He would fold and seal the ravioli, lay them out on cornmeal-dusted kitchen towels, and leave them on the cold back porch until Christmas lunch the next day. It wasn't Christmas until Uncle Fred made his ravioli. It's essential to have heroes like the Similis and Uncle Fred—they go before us and show us the way.

Facing page, clockwise from top left: Valeria and Margherita Simili in the doorway of their cooking school, Corsi di Cucina Sorelle Simili in Bologna, in the 1990s; unbaked cannelloni (page 248); rolling out a sheet of egg pasta (page 236)

FRESH PASTA
makes 1 pound; enough to serve 4

Fresh homemade pasta, rolled out with a hand-cranked pasta machine, couldn't be easier. Follow our step-by-step pictures to help you through the process.

2 cups "00" or unbleached all-purpose flour, plus more for dusting

4 large eggs
Large pinch of salt

December 3rd, 39° pasta pasta pasta!

Put the flour into a medium mixing bowl and make a well in the center of the mound. Add the eggs and salt to the well and beat with a fork (1). Continue gently beating the eggs while gradually stirring in the flour, little by little, from the inside rim of the well (2–4). When the dough is too lumpy to work with the fork, use your hand and knead in the remaining flour and form a rough ball (5).

Transfer the ball of dough to a lightly floured work surface. With clean dry hands, knead the dough, dusting it with flour as you work, until it becomes a smooth supple ball and is no longer tacky. Press your thumb into the center of the dough (6); if the center feels tacky, knead in a little more flour. Cover the dough with an inverted bowl or wrap it in plastic wrap and let it rest at room temperature for at least 30 minutes and up to several hours.

Cut the dough into eighths and keep it covered until ready to use. Working with one piece of dough at a time, flatten the dough a bit into a rectangle, then feed the narrow end through the smooth cylinders of a hand-crank pasta machine set on the widest setting (7). Do this two or three times to make the dough uniform. Decrease the setting on the machine by one notch and feed the narrow end of the dough through the cylinders again. Repeat this process, decreasing the setting by one notch each time. Roll the pasta as thin as you like. We find the thinness of the sheets of pasta rolled through all but the last notch to be the most versatile (8). Lay the sheets of pasta out on a lightly floured surface and cover with clean, damp kitchen towels to keep them from drying out until you're ready to cut them (9).

CUTTING PASTA ~ Just rolled-out sheets of pasta are satiny smooth and soft—perfect for creating a good seal when making stuffed pasta like ravioli. To cut long strands for pappardelle or tagliatelle, you must first let the sheets dry, but only until they are slightly stiff yet still completely pliable. For pappardelle, use a fluted pastry wheel to cut ribbons for pappardelle ¾ to 1 inch wide. To make ¼-inch-wide strands for tagliatelle, run the sheet through the appropriate cutters of your pasta machine's attachment. Or, loosely roll up a sheet crosswise; cut crosswise into ¼-inch-wide strands, and unfurl.

SPINACH PASTA
makes 1 pound; enough to serve 4

Italian wheat flour is graded according to how finely it's ground; "00" is the finest and used to make fresh pasta. Unbleached, all-purpose flour is a perfectly good substitute. Use mature spinach as "baby" leaves are too watery and tender.

1 pound fresh spinach, washed
   and trimmed
Salt

2 cups "00" or unbleached all-purpose flour,
   plus more for dusting
2 extra-large eggs

Blanch the spinach in a large pot of salted boiling water for 1 minute. Transfer it with a slotted spoon to a bowl of ice water to cool, then drain it. Squeeze out as much water as possible with your hands. Finely chop the spinach.

Sift the flour into a mound on a smooth surface and make a well in the center. Add the spinach, then the eggs, and 1 generous pinch of salt to the well and beat with a fork until well combined (1). Continue gently beating the eggs and spinach while gradually stirring in the flour, little by little, from the inside rim of the well. When the dough is too lumpy to work with the fork, use your hands to knead in the remaining flour (2) and form a rough ball.

Clean the work surface and lightly dust it with flour. With clean dry hands, knead the dough, dusting it with flour as you work, until it becomes a smooth supple ball and is no longer tacky. Press your thumb into the center of the dough (3); if the center feels tacky, knead in a little more flour. Cover the dough with an inverted bowl or wrap it in plastic wrap and let it rest at room temperature for at least 30 minutes and up to several hours.

Cut the dough into eighths and keep them covered. Flatten one piece of dough into a rectangle, then feed it through the smooth cylinders of a hand-crank pasta machine set on the widest setting. Do this two or three times. Decrease the setting on the machine by one notch and feed the dough through the cylinders again. Repeat, decreasing the setting by one notch each time. Roll the pasta through all but the last notch (4). Lay the sheets of pasta out on a lightly floured surface and cover with clean, damp kitchen towels until you are ready to cut it.

BALSAMELLA
makes about 4 cups

One of the building blocks of Northern Italian cooking is balsamella, the elegant white sauce used in making classic dishes like lasagne and cannelloni. It's a simple white sauce (béchamel in France) that needs a certain amount of finesse to keep the butter from browning and the roux from taking on any color whatsoever.

8 tablespoons butter
½ cup flour
4 cups hot whole milk

½ cup grated parmigiano-reggiano, optional
¼ whole nutmeg, finely grated
Salt

Melt the butter in a heavy medium saucepan over medium-low heat. Add the flour and cook for 1½–2 minutes, stirring constantly with a wooden spoon to prevent it from taking on any color. Gradually add the hot milk in a slow, steady stream, stirring constantly with a whisk to prevent lumps.

Increase the heat to medium and cook the sauce, stirring constantly with a wooden spoon, until it has the consistency of thick cream, 10–15 minutes. Remove the pan from the heat. Stir in the cheese, if using, and season with nutmeg and salt to taste. Strain the sauce if it's lumpy. Lay a sheet of plastic wrap directly on the surface of the balsamella to keep it warm until ready to use and to prevent a skin from forming.

SIMPLE TOMATO SAUCE
makes about 8 cups

We use the thicker version of this sauce for our Green Lasagne with Tomato Sauce & Fresh Ricotta (page 244), and the thinner version for saucing delicate fresh pasta, ravioli, and gnocchi. Or ladle it into soup bowls, float a fried egg on top, and sop up the goodness with warm crusty bread.

6 cups *passato di pomodoro* (strained tomatoes)
  or tomato purée
1 medium onion, halved
2–3 cloves garlic

4–6 tablespoons really good
  extra-virgin olive oil
Salt and pepper

Put the tomatoes into a heavy medium pot, rinsing out the containers with 4 cups water and adding it to the pot. Add the onion halves, garlic, olive oil, and salt and pepper to taste to the pot. Gently simmer over medium-low heat for about 1 hour for a thin, loose sauce, or 2–3 hours for a richer, thicker consistency. Adjust the seasonings and add a little more olive oil to round out the flavors, if you like. Discard the onions and garlic before using.

RAGÙ BOLOGNESE
makes about 6 cups

Like many long-simmered sauces, this one, perhaps the most delicious of all the Italian meat sauces, is more flavorful and balanced the following day.

2 tablespoons butter
2 tablespoons extra-virgin olive oil
1 onion, finely chopped
1 rib celery, finely diced
1 carrot, peeled and finely diced
2–3 thin slices prosciutto, finely chopped
2 chicken livers, finely chopped
¾ pound ground chuck

¾ pound ground pork
¼–½ whole nutmeg, finely grated
Salt and pepper
½ cup dry white wine
1 cup hot whole milk
One 28-ounce can tomato purée
1 cup chicken, veal, or beef stock

Heat the butter and oil together in a heavy large pot over medium heat. Add the onions and cook, stirring frequently with a wooden spoon, just until soft and translucent, 3–5 minutes. Add the celery and carrots and cook until they begin to soften, about 3 minutes. Add the prosciutto and chicken livers and cook until the livers are pale pink, about 1 minute. Add the ground chuck and pork, season with nutmeg and salt and pepper, and cook, breaking up the meat with the back of the spoon, until there is still a little pink, about 5 minutes. Avoid frying or browning the meat.

Add the wine to the pot and cook until evaporated, 10–12 minutes. Add the milk, and cook over medium-low heat, stirring occasionally, until absorbed, about 20 minutes.

Meanwhile, heat the tomato purée and stock in a medium saucepan until hot, then add it to the meat. Reduce the heat to low and gently simmer, stirring occasionally, until the meat is tender, 6–7 hours. Add water, if needed, to keep the ragù loose and saucy. Season it with salt and pepper.

SPINACH TAGLIATELLE BOLOGNESE ～ Heat 4–6 cups Ragù Bolognese in a wide pan over medium heat until hot. Add 1 pound cooked fresh spinach tagliatelle and a little of the pasta water. Serve with grated parmigiano. —— *serves 4–8*

PAPPARDELLE BOLOGNESE ～ Substitute fresh pappardelle for the spinach tagliatelle.

Overleaf: left, Balsamella; right, Ragù Bolognese

GREEN LASAGNE WITH TOMATO SAUCE & FRESH RICOTTA
serves 8–12

Legendary home cooks Margherita and Valeria Simili, twin sisters from Bologna, taught us the nuances of making pasta and lasagne. Their recipes are the model for ours. Don't be hesitant to make sheets of fresh pasta for this noble layered dish; you need only take one bite of it to understand the difference between ordinary and sublime. If you've only had those clunky lasagne made with thick sheets of dried pasta, the tenderness of fresh pasta will be a revelation.

1 pound Spinach Pasta (page 238)	1¼ cups grated parmigiano-reggiano
Salt	4 cups warm Balsamella (page 240)
2 tablespoons butter	1 cup fresh whole-milk ricotta
3 cups Simple Tomato Sauce (page 240)	

Cook the pasta, 1–2 sheets at a time, in a large pot of salted boiling water until tender, about 30 seconds. Carefully transfer the pasta to a bowl of ice water to cool. Lay the sheets of cooked pasta out on clean, damp kitchen towels in a single layer without touching. Cover with more damp kitchen towels.

Preheat the oven to 400°. Grease a deep 9 × 13-inch baking dish with the butter. Cover the bottom with a layer of pasta, trimming the sheets to fit and patching, if necessary. Spread evenly with 1 cup of the tomato sauce, then sprinkle with ¼ cup of the parmigiano. Add another layer of pasta, cover with 1½ cups of the balsamella, dot with ½ cup of the ricotta, then sprinkle with more parmigiano. Repeat layers again. Finally, add another layer of pasta, cover it with the remaining tomato sauce, then spoonfuls of the balsamella and the parmigiano.

Bake the lasagne until it is bubbling around the edges and browned on top, about 15 minutes. Do not overcook. Let the lasagne rest for 10–15 minutes before serving.

LASAGNE BOLOGNESE
serves 8–12

Traditional *lasagne bolognese* is made with spinach pasta but we use either spinach or plain egg pasta depending on what we have. It's the ragù that matters.

1 pound Spinach Pasta (page 238) or Fresh Pasta (page 236)	4–5 cups warm Ragù Bolognese (page 241)
	1¼ cups grated parmigiano-reggiano
Salt	4 cups warm Balsamella (page 240)
2 tablespoons butter	

continued

Cook the pasta, 1–2 sheets at a time, in a large pot of salted boiling water until tender, about 30 seconds. Carefully transfer the pasta to a bowl of ice water to cool. Lay the sheets of cooked pasta out on clean, damp kitchen towels in a single layer without touching. Cover with more damp kitchen towels.

Preheat the oven to 400°. Grease a deep 9×13-inch baking dish with the butter. Cover the bottom with a layer of pasta, trimming the sheets to fit and patching, if necessary. Spread evenly with 1½ cups of the ragù, then sprinkle with ¼ cup of the parmigiano. Add another layer of pasta, cover it with 1½ cups of the balsamella, then sprinkle with more parmigiano. Repeat layers again. Add the final layer of pasta, cover it with the remaining ragù, then with the remaining balsamella, and sprinkle the last bit of parmigiano on top.

Bake lasagne until it is bubbling around the edges and browned on top, about 15 minutes. Do not overcook. Let lasagne rest for 10–15 minutes before serving.

PAPPARDELLE & MUSHROOMS
serves 4

In Italy's Piedmont region, autumn is the season for mushrooms as well as white truffles, and it's porcini that reign as the king of mushrooms. You can use fresh porcini in this recipe. But usually they're not around in our markets, so we do what the Italians do, and use common (and affordable) cultivated cremini with dried porcini to add deep, earthy mushroom flavor.

1 ounce dried porcini
2 tablespoons butter
2 tablespoons extra-virgin olive oil
2 cloves garlic, minced
2 tablespoons tomato paste

1½ pounds cremini mushrooms, sliced
1 cup finely chopped fresh parsley leaves
Salt and pepper
1 recipe Fresh Pasta (page 236) or
    1 pound dried pappardelle

Put the porcini in a small bowl, cover with boiling water, and let soften for 15 minutes. Meanwhile, heat the butter and oil together in a large skillet over medium-high heat. Add the garlic and sauté for 1 minute. Add the tomato paste and cook for 1 minute. Add the cremini, stir everything together, and cook for 10 minutes.

Chop the porcini and strain the soaking liquid through a coffee filter. Add the porcini, their liquid, and the parsley to the skillet. Season with salt and pepper. Stir to mix everything together. Cook until the sauce thickens slightly, about 2 minutes.

Cut the egg pasta into pappardelle (page 236). Cook the pappardelle in a large pot of salted boiling water over high heat until just cooked, 2–3 minutes for fresh pasta; about 10 minutes for dried pasta. Drain and return to the pot, leaving behind a little of the pasta water. Add the mushroom sauce and mix everything together.

CANNELLONI
serves 4–6

Everyone in our families is crazy for this elaborate stuffed pasta dish. It is always top of the list for holiday meals, birthday dinners, and special occasions.

FOR THE TOMATO SAUCE
One 28-ounce can crushed tomatoes
1 onion, halved
4–6 tablespoons butter
Salt and pepper

FOR THE FILLING
2 tablespoons extra-virgin olive oil
1 small onion, minced
1 clove garlic, minced
1 chicken liver, diced
6 ounces boneless, skinless chicken thighs, diced
6 ounces ground pork
6 ounces ground veal

Salt and pepper
Freshly grated nutmeg

FOR THE BALSAMELLA
4 tablespoons butter
¼ cup flour
2 cups hot milk
¼ cup grated parmigiano-reggiano
Salt and pepper

TO ASSEMBLE THE CANNELLONI
Salt
12 sheets Fresh Pasta (page 236),
    4 × 5 inches each
¼ cup grated parmigiano-reggiano
2–3 tablespoons butter

For the tomato sauce, put the crushed tomatoes into a medium saucepan. Rinse the can with a little water to get the remaining tomatoes out and pour the liquid into the saucepan. Add the onions and butter and season with salt and pepper. Simmer over medium-low heat, stirring occasionally, until the onions soften and the sauce thickens a bit, about 30 minutes.

Taste the sauce. Depending on the acidity of the canned tomatoes you've used, you may want to soften the sauce; the more butter you use, the softer and rounder the flavors. On occasion, we've even added a pinch or two of sugar to balance the acidity. Remove and discard the onions from the sauce before using.

For the filling, heat the oil in a large skillet over medium heat. Add the onions and garlic and cook until soft, 3–5 minutes. Add the chicken livers, and cook until no longer pink. Add the chicken, pork, and veal and season well with salt and pepper. Cook the meat, breaking it up with a fork or the back of a spoon, until it is cooked through and much of the liquid has evaporated, about 10 minutes.

continued

Working in batches, transfer the meat to a cutting board and chop it until its texture is quite fine, like a coarse paste. Or, pulse the meat in a food processor until it just begins to hold together, but avoid turning the meat into a smooth paste. Season the filling with a couple pinches of nutmeg and a little more salt and pepper, if needed. Transfer to a mixing bowl and set aside.

For the balsamella, melt the butter in a medium saucepan over medium-low heat. Sift in the flour and cook, stirring constantly, until the flour loses its raw taste yet has not taken on any color (it should remain white), 1–2 minutes. Gradually whisk in the milk, then stir constantly until the sauce is as thick as heavy cream, about 10 minutes.

Remove the pan from the heat and stir in the cheese. Season with salt and pepper. Add about ½ cup of the balsamella to the meat filling. Cover the surface of the remaining balsamella with a sheet of plastic wrap to prevent a skin from forming and set aside in a warm spot.

To assemble the cannelloni, bring a large pot of salted water to a boil. Cook 2–3 sheets of pasta at a time until tender, about 30 seconds, then transfer them with a slotted spoon to a large bowl of cold water to cool. Lay the sheets of cooked pasta out on clean, damp kitchen towels in a single layer without touching. Cover with more damp towels.

Spread 2 3 tablespoons of the meat filling along the wide edge of a sheet of pasta, then roll it up jelly roll style. Repeat with the remaining filling and sheets of pasta.

Spread about half of the tomato sauce over the bottom of a large baking dish. Nestle the cannelloni, overlapping side down, into the dish in a single layer. Spread the remaining tomato sauce over the cannelloni. Spoon the reserved balsamella over the sauce, making a swath down the center of the dish. Sprinkle the top with the parmigiano and dot with small knobs of the butter. The prepared cannelloni will keep in the refrigerator, covered with plastic wrap, for up to 2 days.

Preheat the oven to 375°. Bake the cannelloni until the sauce is bubbling hot and the top is lightly browned in spots, 15–30 minutes.

Overleaf: left, top, Green Lasagne with Tomato Sauce & Fresh Ricotta; bottom, Lasagne Bolognese; right, Cannelloni

SPINACH TAGLIATELLE WITH TOMATO SAUCE & RICOTTA

Bring a large pot of salted water to a boil. Heat 4–6 cups Simple Tomato Sauce (page 240) in a large skillet over medium heat until gently bubbling. Season with salt and pepper, and round out the flavors with some really good extra-virgin olive oil. Cook 1 recipe Spinach Pasta (page 238) cut into tagliatelle (page 236) or 1 pound dried tagliatelle in the boiling water until just cooked through, 2–3 minutes for fresh pasta, or about 10 minutes for dried pasta. Drain, reserving 1 cup of the cooking water. Toss the pasta in with the tomato sauce until thoroughly coated. Stir in some of the reserved cooking water to loosen it, if you like. Divide the pasta between 4 plates and top with a big spoonful of fresh whole-milk ricotta. Drizzle a little really good extra-virgin olive oil on top of each serving and grate as much parmigiano-reggiano over each as you like. — *serves 4*

BUTTERNUT SQUASH & CANDIED BACON ON FRESH PASTA
serves 8 as a first course

Have your filling ready to go before cooking the sheets of pasta so that the pasta is nice and hot when you assemble the dish.

1 pound slab bacon, trimmed of rind and
  excess layer of fat, diced
½ cup dark brown sugar
4 cups ¼-inch-thick bite size slices
  butternut squash
12 tablespoons butter

Handful fresh parsley leaves, chopped
Salt and pepper
16 sheets Fresh Pasta (see page 236),
  each 4–5 inches long
Parmigiano-reggiano

Preheat the oven to 400°. Toss the bacon with the brown sugar in a bowl. Spread it out on a foil-lined baking sheet. Bake until the pieces are glazed and crisp yet meaty, about 20 minutes.

Put the squash into a large pot of salted water and gently boil over medium heat until tender, 5–10 minutes. Drain and set aside.

Melt the butter in a large skillet over medium heat. When it begins to turn golden, add the squash and cook for a few minutes. Add the parsley and season with salt and pepper.

Bring a large pot of salted water to a boil. Cook the pasta, a few sheets at a time to keep them from sticking to each other, until tender, about 1 minute. Transfer them with a slotted spoon to a clean kitchen towel, laying them out so they don't touch, and blot dry.

For each serving, place a sheet of hot pasta on a warm, deep plate. Spoon some of the squash and the butter in the center of the pasta. Add a spoonful or two of the candied bacon. Drape another sheet of pasta over the filling and spoon a little more butter on top. Grate parmigiano over the pasta.

MILK PUNCH
serves 8

We make this frosty deliciousness by the pitcherful, letting it get nice and icy in the freezer just before serving it. It's better than eggnog.

1 quart whole milk
1 cup half-and-half
1½ cups bourbon, whiskey,
    or brandy

1 cup powdered sugar, sifted
1 tablespoon vanilla extract
Freshly ground nutmeg

December 24th, 31°
light powdery snow

Put the milk, half-and-half, booze, sugar, and vanilla into a pitcher and stir well. Put the pitcher into the freezer and chill the milk punch until it is quite slushy, 3–4 hours. Stir well and serve in chilled pretty glasses, garnished with a dash of nutmeg.

CHEESE STRAWS
makes about 20

These elegant crispy straws are perfect with cocktails before a big holiday meal. Sometimes we serve them sprinkled with black pepper, cayenne, or pimentón. If you're using store-bought frozen puff pastry, be sure that it that has butter listed in the ingredients.

1 cup finely grated parmigiano-reggiano

1 sheet Simple Puff Pastry (page 155), or
    frozen puff pastry, defrosted but not
    unfolded

Preheat the oven to 375°. Dust a clean work surface with about ½ cup of the grated cheese. Put 1 unfolded sheet puff pastry on top of the cheese and dust it with another ½ cup of the cheese. Roll the pastry out with a rolling pin into a rectangle about ⅛ inch thick, dusting it with more cheese, if necessary.

Using a sharp knife or a pastry cutter, cut the pastry into long ½-inch-wide strips. Twist each strip several times into the shape of a corkscrew and lay them on a parchment paper–lined baking sheet about ½ inch apart.

Bake the cheese straws until they are puffed and golden, about 10 minutes. Let them cool to room temperature before peeling them off the paper.

PICKLED SHRIMP & CELERY
serves 4–6

We prefer first to poach the shrimp, then to peel and devein them. That way they maintain their shape rather than curling and flaring into a "butterfly".

For THE PICKLING BRINE
½ cup rice wine vinegar
½ cup mirin
2 tablespoons sugar
2 thick slices fresh ginger
5 black peppercorns
5 juniper berries
1 cinnamon stick

2 whole celery hearts, some leaves reserved
   for garnish
1 cup white wine
8 black peppercorns
2 bay leaves
Salt
24–32 medium unpeeled shrimp
Really good extra-virgin olive oil
Pepper
2 tablespoons chopped fresh chives

For the pickling brine, put the rice wine vinegar, mirin, sugar, ginger, peppercorns, juniper berries, and cinnamon stick, along with 1 cup water, in a pot and cook over medium heat, stirring from time to time, until the sugar has dissolved. Pour the brine into a wide shallow dish. This brine can be made up to 1 week in advance. Keep refrigerated.

Remove any large ribs of celery from the hearts. Keep the hearts whole and put them into

continued

a large pot with the wine, peppercorns, bay leaves, and a generous pinch of salt. Add just enough water to cover the celery. Cover and simmer over medium heat until the celery is crisp-tender when pierced with a paring knife, 25–30 minutes. Transfer the celery to a cutting board. Cut the hearts crosswise into ½-inch-thick pieces and add them to the pickling brine.

Using the same pot and liquid in which you cooked the celery, poach the shrimp until just cooked, about 3 minutes. Drain the shrimp in a colander. Peel and devein the shrimp and put in a bowl. Pour the celery and the pickling brine over the shrimp. Make sure everything is submerged. If there isn't enough brine to cover everything completely, just give the celery and shrimp a turn every now and then. Cover with plastic wrap, refrigerate, and allow the shrimp and celery to "pickle" for about an hour.

Use a slotted spoon to transfer the shrimp and celery to plates. Drizzle with olive oil, season with salt and pepper, and garnish with celery leaves and chopped chives. Serve cold.

LOBSTER STEW
serves 4–6

Ask at your fish market to have them steam and crack the lobsters just before you pick them up. If they have good fish stock, pick that up, too.

Two 1½-pound lobsters
Salt
4 tablespoons butter
1 onion, finely chopped
2 ribs celery, diced
2 sprigs fresh tarragon

Pepper
2–3 russet potatoes, peeled and diced
1 cup white wine
1 cup good fish stock
1 cup heavy cream
Chopped fresh chives

Plunge the tip of a large sharp knife into the heads of the lobsters just behind the eyes. (This is the hardest part of the whole recipe.) Drop the lobsters into a large pot of salted boiling water over high heat and cook for about 8 minutes. Remove the lobsters from the pot and set them aside until they are cool enough to handle. Remove the meat from the lobsters, reserving the shells and any juices. Cut the lobster into large bite-size pieces, leaving the claw meat whole.

Melt the butter in a heavy large pot over medium-low heat. Add the onions, celery, and tarragon. Season with salt and pepper. Add the large pieces of lobster shells along with any juices, and cook, stirring from time to time, for 10 minutes. Remove and discard the tarragon and lobster shells. Add the potatoes, wine, and fish stock, cover, and gently simmer until the vegetables are just soft, about 15 minutes. Add the cream and the lobster meat and cook until the lobster is just heated through, about 5 minutes. Adjust seasonings. Ladle into bowls; garnish with chives.

ROAST PRIME RIB OF BEEF
serves 8–10

We favor roasting large cuts of meat at a low temperature; the gentle heat cooks them evenly throughout (which means beautifully rosy-pink slices of beef).

1 prime rib roast of beef, 8–12 pounds,
  tied between the ribs

Salt and pepper

December 25th, 31°
a snowy Christmas day

Preheat the oven to 200°. Generously season the roast all over with salt and pepper. Heat a heavy skillet large enough to accommodate the roast and sear the meaty sides until they are nicely browned, 5–10 minutes.

Transfer the roast to a large roasting pan, rib side down, and roast in the oven until the internal temperature reaches 120° for rare, 130°–135° for medium-rare, or 140° for medium, 3–4½ hours. Transfer the roast beef to a carving board or a warm serving platter and let it rest for 30 minutes. Remove the string before carving.

LITTLE YORKSHIRE PUDDINGS
makes 8

Traditionally, Yorkshire pudding is made right in the hot roasting pan with the pan drippings while the prime rib rests on a cutting board before slicing. But we like using popover molds or a muffin pan so that everyone gets a lovely crispy individual pudding.

1 cup flour
½ teaspoon salt
2 eggs, lightly beaten

1 cup whole milk
3–4 tablespoons roast beef pan
  drippings or melted butter

Whisk together the flour and salt in a medium bowl. Add the eggs and milk, whisking until the batter is well mixed (it's okay if there are a few lumps). Cover and refrigerate the batter for at least 1 hour or as long as overnight.

Preheat the oven to 425°. Put a small spoonful of pan drippings or butter into each cup of an 8-cup popover or muffin pan and put the pan into the oven until it is hot. Give the batter a stir, then pour it into the hot cups, filling them no more than three-quarters full. Quickly return the pan to the oven and bake for 15 minutes. Reduce the heat to 350° and continue baking until puffed and browned, about 20 minutes (resist the urge to open the oven door and peek; the puddings will deflate). Tip the puddings out of the cups and poke their sides with a toothpick to let steam escape. Serve hot.

ROAST GOOSE WITH TEN LEGS
serves 10–12

While a whole glorious golden goose makes a beautiful presentation, the legs are where you find the real meat and delicious flavor. Schiltz Goose Farm, in South Dakota, sells beautiful big birds and also whole legs, four to the package. We roast one big bird for the "tah-dah!" factor, along with eight legs—and everyone is well fed and happy.

1 whole goose, 8–10 pounds
Salt and pepper
1 large handful fresh thyme leaves

3 tablespoons juniper berries, crushed
8 whole goose legs (thigh and drumstick attached)

Preheat the oven to 400°. Remove the neck and giblets from the goose and save to make stock, if you like. Remove any excess fat and save to make rendered fat, if you like. Rinse and pat the goose dry with paper towels. Use a wooden spoon to mix and crush together 1 tablespoon salt, 2 teaspoons pepper, the thyme leaves, and juniper berries in a small bowl. Rub the bird inside and out with the mixture, and also on the goose legs. Use a sharp fork to prick the goose and the legs all over to release fat while they cook. Bend the wings behind the bird's back and tie its legs together.

Put the goose on a rack in a roasting pan. Pour 1 cup water into the pan to keep the fat from burning. Arrange the legs in a single layer in another large roasting pan and add a little water. Cover both pans with foil and roast for 45 minutes. Reduce the temperature to 325°, uncover both pans, and roast until a meat thermometer inserted into a thigh registers 180° and the skin is brown and crisp, 1–2 hours. If the legs are cooked before the goose, remove them from the oven. You can pop them back in for a few minutes to warm them before serving. Season with salt and pepper.

Transfer the goose along with the legs to a platter and serve with Apples Cooked with Cumin.

APPLES COOKED WITH CUMIN

Fall is the season for apples and we are lucky to have beautiful orchards all around us. Branch out and try an heirloom variety that is a cooking apple. The apples will hold their shape but have a nice tender texture. You can make a smaller batch of this recipe using fewer apples, but don't cut down on the butter, sugar, and cumin.

Melt 8 tablespoons butter over medium heat in a large skillet with a lid. Add 1 tablespoon ground cumin and 2 tablespoons sugar, then add 10 peeled, cored whole apples. Cook, basting and turning the apples to coat them in the butter. Reduce the heat to low, cover, and cook, basting from time to time, until the apples are tender, about 1 hour. — *serves 10*

MARMALADE CAKE

makes one 8-inch cake

You can use a skewer to poke holes in the cake as it cools, and brush it with Grand Marnier for a delicious boozy cake. Or spoon the syrup and candied orange peel over slices of the cake.

FOR THE CANDIED ORANGE PEEL

1 navel orange, scrubbed

1 cup sugar

1 whole star anise

½ vanilla bean, split lengthwise

FOR THE CAKE

10 tablespoons unsalted butter, at room temperature, plus more for the pan

¾ cup packed light brown sugar

¾ cup dried currants

½ cup Grand Marnier

1½ cups cake flour

1 teaspoon baking powder

½ teaspoon kosher salt

½ cup fresh orange juice

3 generous tablespoons orange marmalade

2 tablespoons finely grated fresh orange zest

2 large eggs

¼ cup whole milk or half-and-half

For the candied orange peel, use a sharp knife to cut all the rind and white pith off the oranges in wide strips. Trim off any flesh still clinging to the white pith. Put the peel into a heavy small saucepan. Add cold water to cover and bring to a boil over high heat. Drain. Repeat with cold water. Drain, reserving the peel.

Combine the sugar and 2 cups cold water in the same saucepan. Stir over medium heat until the sugar dissolves. Add the orange peel, star anise, and vanilla bean. Bring to a boil. Reduce the heat to low and simmer, partially covered and stirring occasionally, until the peel is soft, 50–60 minutes. Cool slightly. Transfer the peel to a cutting board and thinly slice. Return the peel to the syrup. The peel will keep in the syrup covered and refrigerated for up to 2 weeks.

For the cake, preheat the oven to 350°. Butter an 8-inch round springform cake pan. Line the bottom with a piece of buttered parchment paper. Bring the currants and Grand Marnier to a simmer in a small saucepan over medium heat. Remove from the heat and set aside to macerate.

Meanwhile, sift the flour, baking powder, and salt together into a medium bowl. Using a mixer, beat the butter and sugar together in a large mixing bowl on medium speed until light and fluffy, about 3 minutes. Beat in the orange juice, marmalade, and orange zest. Beat in the eggs one at a time, beating well after each addition (don't worry if the mixture looks curdled). Add the flour mixture in three parts and the milk in two parts, alternating and beginning and ending with the flour mixture, and beating well after each addition. Beat in any Grand Marnier not absorbed by the currants. Fold in the currants. Use a rubber spatula to scrape the batter into the prepared pan and smooth the top. Bake the cake until the top is golden and a wooden skewer inserted into the center comes out clean, 40–45 minutes. Let the cake cool in the pan on a wire rack. Remove the outer ring and invert the cake onto a serving plate. Serve the cake with the candied orange peel and syrup.

GINGER SPICE CAKE WITH DRIED CHERRIES
serves 10

Sometimes we bake this moist, spicy cake in an 8-inch springform pan, or for a more festive occasion, we divide it between small decorative molds. Serve glazed with chocolate icing or simply dust the cake with powdered sugar.

1 cup dried tart cherries, finely chopped
½ cup finely chopped crystallized ginger
1 tablespoon grated peeled fresh ginger
1 tablespoon Dijon mustard
1 cup hot espresso or very strong coffee
2½ cups all-purpose flour, plus more
   for the pan
1 tablespoon ground ginger
2 teaspoons baking soda
1½ teaspoons kosher salt
1 teaspoon ground allspice

1 teaspoon ground cinnamon
½ teaspoon ground black pepper
8 tablespoons unsalted butter, at room
   temperature, plus more for the pan
½ cup packed dark brown sugar
3 large eggs
1 cup light molasses

FOR THE CHOCOLATE ICING
½ cup heavy cream
2 tablespoons hot espresso or strong coffee
8 ounces semisweet chocolate, chopped

Preheat the oven to 350°. Combine the dried cherries, crystallized ginger, grated ginger, and mustard in a medium bowl. Pour the hot espresso over it and set aside. Whisk together the flour, ground ginger, baking soda, salt, allspice, cinnamon, and black pepper in a large bowl and set aside. Butter a 6–8-cup Bundt pan (an 8-inch springform pan or 2 small decorative molds). Dust it with flour, tapping out any excess.

Beat the butter in a large mixing bowl with a mixer on medium speed until light and fluffy, about 2 minutes. Add the brown sugar and continue to beat for another 2 minutes. Beat in the eggs one at a time. Beat in the molasses.

Strain the cherry mixture into a small bowl, reserving the soaking liquid. Add the dry ingredients to the butter mixture in three parts, and the soaking liquid in two parts, beginning and ending with the dry ingredients, and beating well after each addition. Fold in the cherry mixture. Using a rubber spatula, scrape the batter into the prepared cake pan.

Bake until the top springs back when lightly pressed in the middle and a wooden skewer inserted in the center comes out clean, about 1 hour. Let the cake cool completely in the pan on a wire rack before removing it from the pan.

For the chocolate icing, heat the cream in a small saucepan over medium heat until tiny bubbles form around the edges. Stir in the hot espresso. Put the chocolate in a medium bowl. Add the hot cream and let stand for 1 minute, then stir until the icing is smooth and melted. Spoon over the cake, allowing it to drip down the sides. Cut into slices.

winter

❧ January Recipes ❧

limonada ∾ 270

winter margarita ∾ 270

ham & bacon with mustard & brown sugar sauce ∾ 272

buttermilk love cakes ∾ 272

ian's healthy pancakes ∾ 273

the sensible cleanse ∾ 274

restorative beef broth ∾ 276

everyday vegetable tonic ∾ 276

cleansing ginger-chicken soup ∾ 277

avocado love ∾ 279

avocado mash on multigrain toast ∾ 279

fire-toasted corn tortilla with mashed avocado ∾ 279

ruby red grapefruit, avocado & escarole salad ∾ 280

white sweet potato soup with pickled scallions ∾ 280

borlotti beans with sautéed baby kale ∾ 283

beef tenderloin with parsley-tarragon butter ∾ 284

chopped celery salad ∾ 284

no-knead bread ∾ 286

little chocolate turnovers ∾ 289

little gianduia turnovers ∾ 289

puff pastry jam tartlets ∾ 290

chocolate-covered boozy prunes ∾ 290

We do not want granite kitchen countertops. We do not need an expensive mega-Btu stovetop or convection oven or a glass-front, built-in Sub-Zero. We don't have a microwave. We barely use the food processor that we just bought. And we do not own a proper pepper mill. But someday we hope to have a walk-in refrigerator.

It doesn't need to be big. It could be the size of a walk-in clothes closet or a wide, deep broom closet, just as long as it's lined with broad shelves that can hold the following: platters of leftovers, jars of brandied fruit and preserved lemons, tubs of refrigerator pickles, crocks of duck confit, broths cooling in their stockpots, a bushel basket of crisp apples, a big hunk of Parmigiano-reggiano, a few cases of wine and Champagne.

If there is enough room to fit a 26-pound turkey soaking in brine, a few hooks to hang some strings of homemade fresh sausages and dry-age a roast of beef, our dreams would come true. But for now, we just open the door to the great outdoors and use it as our walk-in refrigerator/freezer from early fall through late spring, when the temperature outside drops below 40 degrees.

There's definitely an art to using the outdoors to keep things cool—just as there is an art to cooking over a big bed of fire and hot coals. You can't control the temperature with a dial, so you've got to work with it. It's one thing to put a case of wine outside overnight to chill, but if the temperature unexpectedly plummets into the teens, well, that case is ruined. We cool pots of stock out on our balcony, and wrap large leftover roasts or a big smoked ham in foil to keep outside—they're just too big for our narrow fridge. At the end of a meal, when we can't be bothered with dividing leftovers into plastic containers and washing the pots and platters, we cover them up and find a spot for them outside.

We've lost good food to the cold—some live lobsters and an untossed salad we never got around to serving. Occasionally there are pots of leftovers we forget about; by the time we remember, what was once worth saving for another meal has turned into what looks like a nasty science experiment. Sometimes, pots get buried in the snow. We dig them out, brush the snow off, and gently reheat the frozen leftovers over the lowest heat on top of the stove. The frostiness on the outside of the pot melts and sizzles as it hits the burner plate. Eventually, we have another good meal, sometimes even more flavorful after its cold repose. So, until we have the room and money for a custom-built walk-in fridge, we'll continue to use what we've got—the great, free outdoors.

January 1st, 33°
calm & overcast

OVER THE YEARS, WE'VE CELEBRATED New Year's Eve every which way. But New Year's Day is always a quiet and relaxed day spent with a collection of family and friends. And, of course, there's always food, typically a lunch. It could be a big smoked ham, great home-made bread, and a big salad, or pans of cannelloni, or hot soups on the stove. Whatever it is, it's casual—easy recuperative food that leaves time to sit and eat and talk. Around the table, you can feel a collective sigh of relief that the holidays are over. It's a day for looking back, but also for moving forward and embracing hope, the great human drive.

LIMONADA
makes about 7 cups

We're not sure whether limes ward off evil, as purported by some, but we do know that this limeade has the power to revive—whether we're drinking it on the day after a long New Year's Eve or in the summer when it's 100 degrees in the shade and we can barely move.

1 cup sugar   2 cups fresh lime juice (8–10 large limes)

Put the sugar and ½ cup cold water into a medium saucepan. Heat over medium heat, gently swirling the pan over the heat to help dissolve the sugar. When the syrup comes to a boil, cover the pan to let the steam run down the sides, washing away and dissolving any sugar granules left on the side of the pan. Boil until the sugar is completely dissolved and the syrup is clear, 2–3 minutes. Remove the pan from the heat. Allow the syrup to cool to room temperature. This makes about 1 cup simple syrup. Store it in the refrigerator until ready to use.

Combine the simple syrup, lime juice, and 4 cups cold water in a pitcher. Serve in tall glasses over ice, garnished with fat wedges of lime and fresh sprigs of mint, if you like.

WINTER MARGARITA

This is our holiday brunch and/or lunchtime version of the classic lime juice–tequila cocktail—it's lighter and more refreshing. We set out a pitcher of the Limonada and a bottle of 100 percent blue agave tequila and let our imbibing guests make their own drinks.

Combine 2 tablespoons superfine sugar and 1 tablespoon flaky sea salt, such as Maldon, in a saucer. Rub the rims of two short glasses with the cut side of a fat lime wedge, then roll the wet rims in the saucer, rimming the glasses with the sugar and salt. Fill the glasses with crushed ice. Pour 1½ ounces premium tequila and ½ cup Limonada (recipe above) into each glass. Stir gently. Garnish the cocktails with a fat lime wedge. —— *makes 2*

Clockwise from top left: Winter Margarita; Ham & Bacon with Mustard & Brown Sugar Sauce (page 272); Buttermilk Love Cakes (page 272)

HAM & BACON WITH MUSTARD & BROWN SUGAR SAUCE
serves 4–6

We joke that if we ever open up a lumberjack canteen, we'll never be able to take this dish off the menu. It's a natural with a stack of pancakes—tall or short.

6 slices thick-cut bacon
1 ham steak, about ¾ inch thick
½ cup Dijon mustard
¼ cup brown sugar

1 cup heavy cream
½–1 teaspoon apple cider vinegar
Salt and pepper

Preheat the oven to 200°. Heat a heavy large skillet over medium heat. Cook the strips of bacon until browned and crisp on both sides, about 15 minutes. Drain on paper towels, leaving the rendered bacon fat in the skillet. Keep the bacon warm in the oven.

Return the skillet with the bacon fat to medium-high heat. Add the ham steak and cook until browned on both sides, 8–10 minutes. Transfer to a serving platter and keep it warm in the oven.

Return the skillet to medium-low heat. Add the mustard and brown sugar and cook, whisking, until the sugar dissolves into the mustard. Whisk in the cream, then the vinegar, and cook for 1–2 minutes. Taste the sauce and season it with salt and pepper. The ham and bacon are salty, so you'll want to season the sauce judiciously with salt, but with lots of pepper. Thin the sauce with a splash of water. Spoon the sauce over the ham and serve with the bacon.

BUTTERMILK LOVE CAKES
makes about 1½ dozen 4-inch love cakes

You may call these delicate pancakes by another name—flapjacks, hotcakes, griddle cakes—but in honor of the dearly beloved relative who always turned these out with tender care and passed her recipe on to us, they're love cakes to us.

2 large eggs, separated
1 cup buttermilk
2 tablespoons melted butter
1 cup cake flour
1 tablespoon sugar
½ teaspoon baking powder

½ teaspoon baking soda
¼ teaspoon salt
Vegetable oil
Butter, at room temperature
Maple syrup

Whisk the egg yolks into the buttermilk in a medium mixing bowl. Whisk in the butter. Put the flour, sugar, baking powder, baking soda, and salt into a sieve and sift it into the buttermilk. Lightly whisk the batter until it is just mixed (a few lumps won't hurt).

continued

Put the egg whites in a clean mixing bowl and beat with a whisk until soft peaks form. Use a rubber spatula to fold them into the batter. Don't overwork the batter; you want to keep it light and fluffy.

Pour a little oil onto a nonstick griddle or large skillet. Wipe out the excess with a paper towel, leaving only the thinnest film. Heat the griddle over medium-high heat until hot. Pour about ¼ cup of the batter on the griddle for each pancake. Cook until little holes appear on the surface and the cooked side of the pancake is golden brown (lift the edge to check), about 1 minute on each side. Serve the warm pancakes slathered with soft butter and a few good glugs of true maple syrup, if you like. How could you not?

IAN'S HEALTHY PANCAKES
makes about a dozen 4-inch pancakes

For the last couple of years, we've spent New Year's Eve as the guests of relatives who have a big house and a wonderful over-the-top sensibility (they like to say, "It's not done until it's overdone"). We sit down to a feast. The table can barely contain the New Year's–themed tablescape, let alone the food. After dinner they set off fireworks, and the Champagne and laughter flow into the wee hours of the morning. We spend the night, wake a few hours later in the proper light of morning, and find our way down to the breakfast table, which nearly tops the previous night's display. There's freshly squeezed juice and good coffee, eggs, bacon, muffins, toast, and homemade preserves. But it's these toothsome, delicious pancakes that we crave most. They restore us on New Year's Day.

1¼ cups rolled oats	1½ teaspoons baking soda
2 cups buttermilk	1 teaspoon salt
1 teaspoon honey	2 large eggs
¼ cup whole wheat flour	Butter, at room temperature
¼ cup cornmeal	Maple syrup

Stir together the oats, buttermilk, and honey in a large mixing bowl. Combine the flour, cornmeal, baking soda, and salt in a small bowl, then add to the oats. Lightly beat the eggs in the same small bowl (there's no need to wash it out first), then add them to the oats and mix well. Set the batter aside to rest at room temperature for 15 minutes.

Melt 1 tablespoon butter in a large griddle or heavy skillet over medium heat. Working in batches, drop a scant ¼ cup of the batter onto the griddle for each pancake. Cook until little holes appear on the surface and the cooked side of the pancake is golden brown (lift the edge to check), about 3 minutes on each side. Brush the griddle with more butter as needed. Serve the pancakes warm, slathered with butter and doused with maple syrup.

THE SEASON FOR INDULGING BEGINS EARLY FOR US. It starts in October with a slew of birthdays, and then sails right into November and on through January with the big three holidays: Thanksgiving, Christmas, and the New Year. We loosen our purse strings and splurge on some of our favorite foods—salty fish roes, fatted livers, plump birds, meaty roasts, and twirled-up confections. We down bottles of good bubbly and hearty big reds, and cook and eat with our families and friends. By January we're ready for a change. We want clean food, clean living. Resolutions are made. We'll take long walks every day, keep the knives in the drawer sharpened, our freezers full of stews and soups, our linen closets straight, we'll pat the dog on the head, brush the cats, give the children a hug, take meals to the elderly, and make trips to expand our minds. And we'll begin this year with a cleanse.

But not like the kind of cleanse our friend went on for a month when he ate nothing but white grapes and carrots. Although his skin looked flawless, he was glowing orange by week four. Or the regime our sweet neighbor carefully, painstakingly wrote out for us a few years ago, six pages long, with the pre-fasting, fasting, and post-fasting details. Not for us. We won't be radical and become breatharians, living on light and air, or swallow a strip of gauze, or attempt a coffee high colonic. We prefer our coffee the old-fashioned way—we drink it.

So, at the beginning of each year when we come to our senses we do what we always do. We keep cooking and eating, but we do it very simply. We remind ourselves that we're not about the No, but rather the Yes! Good wholesome food nourishes us, so we make broths and soups with ingredients that are full of *prana* or life-energy. We always return to our favorites—rich, deep Restorative Beef Broth (page 276) to build us up and Everyday Vegetable Tonic (page 276), a version of a famous recipe by Henry G. Bieler, the physician who wrote *Food Is Your Best Medicine* (Random House, 1966). The broth was considered magic; Raquel Welch apparently has a cup of it every morning and credits it with giving her youthful vitality—if it's good enough for Raquel, we'll drink to that! And there's Cleansing Ginger-Chicken Soup (277), its very name promising a whole lot of good.

We like the New Year's tradition of turning over a new leaf. We've always got a couple of resolutions ready that we hope will stick—to enjoy life more, to simplify, and to feed our minds as well as our bodies. Oh yes, and if we drop ten pounds along the way, that would be dandy. The very thought of it already makes us feel healthier.

Clockwise from top left: healthy ingredients for broths; Restorative Beef Broth; Everyday Vegetable Tonic; Cleansing Ginger-Chicken Soup

RESTORATIVE BEEF BROTH
makes about 9 cups

Drink this faintly sweet, beefy broth as is, or simmer diced root vegetables and/or little pastas in it.

3–4 pounds beef short ribs (about 9 pieces)
1 onion, halved

2–3 cloves garlic
1 cup pitted prunes
Salt

January 2nd, 28° a clear sunny day

Put the short ribs, onions, garlic, and prunes into a large heavy pot and add enough cold water (about 16 cups) to cover the meat by about 3 inches. Bring to a boil over medium-high heat, skimming any foam that rises to the surface. Reduce the heat to low and simmer very gently, skimming any foam on the surface from time to time, until the meat is tender, about 5 hours.

Strain the broth through a fine-mesh sieve into a clean pot, discarding the solids. Season with salt, if you like. Heat the broth before serving.

EVERYDAY VEGETABLE TONIC
makes about 6 cups

This vegetable soup is based on the famous Doctor Bieler's Broth, which made its debut in Doctor Henry G. Bieler's *Food Is Your Best Medicine* (Random House, 1966). It was considered magic and was very popular with the In Crowd.

1 pound green beans, diced
1 pound zucchini, diced
1 medium onion, diced
2 ribs celery, diced

1 clove garlic, minced
1 quart spring water
Salt and pepper
Really good extra-virgin olive oil

January 4th, 24° gusty

Put the green beans, zucchini, onions, celery, and garlic in a large pot and add the spring water. Cover and bring to a boil over medium-high heat. Reduce the heat to medium-low and gently boil until the vegetables are very tender, about 20 minutes.

Remove the pot from the heat. Season the broth and vegetables to taste with salt and pepper. Serve with a good drizzle of the olive oil, or purée the soup in a blender or food processor first.

CLEANSING GINGER-CHICKEN SOUP
serves 6

Ginger has long been known for its health benefits. Prized for its anti-inflammatory proper-
ties, it is also known to calm an upset stomach. We love the heat it adds to this rich, satisfying
broth. We remove the chicken breast halfway through cooking to keep it tender and juicy.
The purity of this broth needs little else, but if you want more substance, add rice or noodles.

1 onion, sliced

2 ribs celery, chopped

1 big hand fresh ginger (about 8 ounces),
  unpeeled and sliced into big pieces

1 clove garlic

10 black peppercorns

1 organic chicken, cut into 7 pieces
  (2 breasts, 2 thighs and legs, 2 wings,
  and the back)

Salt

Handful fresh cilantro leaves

Put the onions, celery, ginger, garlic, and peppercorns in a heavy large pot, then add the
chicken pieces, placing the breasts on top so they will be easier to remove from the hot broth
halfway through the cooking. Cover with 4 quarts cold water and bring just to a boil over
medium-high heat. Reduce the heat to low. Skim off any foam that rises to the surface. After
about 30 minutes, remove the chicken breasts and set them aside to cool. Continue to gently
simmer the soup for 1½ hours.

January 6th, 23°
all clear

Remove all the chicken from the broth and set it aside until it is cool enough to handle.
Pull off and discard the skin, bones, and gristle. Strain the broth through a fine mesh sieve
into a bowl then return the broth to the pot.

Boil the broth over high heat until it has reduced to about 8 cups. Season with salt to taste.
Put a handful of chicken in each of 6 individual bowls then ladle in the hot broth. Serve
garnished with cilantro leaves.

— AVOCADO LOVE —

WE HAVE A FRIEND WHO LIVES on a property in California with a garden full of Hass avocado trees. A couple times a year he packs up one of those large U.S. Postal Service flat-rate mailing boxes—"If It Fits, It Ships"—with as many avocados as will safely fit and sends it off to us. They arrive in pristine condition, still hard as rocks, their pebbly skins dark green. It is an incredible gift. We set them out in the studio on a few platters to finish ripening, checking them each day as the color of their skins deepens to see if the flesh has begun to yield under the gentle pressure of our thumbs. We feel like avocado *affineurs*, coaxing the fruits to ripe perfection. Within a few days they're ready—their skins have turned a midnight green and they're softer now, just barely firm, with a rich, creamy flavor. We eat one after another: breakfast, lunch, and dinner. Heaven while they last.

AVOCADO MASH ON MULTIGRAIN TOAST
serves 2–4

We try to keep ripe avocados on hand. They come to our rescue when we're hungry and don't have much time to cook. These toasts have served us well for a late-morning breakfast, lunch, or a quickly made supper. But we could find an excuse to eat them anytime.

4 slices multigrain bread
Really good extra-virgin olive oil
4 ripe Hass avocados, halved,
   pitted, and peeled

1–2 lemons, preferably Meyers, halved
Aleppo pepper or other crushed red
   pepper flakes
Salt, preferably flaky sea salt like Maldon

Toast the bread, then drizzle one side with the olive oil while still warm. Put 2 avocado halves on each piece of toast and mash them with a butter knife or fork, spreading the soft fruit to the edges of the toast. Drizzle the avocados with some olive oil. Squeeze some lemon juice over the toasts, sprinkle with a pinch or two of Aleppo pepper, and season with salt. Serve with lemon halves.

{ January 9th, 15°
bitter cold

FIRE-TOASTED CORN TORTILLA WITH MASHED AVOCADO

Toast both sides of a good corn tortilla directly over the flame turned to medium-high on top of the burner plate of a gas stove or directly on the coil of an electric stove top on medium-high heat until warmed through and slightly charred in places, turning it frequently back and forth with tongs. Mash ½ ripe, peeled, pitted Hass avocado on the toasted tortilla with a fork. Squeeze fresh lime juice on top and sprinkle with coarse salt. —— *makes 1*

{ January 10th, 18°
azure sky

RUBY RED GRAPEFRUIT, AVOCADO & ESCAROLE SALAD

It's really the juicy, sweet, grapefruit segments we're after for this classic salad and not so much the juice—it's too mild for the vinaigrette. But don't waste what's left after cutting out the segments. Squeeze the extra juice into a glass and drink up.

January 11th, 21°
sunny & "mild"

Slice the ends off 1 Ruby Red grapefruit. Steady the grapefruit on one end and slice off the rind and white pith, exposing the flesh. Working over a bowl, cut along both sides of each segment to release it from the membrane, letting it drop into the bowl. Add 1 tablespoon wine vinegar and 2–4 tablespoons really good extra-virgin olive oil to the bowl. Season with a 1–2 pinches of dried red chile flakes or Aleppo pepper and salt and pepper. Swirl the bowl to combine the segments with the vinaigrette. Pile about 4 cups pale green escarole leaves onto a serving platter. Arrange 1 quartered, peeled, and pitted ripe Hass avocado on the platter and spoon the grapefruit segments and vinaigrette over the salad. Drizzle with a little more olive oil and season with salt and pepper. Scatter a small handful chopped fresh chives on top. —— *serves 2*

WHITE SWEET POTATO SOUP WITH PICKLED SCALLIONS
serves 4–6

We're crazy for little white sweet potatoes—they're starchier and drier than the orange-fleshed variety, giving them a dense texture that we love. They also make such a silky-smooth soup. Japanese in its inspiration, this soup is a perfect foil for the pickled scallions.

3 bunches scallions
1 small clove garlic, finely grated or minced
¼ cup rice wine vinegar
¼ cup extra-virgin olive oil
1 teaspoon Asian sesame oil

Salt
1 large hand of fresh ginger (about 6 ounces), unpeeled, coarsely chopped
6 cups chicken or turkey broth
2 pounds small white sweet potatoes

January 16th, 32°
a wet heavy snow

Chop 1 bunch of the scallions and put them in a small bowl. Add the garlic. Stir in the vinegar, olive oil, and sesame oil and season with salt. Set aside to pickle.

Coarsely chop the remaining 2 bunches of scallions and put them with the ginger in a medium pot. Add the broth and gently boil over medium heat for 30 minutes. Strain the broth through a fine-mesh sieve, return it to the pot, and keep warm over low heat.

Put the unpeeled potatoes in a medium pot of cold water and add a pinch of salt. Boil over medium heat until tender, 15–20 minutes. Drain and peel the potatoes. Drop them into a blender or food processor. Purée the potatoes with 5 cups of the broth until very smooth, thinning it with more broth if needed. Serve in warm bowls with a spoonful of the pickled scallions floating on top. Garnish with a few tiny nasturtium leaves if you have any on hand.

BORLOTTI BEANS WITH SAUTÉED BABY KALE
serves 4–6

We often keep a pot of brothy beans in the refrigerator (they'll keep nicely for up to 4 days). It gives us an instant leg up on putting a meal together. We eat them with good thick toast and olive oil, or stirred into a vegetable soup, or served alongside a pork roast or pan-fried lamb chops or duck legs. The list of possibilities is endless. Canned beans are okay in a pinch, of course, but don't really have the fresh sweet flavor and just-tender, somewhat toothsome texture of beans that you've cooked yourself. You get the point. Keep some cooked beans on hand. You'll thank yourself every time you tuck into them.

2 cups dried borlotti beans, soaked for 4 hours or overnight, or 6–7 cups cooked beans

1 medium onion, halved

2 bay leaves

Salt

Really good extra-virgin olive oil

2 cloves garlic, thinly sliced

1–1½ pounds baby kale

Cracked black pepper

4–8 thick slices country bread, toasted

If using dried beans, put them and their soaking water into a heavy medium pot. Add more cold water, if necessary, to cover them by 2–3 inches. Add the onions and bay leaves. Bring the beans just to a simmer over medium heat, stirring occasionally. Reduce the heat to low and very gently simmer them until they are swollen and tender. Depending on the freshness of the dried beans this can take 30–90 minutes (or more). Fish out and discard the onions and bay leaves. Stir in a generous pinch or two of salt and a glug of the olive oil.

January 18th, 34°
glazing rain

If using cooked beans, put them in a medium pot with a spoonful or two of water and a splash of olive oil. Cover and warm them over medium-low heat.

Put 3 tablespoons of the olive oil along with the garlic in a heavy medium pot and warm together over medium heat. Rinse the kale and add it to the pot with the water still clinging to its leaves. Sauté the kale, stirring and turning the leaves in the oil, until wilted and tender, 5–10 minutes, adding a splash of water if the kale begins to dry out. Season with salt and pepper.

To serve, use a slotted spoon to put a generous spoonful or two of the beans in each shallow bowl. Top with a tangle of kale. Drizzle the beans and kale with olive oil, season with salt and pepper, and serve with the toast.

BEEF TENDERLOIN WITH PARSLEY-TARRAGON BUTTER
serves 4

We had a whole beef tenderloin in the fridge, intending to grill it for a weekend gathering, but the plans changed at the last minute and there we were, heading into a busy work week, stuck with a whole filet—an expensive piece of meat large enough to feed a crowd. In the beginning of the week, we cut a roast from the thick end, tied kitchen twine around its waist to cinch it into a uniform shape, and roasted it in the oven for a supper for four. A couple of days later we made another meal. The evenly thick center of the tenderloin—the châteaubriand—we portioned into thick medallions and poached in beef broth with root vegetables. By the end of the week, we were left with the skinny tenderloin tip and a nearly empty refrigerator. Luckily, we still had a hunger for red meat. We pulled Irish butter and a head of celery out of the refrigerator and made a last meal of the tenderloin like this. Now you know the winding path of this recipe, with several good meals along the way. May you have the fine fortune to be stuck with a whole beef tenderloin.

FOR THE BUTTER
8 tablespoons softened butter
1 clove garlic, finely minced
1 handful fresh parsley leaves, chopped
1 sprig fresh tarragon, leaves chopped
1–2 teaspoons fresh lemon juice
Salt and pepper

FOR THE BEEF
4 beef tenderloins or other steaks,
 4–6 ounces each
1 tablespoon extra-virgin olive oil
Salt and pepper

January 19th, 30°
ice-crystal wonderland

For the butter, beat the butter, garlic, parsley, and tarragon in a bowl with a wooden spoon until well combined. Beat in the lemon juice and season with salt and pepper. The butter can be used right away, or covered and refrigerated for up to 3 days or frozen for up to 1 month.

For the beef, rub the meat all over with the olive oil and season well with salt and pepper. Heat a heavy large grill pan over medium-high heat. Sear the meat until well browned on both sides, about 5 minutes. Reduce the heat to medium and cook until the internal temperature reaches 120° for rare and 130° for medium-rare. Serve the meat slathered with some of the butter accompanied by Chopped Celery Salad.

CHOPPED CELERY SALAD

Chop the tender inner ribs and the leaves from 1 head of celery and put them in a bowl. Add 4–6 chopped anchovy filets, chopped rind of ½ preserved lemon, and 3–4 tablespoons really good extra-virgin olive oil and toss well. Season with salt and cracked black pepper and with enough juice from 1 lemon to suit your taste. Refrigerate until well chilled. — *serves 2–4*

NO-KNEAD BREAD
makes 1 big loaf

This recipe is an adaptation of one we think must be the most famous bread recipe in the world. When Jim Lahey's original recipe was first published in the *New York Times* Dining section on November 8, 2006, it was like the shot heard around the world. Everybody was talking about it, and everybody was making it. Could it be true? A professional-quality, chewy, European-style loaf of bread made in a home oven requiring no special equipment? And here's the clincher—no kneading the dough! The first loaves we made were good enough to hook us, but the recipe needed fiddling around with (everyone we knew who made it was doing the same thing). Here's our adapted recipe for this wonderful loaf of bread.

3 cups all-purpose or bread flour,   ¼ teaspoon instant yeast
  plus more for dusting   1¼ teaspoons salt

January 23rd, 18°
cold snap

Using a whisk, mix together the flour, yeast, and salt in a large bowl (1–2). Add 1½ cups plus 2 tablespoons water, and use a wooden spoon to stir until blended (3); the dough will be shaggy and sticky. Cover the bowl with plastic wrap (4). Let the dough rest for 18 hours at a warm room temperature, about 70°.

The dough is ready when its surface is dotted with bubbles. Lightly flour a work surface and place the dough on it. Sprinkle it with a little more flour and fold it over on itself once or twice (5). Loosely cover the dough with plastic wrap and let it rest for about 15 minutes.

Sprinkling the work surface with just enough flour to keep the dough from sticking, use a pastry/dough scraper or your fingers to gently and quickly shape the dough into a ball. Generously coat a smooth kitchen towel (not terry cloth) with flour. Put the dough seam side down on the towel and dust it with more flour (6). Cover the dough with another kitchen towel and let it rise undisturbed for about 2 hours. When it is ready, the dough will have more than doubled in size and will not readily spring back when poked with a finger.

At least 30 minutes before the dough is ready, put a 4-quart heavy covered pot (cast iron, enamel, Pyrex, or ceramic) in the oven and preheat the oven to 450°. When the dough is ready, carefully remove the pot from the oven. Slide your hand under the towel and turn the dough over into the pot seam side up (7). It may look like a mess, but that's okay. Shake the pot once or twice if the dough is unevenly distributed (it will straighten out as it bakes).

Cover the pot with the lid and bake for 30 minutes. Remove the lid and bake until the loaf of bread is beautifully browned, 15–30 minutes (8). Remove the loaf from the pot and let it cool on a wire rack. Serve the bread in slices (9).

LITTLE CHOCOLATE TURNOVERS
makes 8

We make our own puff pastry (page 155) and if we're not using the dough right away, we'll roll it out, gently fold the sheets into thirds like a business letter, wrap them up, and store them in the freezer so the delicious buttery dough is ready to use at a moment's notice, relatively speaking. The pastry defrosts in the time it takes to heat up the oven, so a batch of cheese straws or a savory or sweet tart can be put together quite spontaneously. These dainty chocolate turnovers came to our rescue once when dessert had been left as an afterthought. Not a bad save. Serve them at dinner or, if something sweet is your thing in the morning, at breakfast.

1 recipe Simple Puff Pastry (page 155) or
   1 sheet store-bought puff pastry
Flour
2 ounces good chocolate from a thin bar,
   broken into 8 triangles, or ½ cup
   chocolate chips

¼ cup heavy cream
2–3 tablespoons granulated sugar
Powdered sugar

Preheat the oven to 400°. Line a baking sheet with parchment paper and set aside.

{ January 24th, 20°
clear as a bell

Lay the puff pastry on a lightly floured work surface and dust the top with a little flour. Roll the pastry out to a ⅛-inch-thick rectangle. Cut the pastry into eight 3-inches squares. Lay a piece of chocolate just inside one of the corners or quadrants of each pastry square (or fill a quadrant with about 1 tablespoon of the chocolate chips). Brush the edge of the pastry with some of the heavy cream. Fold the pastry in half over the chocolate, forming a nice little triangle or turnover. Crimp the edges together. Repeat with the remaining pastry squares and chocolate.

Arrange the turnovers on the prepared baking sheet at least 1 inch apart. (The turnovers can be frozen at this point and baked later, if you like. Once they are frozen solid, transfer them to a resealable plastic bag. They'll keep in the freezer, frozen, for up to 1 month. They do not need to be defrosted before continuing with the recipe.)

Brush the turnovers with some heavy cream and sprinkle each with some of the granulated sugar. Bake until puffed and golden, about 15 minutes. Cool slightly before dusting with powdered sugar. Serve warm.

LITTLE GIANDUIA TURNOVERS

Follow the directions for Little Chocolate Turnovers, substituting 1–2 teaspoons Gianduia (page 203) per turnover for the chocolate.

PUFF PASTRY JAM TARTLETS
makes 1 dozen

Any good fruit preserve or jam is delicious in these buttery tartlets, but if we had to pick a favorite, it might just be apricot. Make these the day you plan to eat them.

1 recipe Simple Puff Pastry (page 155) or
   1 sheet store-bought puff pastry

Flour
½ cup good fruit preserves or jam

January 25th, 28°
sunny & warming

Preheat the oven to 400°. Line 2 baking sheets with parchment paper and set aside.

Lay the puff pastry on a lightly floured work surface and dust the top with a little flour. Roll the pastry out to a ⅛-inch-thick rectangle. Cut the dough in half. Transfer each half to one of the lined baking sheets. Cut each sheet of dough into 6 pieces. (To keep the dough cold, put one baking sheet in the refrigerator while preparing the other.) Using the tip of a paring knife, lightly score a border about ½ inch from the edge of each piece of dough. Prick the dough inside the border all over with the tines of a fork to prevent it from puffing up too much during baking.

Put a generous spoonful (1½–2 teaspoons) of the preserves within the border of each pastry. Bake the tartlets, one sheet at a time, until the pastries are golden brown, 15–20 minutes. Let the tartlets cool slightly before eating. They are also delicious eaten at room temperature.

CHOCOLATE-COVERED BOOZY PRUNES
makes 2 dozen

The boozy prunes are a good staple that go well with pork or duck, or spooned over vanilla ice cream. We gild the lily by stuffing them with an almond and bathing them in chocolate.

¾ cup cognac or brandy
24 pitted prunes
24 almonds, toasted

3 ounces semisweet chocolate, melted
2 tablespoons unsalted butter, melted
3 tablespoons heavy cream

January 30th, 35°
sunny & springlike

Warm the cognac in a small saucepan over low heat. Put the prunes into a glass jar, then pour the cognac over them. Once they've cooled down, screw the jar lid on and set aside to macerate at least overnight, or store them in the refrigerator for up to 6 months (the longer they macerate, the boozier they become).

Lay the prunes out on a rack to dry slightly. Stuff each one with an almond. Stir the warm melted chocolate and butter together in a small bowl. Whisk in the cream. Set aside to cool until slightly thickened. Dip one prune at a time in the chocolate and set it on a cookie tray or plate to cool.

❧ February Recipes ❧

preserved lemons ~ 294

shrimp roast ~ 296

curd rice ~ 296

chicken thighs with pancetta & caperberries ~ 299

hearts of romaine with mimosa dressing ~ 299

braised beef brisket with onions & currants ~ 300

sliced brisket with onions on a soft potato roll ~ 300

pizza dough ~ 304

prosciutto, lemon & green olive pizza ~ 304

escarole, fontina & black olive pizza ~ 305

potato & onion pizza ~ 305

white clam pizza ~ 305

baked ham with golden bread crumbs ~ 306

sliced ham on baguette ~ 306

red velvet cupcakes with meringue frosting ~ 308

chocolate sponge cake ~ 310

fallen chocolate soufflé cake ~ 311

pimentón & caraway short ribs with egg noodles ~ 312

waldorf chicken salad ~ 314

buckwheat crêpes with ham & cheese ~ 314

melba toasts ~ 316

potted crab ~ 316

blue cheese with black pepper ~ 316

smoked salmon butter ~ 316

anchovy & lemon butter ~ 316

It started with a gift. A cardboard box arrived in the mail from a friend of ours in California who had picked a half-bushel of Meyer lemons from the trees in his backyard and sent them to us. The box was packed solid. Some of the lemons were still attached in pairs to the branch, and the branches still had their leaves. Resting on top were lavender and flowering rosemary wrapped in wet newspaper, the bouquet slightly crushed, like pressed flowers in a book. They were still rare in our area; we could only find them occasionally during the winter in the specialty produce section, and we always loaded up whenever we were lucky enough to spot them.

The first thing you notice about a Meyer lemon—most likely a cross between an orange and a lemon—is its smooth, shiny skin, then its striking color, which can be a soft creamy yellow but more often is a rich golden. Its skin is thin, with little pith underneath, and it's practically all flesh inside. Its juice is pure lemon, but sweet and floral.

What were we to do with all these golden treasures? We could squeeze the juice into only so many gins on the rocks or vinaigrettes. And diluting the juice to make lemonade seemed a bit of a waste. So we decided to preserve them the way the Moroccans do with regular lemons. We cut them into quarters, keeping them attached at the stem end, and tamped their insides with kosher salt. Then we packed them into a wide-mouthed glass jar, layering with more salt as we worked. Over it we poured juice we squeezed from regular lemons (we didn't want to sacrifice the Meyers) and stashed the jar in the refrigerator. Within a month, the lemons had collapsed into the salty brine. They were ready, with plump supple rinds and soft flesh.

Typically, the lemons are rinsed before they're added to stews, tagines, soups, and couscous dishes, and only the rind is used—the pulpy flesh gets discarded. When our own preserved lemons are still new (up to about four months), we never bother to rinse the lemons, and use both rind and flesh. The longer the lemons cure, the saltier they get. So we taste them first to decide how to treat them. We've come to think of our preserved lemons as money in the bank: their deep, salty-sour flavor can brighten up practically any dish. They go into our salads and flavored butters, our lemon meringue tart, even into our gin martinis in place of the olive. You could say that we've become a little obsessed.

Over the years, boxes of Meyer lemons have continued to find their way to the studio doorstep from an ever-expanding group of West Coast friends. And each time one does, we thank our lucky stars for the friendship and the gift. Then we set to work making a new batch of preserved lemons that will carry us through the year and who knows, end up flavoring our lives in unexpected ways.

Clockwise from top left: packing kosher salt into an almost quartered lemon; Meyer lemons; two jars of preserved lemons, the one on the left has just been prepared, and the one on the right has been curing for two months; a small batch of just-made preserved lemons

SHRIMP ROAST
serves 4–6

Our dear friend Maya Kaimal sent us this recipe for her curry. It gets its heat from ground Kashmiri chile and its wonderful complex flavor from a masterful blend of spices. Her delicious, ready-to-heat curry sauces of the same name are always in our fridges.

FOR THE SPICE BLEND
2 teaspoons ground coriander
½ teaspoon Kerala-style garam masala
¼ teaspoon lightly crushed fennel seeds

FOR THE SHRIMP
5 small dried red chiles, preferably
  bright red in color
1½ pounds medium shrimp, peeled
  and cleaned
1 teaspoon Kashmiri chile powder
¼ teaspoon coarsely ground black pepper

¼ teaspoon ground turmeric
¾–1 teaspoon salt
¼ cup coconut oil
1 medium onion, diced
4 cloves garlic, minced
1 teaspoon peeled and finely
  minced fresh ginger
1 tablespoon tomato paste

FOR THE TARKA
2 tablespoons coconut oil
20 fresh curry leaves

February 1st, 28°
light freezing rain

For the spice blend, mix together the coriander, garam masala, and fennel seeds in a bowl. Set aside.

For the shrimp, put the chiles in a small saucepan with 1 cup of water. Boil for 1 minute, remove from the heat, and allow to sit for 5 minutes. Drain the chiles and mince them; you should have about 2 teaspoons. Set aside. Pat the shrimp dry and put them in a medium bowl. Add the chile powder, pepper, turmeric, and salt and toss to coat. Set aside.

Heat the coconut oil in a large wide skillet or wok over medium heat. Add the onions and sauté until they begin to brown around the edges, about 8 minutes. Add the garlic, ginger, tomato paste, and reserved minced red chiles, and fry for 1 minute. Add the spice blend and fry briefly until fragrant. Increase the heat to high and add the shrimp, stirring constantly until the shrimp are cooked through, about 5 minutes. Transfer to a serving dish.

For the tarka, heat the coconut oil in a small skillet over medium-high heat. Add the curry leaves and fry briefly until they crackle. Pour the tarka over the shrimp. Serve with Curd Rice.

CURD RICE

Put 1 cup jasmine rice, 1 teaspoon salt, and 2 cups water in a medium saucepan. Bring to a boil, cover, and reduce the heat to low. Cook undisturbed for 25 minutes. Fluff the rice with a fork and transfer to a large bowl to cool. Combine ¼ cup milk, ¾ cup whole-milk yogurt, 1½ teaspoons peeled and minced fresh ginger, ¾ teaspoon green chile, 2 tablespoons chopped fresh cilantro, and salt to taste. Add the rice and stir well. Moisten the rice with a little extra milk and yogurt if needed. Serve at room temperature. — *makes 4 cups*

CHICKEN THIGHS WITH PANCETTA & CAPERBERRIES
serves 4

Marble-size caperberries are the mature fruit of the caper bush, *Capparis spinosa*. Capers are the pickled flower buds of the same shrub and have a more intense, tart flavor than the berries. We like the meatiness of caperberries for this dish.

8 whole chicken thighs	6 ounces pancetta, diced
Salt and pepper	1 clove garlic, sliced
1 tablespoon olive oil	1 cup caperberries, stemmed and halved

Season the chicken thighs with salt and pepper and set aside. Put the olive oil and pancetta into a heavy large skillet and cook over medium-high heat, stirring frequently, until the fat begins to render, 2–3 minutes. Push the pancetta to the edge of the skillet and add the chicken thighs skin side down. Cook without moving them until the fat has rendered out and the skin is deep golden brown and crisp, 15–20 minutes. Adjust the heat, reducing it to medium-low if the skin begins to burn before it browns evenly.

February 2nd, 36°
heavy fog on the river

Turn the thighs over. Add the garlic around the thighs and cook until soft, about 1 minute. Add the caperberries and a splash of their pickling juices from the jar and stir them around the skillet to combine them with the pancetta. Continue cooking the thighs until they are cooked through and the juices run clear when pierced, 10–15 minutes.

Serve the thighs on a platter and spoon the pancetta and caperberries on top. Season with a little salt and some pepper, if you like.

HEARTS OF ROMAINE WITH MIMOSA DRESSING

When we serve this crunchy salad with sliced ham and good crusty bread it makes us feel like we're on a picnic—even if it's the dead of winter!

February 6th, 27°
light snow

Use a wooden spoon to mash together 4 chopped anchovy filets, 1 small clove garlic, and salt and pepper to taste in the bottom of a wooden salad bowl. Stir in 1 tablespoon seasoned rice wine vinegar. Add 3–4 tablespoons really good extra-virgin olive oil, stirring constantly. Add 2 coarsely chopped hard-boiled eggs and 1 tablespoon capers and stir the dressing together. Adjust the seasonings. Chop 1 large or 2 small hearts of romaine lettuce and toss with the dressing. Pile the salad onto a platter and serve. — *serves 2–4*

BRAISED BEEF BRISKET WITH ONIONS & CURRANTS
serves 4–6

We're often looking for ways to add saltiness or sweetness to a dish by using more complex ingredients than straight-up salt or sugar. Anchovies, capers, preserved lemons, and pancetta are some of our favorite saline seasonings. In this recipe, we add sweetness to the beef brisket and its rich, silky braising sauce with onions, ketchup, sherry vinegar, and dried currants. This is how we build flavor. The trick to cooking is learning how to balance flavors and seasonings while keeping them from getting murky. We've been cooking a long time and we're still learning constantly. It's one of the reasons we love to cook.

2 tablespoons olive oil
4 medium onions, sliced into
   thick rounds
3 cloves garlic, peeled and crushed
One 3-pound beef brisket with a
   nice layer of fat

1 tablespoon pimentón
Salt and pepper
1 cup ketchup
2 tablespoons sherry or red wine vinegar
1 cup dried currants or raisins

February 7th, 26°
blizzard

Preheat the oven to 300°. Heat the olive oil in a large enameled cast-iron or other heavy ovenproof pot with a lid over medium-high heat. Add the onions and garlic and cook until softened and slightly collapsed, about 5 minutes. Remove the pot from the heat.

Rub the brisket all over with the pimentón and a generous seasoning of salt and pepper. Put the brisket in the pot fat side up on top of the onions. Stir together the ketchup, ½ cup water, the vinegar, and currants in a small bowl, and pour over the brisket. Cover the pot and transfer it to the oven.

Braise the meat until it is very tender, about 3 hours. Remove the pot from the oven, then transfer the meat to a cutting board. Skim off the fat from the sauce. Slice the meat and serve with the sauce.

SLICED BRISKET WITH ONIONS ON A SOFT POTATO ROLL

February 8th, 32°
more light snow

The best thing about leftover braised brisket is having it for lunch on a soft potato roll. Its encore may be an even better performance than the one the night before!

Pile slices of warm Beef Brisket with Onions & Currants on the bottom half of a soft potato roll. Spoon some of the warm sauce on top of the meat and add a few rings of braised onions. Add the top half of the roll. — *makes 1*

Top left, White Clam Pizza; top right, Prosciutto, Lemon & Green Olive Pizza; bottom, left to right: Escarole, Fontina & Black Olive Pizza,
Potato & Onion Pizza, White Clam Pizza, Proscuitto, Lemon & Green Olive Pizza

PIZZA DOUGH
makes enough to make 4 10-inch pizzas

This pizza dough can be made early in the day and left to slowly rise in the refrigerator until the evening; you can even leave it overnight. Use this dough with your own pizza toppings or with any of the following recipes. (See page 302 to follow the numbered steps below.)

One ¼-ounce envelope active dry yeast
  (2¼ teaspoons)
3 tablespoons really good extra-virgin
  olive oil, plus more for the crust

4 cups bread flour, plus more for kneading
2 teaspoons salt, plus more for the crust
Cornmeal

February 9th, 18°
crystal clear

For the dough (1), dissolve the yeast in ½ cup warm water in a small bowl. Stir in 1¼ cups water and 2 tablespoons of the olive oil.

Pulse the flour and salt together in a food processor. Pour the yeast mixture through the feed hole in the lid while the processor is running (2) and process until the dough comes together and forms a sticky ball, about 1 minute. Turn the dough out on a floured work surface (3) and briefly knead into a smooth ball (4). Put the remaining 1 tablespoon oil in a large bowl. Roll the dough around in the bowl until coated all over with oil (5). Cover the bowl with plastic wrap and let the dough rise in a warm spot until it has doubled in size, about 2 hours.

Divide the dough into 4 equal pieces on a lightly floured surface and shape each into a ball. Place the balls at least 5 inches apart, loosely cover them with a clean, damp kitchen towel, and let them rise until nearly doubled in size, 30–60 minutes (6).

Place a pizza stone on the upper rack in the oven and preheat the oven to 500°. Working with one ball at a time, stretch the dough into a 10-inch round on a floured surface (7), letting it rest and relax if resistant. Lay the dough out on a cornmeal-dusted pizza peel (8) or a rimless cookie sheet. Prick the surface with a fork, brush with some olive oil, and sprinkle with salt. Arrange the pizza toppings of your choosing over the dough (9). Slide the pizza off the peel onto the hot pizza stone in the oven. Bake until the crust is puffed and golden around the edges and the topping is bubbling hot, 6–8 minutes. Use the peel to remove the pizza from the oven.

PROSCIUTTO, LEMON & GREEN OLIVE PIZZA

Arrange 3 ounces torn fresh mozzarella and 8 paper-thin lemon slices over the prepared pizza dough. Scatter 6–8 halved, pitted green olives and the leaves of 1 sprig fresh rosemary on top and sprinkle with a pinch of Aleppo pepper. Bake the pizza until the cheese is melted and bubbling, 6–8 minutes. Remove the pizza from the oven. Drape 3 slices of prosciutto over the hot pizza, drizzle with a little really good extra-virgin olive oil, and cut into wedges. —— *makes 1*

ESCAROLE, FONTINA & BLACK OLIVE PIZZA

Rinse ¼ head of escarole. Coarsely chop the wet leaves (you should have about 4 cups). Heat 1 tablespoon extra-virgin olive oil in a medium skillet over medium heat. Add the wet leaves, season to taste with salt, and cook, stirring often, until they are limp, 2–3 minutes. Drain the escarole, then scatter the leaves, about ¼ cup grated Italian fontina, and a small handful of pitted black oil-cured olives over the prepared pizza dough. Bake the pizza until the cheese is melted, 6–8 minutes. Remove the pizza from the oven. Drizzle with a little really good extra-virgin olive oil, and cut into wedges. —— *makes 1*

POTATO & ONION PIZZA

Use a mandoline to thinly slice 2 Yukon gold potatoes. Wash the potato slices in several changes of cold water until the water runs clear. Drain the potatoes, toss with a generous pinch of salt, and transfer to a colander to drain and soften for about 10 minutes. Transfer the potatoes to a medium bowl. Add 1 small onion, sliced lengthwise. Add 2 tablespoons really good extra-virgin olive oil, season to taste with salt, and toss with your hands until the potatoes and onions are well coated. Set aside for about 5 minutes. Arrange the potatoes in overlapping circles over the prepared pizza dough, tucking slices of onion in between. Sprinkle a big pinch of red pepper flakes over the pizza, then brush the edges of the dough with more olive oil. Bake the pizza until the cheese is melted, 6–8 minutes. Remove the pizza from the oven. Drizzle with a little more olive oil, and cut into wedges. —— *makes 1*

WHITE CLAM PIZZA

Heat 2 tablespoons extra-virgin olive oil, 2 thinly sliced cloves garlic, and a pinch of red pepper flakes in a small skillet over medium heat until everything begins to sizzle, about 2 minutes. Stir in ¼ cup drained, canned baby clams and a splash of the juice from the can, and season with salt to taste. Set aside. Using a vegetable peeler, make long shards of cheese from a 1-ounce hunk of parmigiano-reggiano. Scatter the cheese over the prepared pizza dough, then spoon the seasoned clams evenly over the top. Brush the edges of the dough with more olive oil. Bake the pizza until the cheese is melted and the clams are bubbling, 6–8 minutes. Remove the pizza from the oven. Drizzle with a little more olive oil, and cut into wedges. —— *makes 1*

BAKED HAM WITH GOLDEN BREAD CRUMBS
makes enough for a village

The sweet, crunchy bread-crumb crust is the part everyone always wants when we serve this ham. Make extra toasted bread crumbs to serve sprinkled on the sliced ham or serve the ham with Golden Bread Crumbs with Pancetta & Prunes (page 213). A bone-in ham will feed 3–4 people per pound.

One 16-pound bone-in smoked ham
2 cups packed dark brown sugar
½ cup Dijon mustard

¼ cup extra-virgin olive oil
3 cups coarse fresh bread crumbs made
   from rustic white bread

February 10th, 32°
sunny & blustery

Preheat the oven to 300°. Using a sharp knife, remove the rind from most of the ham, leaving a band around the end of the shank bone and a thin layer of fat all over. Score the fat on top of the ham in a ¾-inch diamond pattern. Place the ham in a large roasting pan. Pour 3 cups of water into the pan. Bake the ham for 2 hours.

Meanwhile, stir the brown sugar and mustard in a medium bowl to make a thick paste and set aside.

Heat the olive oil in a large skillet over medium heat. Add the bread crumbs and toast, stirring frequently, until crisp and golden, 5–10 minutes. Set the bread crumbs aside.

Remove the ham from the oven and increase the oven temperature to 350°. Spread half of the sugar-mustard paste over the scored top of the ham. Bake the ham for 1 hour.

Remove the ham from the oven and increase the oven temperature to 400°. Spread the remaining half of the sugar-mustard paste over the ham and pack the bread crumbs all over the top. Add 1 cup water to the roasting pan if the pan juices have dried out.

Return the ham to the oven to bake until the bread crumbs are deep golden brown, about 15 minutes. Transfer the ham to a serving platter or a carving board and let it rest for about 10 minutes before carving.

SLICED HAM ON BAGUETTE

February 13th, 36°
cold hard rain

It seems we never tire of a good ham sandwich. Lucky for us, as there's always ham left over after baking a big beauty like the one above, no matter how many people we've fed. We like our ham sandwiches on any good bread, but a chewy baguette takes it out of the deli realm and into a classic French one. The bread gets slathered with mayonnaise or buttered with flavorful Irish butter. Mustard has a minor role, if any, and sliced tomato or lettuce never do. Gosh, for such a simple sandwich, it certainly has its rigor!

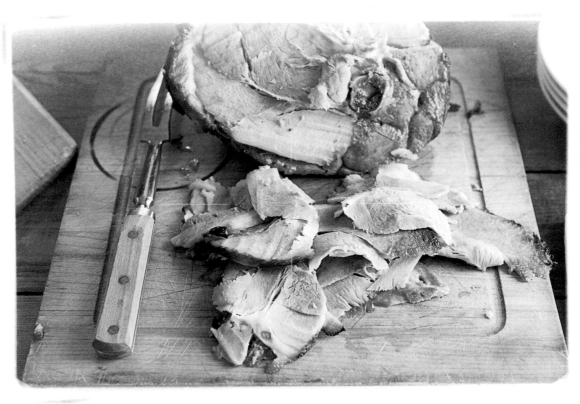

RED VELVET CUPCAKES WITH MERINGUE FROSTING
makes 24–28

We make these every Valentine's Day for all our sweethearts. The meringue frosting—light, silky-smooth, and sweet—beats all the others we've tried, hands down.

FOR THE CUPCAKES
12 tablespoons unsalted butter, softened
2 cups sugar
3 large eggs, at room temperature
¼ cup red food coloring
2 tablespoons good unsweetened
  cocoa powder
1 teaspoon vanilla extract
3½ cups cake flour, sifted

1½ teaspoons salt
1½ cups buttermilk
1½ teaspoons white vinegar
1½ teaspoons baking soda

FOR THE MERINGUE FROSTING
1½ cups sugar
4 large egg whites, at room temperature
Pinch of salt
Large pinch of cream of tartar

February 14th, 35°
hazy

For the cupcakes, preheat the oven to 350°. Line muffin pans with paper with 24–28 cupcake liners and set aside. Beat the butter and sugar together in a large mixing bowl with a mixer on medium-high speed until pale yellow and very fluffy, about 5 minutes. Beat in the eggs one at a time, beating well after each addition. Add the food coloring, cocoa, and vanilla, and beat on medium speed until well combined.

Combine the flour and salt in a bowl. Add the flour and buttermilk to the butter-egg mixture alternately in thirds, beating after each addition until just combined. Mix the vinegar and baking soda together, then add to the batter. Beat until the batter is smooth and well combined.

Divide the batter between the cupcake liners, filling them about three-quarters full. Bake until a skewer inserted into the center of the cupcakes comes out clean, about 20 minutes. Tip the cupcakes out of the pans, transfer them to a wire rack, and let cool completely.

For the meringue frosting, put the sugar and ½ cup cold water into a medium saucepan. Heat over medium heat, gently swirling the pan to help dissolve the sugar. When the syrup comes to a boil, cover the pan to let the steam run down the sides, washing away and dissolving any sugar granules clinging to the sides. Boil until the sugar is completely dissolved and the syrup is clear. Uncover, and continue boiling until the temperature registers 238° on a candy thermometer.

Meanwhile, put the egg whites, salt, and cream of tartar in a large mixing bowl. Beat with a mixer on medium speed until soft peaks form, about 2 minutes. Increase the speed to high and gradually pour in the hot syrup. Continue to beat until the whites are stiff, glossy, and have cooled to room temperature, about 15 minutes. Ice the cupcakes with the meringue frosting. (There may be frosting left over; unfortunately it doesn't keep.)

Top, Red Velvet Cupcakes with Meringue Frosting; bottom, Chocolate Sponge Cake (page 310)

CHOCOLATE SPONGE CAKE
serves 4–6

We serve this cake as a triple-decker—we like the proportion of icing to cake. But feel free to cut it into any shape you want—circles, diamonds, whatever you like. Sometimes we spread jam between the layers and other times we just eat it plain with a dusting of powdered sugar.

FOR THE SPONGE CAKE
1 tablespoon butter, softened
¼ cup good unsweetened cocoa powder, plus a little for dusting the pan
¼ cup cake flour
4 eggs, at room temperature

½ cup plus 2 tablespoons sugar
1 teaspoon vanilla extract

FOR THE CHOCOLATE ICING
¾ cup heavy cream
1 cup bittersweet chocolate chips

For the sponge cake, preheat the oven to 400°. Butter an 8 × 13-inch sheet pan and line the bottom with buttered parchment paper. Dust it with a little cocoa, then tap out any excess. Triple-sift the cocoa and flour together through a fine-mesh sieve into a mixing bowl. Set aside.

Crack 2 of the eggs into a deep mixing bowl. Separate the remaining 2 eggs, adding the yolks to the whole eggs and putting the whites into another deep mixing bowl. Set the whites aside. Beat the eggs with a mixer on low speed for about 1 minute. Increase the speed to medium and gradually add ½ cup of the sugar, beating until the eggs are thick and pale yellow, about 3 minutes. Beat in the vanilla.

Using a clean whisk attachment, beat the egg whites on medium-high speed until foamy, then sprinkle in 1 tablespoon of the sugar, continuing to beat until soft peaks form, about 1 minute. Sprinkle in the remaining 1 tablespoon of sugar and beat until the whites are thick and glossy, about 30 seconds.

Using a rubber spatula, fold about half of the beaten whites into the sugar-yolk batter. Sift half of the flour-cocoa mixture over the batter, then fold it in. Fold in the remaining whites and then the remaining flour-cocoa mixture. Pour the batter into the prepared pan, spreading it evenly to the pan's edges. Bake for 6 minutes. Press the center of the cake with your fingertip; if it springs back, it is done. If not, bake for 1–2 minutes. Cool the cake on a wire rack for about 15 minutes. Then place a cutting board on top of the sheet pan, turn it upside down, and unmold the cake. Carefully peel off the parchment.

For the chocolate icing, heat the heavy cream in a pot over medium-low heat. Add the chocolate chips and stir until the chocolate melts and the icing is smooth and glossy. Using a serrated bread knife, trim off the edges of the cake. Pour about half of the icing down the middle of the cake, then use an offset spatula to smooth the icing evenly to the edges. Cut the cake across the length into three even pieces. Stack one piece on top of the other, then ice the sides of the cake.

FALLEN CHOCOLATE SOUFFLÉ CAKE
serves 8

Like most chocolate lovers, we think that if you are going to the trouble of cooking with chocolate rather than just eating it in its pure and heavenly state, you better make it really good. If memory serves us, we first had this cake at Maida Heatter's Miami house overlooking Biscayne Bay. No one can bake like Maida—she just has the touch. And this flourless chocolate cake was no exception. It had a crisp sugary crust that collapsed over its rich mousselike filling. Maida got the recipe from pastry chef Mark Allen, of the long-gone New York City restaurant Foodworks. He learned to make the cake at the Culinary Institute of America. And now we make it. Good recipes pass round and round, year after year. Every time we make this cake, we think of wonderful Maida.

8 ounces unsalted butter, at room temperature (plus some for greasing the pan)

1 cup granulated sugar, plus ¼ cup for the pan

10 ounces semisweet or bittersweet chocolate, chopped

¼ cup espresso or very strong black coffee

8 eggs, separated

1 teaspoon vanilla extract

¼ teaspoon salt

Powdered sugar

Preheat the oven to 300°. Grease a nonstick tube or bundt pan liberally with butter. Sprinkle the ¼ cup of sugar into the pan and shake to coat the bottom and sides with the sugar. Some sugar will fall to the bottom of the pan, that's just fine.

Heat the chocolate and coffee together in a heavy small saucepan set over a larger pan filled with simmering water over medium heat, and whisk until melted and smooth. Remove from the heat and set aside to cool for about 10 minutes.

Meanwhile, beat the butter with ¾ cup of the sugar in the bowl of a standing mixer or with an hand mixer on medium speed until pale yellow and very fluffy, about 5 minutes. Beat in the egg yolks one at a time, beating until very fluffy, about 5 minutes. Add the vanilla. Fold the cooled melted chocolate into the batter. Set aside.

In a clean bowl with clean beaters, beat the egg whites and salt together on medium speed until frothy, about 1 minute. Continue beating, gradually adding the remaining ¼ cup of sugar, until the whites are thick and hold a peak, about 5 minutes. Fold one-third of the whites into the chocolate batter, then fold in the remaining whites in 2 batches, taking care not to deflate the batter. Pour the batter into the prepared pan and bake for 2 hours. The cake will rise, then fall.

Cover the pan with a serving plate, turn the pan over, and unmold the cake onto the plate. It may collapse and look a bit messy, but that's the nature of this cake. Serve warm, dusted with powdered sugar, if you like.

PIMENTÓN & CARAWAY SHORT RIBS WITH EGG NOODLES
serves 4–6

On cold, dreary winter days, the first thing we do when we get to the studio is make a fire in the little Franklin stove to warm the place up. Then we'll make a pot of something like these short ribs, which need to braise in the oven a long time to make them tender. The payoff is threefold: The oven helps warm up the space; the room is filled with the aroma of delicious cooking; and we've got something to eat by lunchtime. It's a win, win, win.

FOR THE SHORT RIBS
4 pounds meaty short ribs
Salt and pepper
2 tablespoons olive oil
2 large onions, thickly sliced
3 cloves garlic, sliced
2 tablespoons pimentón
2 teaspoons caraway seeds

2 tablespoons tomato paste
1 cup dry red wine
FOR THE NOODLES
½ pound egg noodles
1–2 tablespoons butter
2 tablespoons chopped fresh parsley leaves
Salt

February 16th, 29°
freezing drizzle

For the short ribs, preheat the oven to 300°. Season the short ribs all over with the salt and pepper. Heat the olive oil in a large enameled cast-iron or other heavy ovenproof pot with a lid over medium-high heat. Working in batches, add the short ribs and brown all over, about 5 minutes per batch. Transfer the short ribs to a plate as they brown.

Reduce the heat to medium. Add the onions, garlic, pimentón, and caraway seeds to the pot and cook, stirring occasionally, until the onions have softened, about 15 minutes. Push the onions and garlic to the side of the pot. Add the tomato paste and cook, stirring constantly, until it turns a shade darker, 1–2 minutes. Stir the onions and tomato paste together. Return the short ribs, along with any accumulated juices, to the pot. Add the wine and enough water so that the meat is half-submerged. Increase the heat to medium-high and bring to a simmer.

Cover the pot and braise the short ribs in the oven until the meat is fork-tender, about 3 hours. Remove the pot from the oven. Skim off the fat from the sauce. (If making this ahead of time, remove the short ribs from the pot and chill the sauce to make removing the fat easier.)

For the noodles, bring a large pot of salted water to a boil. Add the noodles and cook until tender. Drain the noodles, then return them to the pot. Stir in the butter and parsley, adding a splash of water, if needed. Season with salt.

To serve, arrange the short ribs and sauce on a platter and serve with the buttered noodles.

WALDORF CHICKEN SALAD

The original Waldorf salad, created in 1893 at the Waldorf Hotel in New York City, did not have chunks of chicken, but we think it's a perfectly acceptable face-lift for an old classic.

February 21st, 35°
melting snow

Mix together 1 pound cooked chicken torn in small pieces, 2 diced celery ribs, 1 crisp cored and diced apple, ½ cup chopped toasted pecans, ¼ cup dried currants, and 1 tablespoon capers in a large bowl. Add ½ cup mayonnaise and the juice of 1 lemon and fold together with a rubber spatula. Season with salt and pepper. Before serving, garnish with chopped fresh chives. Serve with Escarole Salad (page 333) and a few nasturtium leaves or fresh herbs, if you like. — *serves 4*

BUCKWHEAT CRÊPES WITH HAM & CHEESE
makes 10–12

Serve these traditional Breton crêpes with a good bottle of chilled hard apple cider.

FOR THE CRÊPES
1 cup pure buckwheat flour
½ cup all-purpose flour
¼ teaspoon salt
¼ teaspoon black pepper
3 eggs
Butter

FOR THE TOPPING
Butter
12 thin slices ham
10–12 eggs
3 cups grated Gruyère cheese
Chopped fresh chives

February 23rd, 36°
slushy

For the crêpes, combine the flours, salt, and pepper in a large mixing bowl. Whisk in the eggs and 1½ cups water. Whisk until smooth. Cover and let rest for 1–2 hours.

Heat a seasoned crêpe pan or medium nonstick skillet over medium-high heat. Grease the pan with a little butter. Stir the batter, then pour about ¼ cup batter into the pan, tilting and rotating it the minute the batter hits the pan so it coats the bottom of the pan in a very thin, even layer. Pour any excess batter back into the bowl. When the crêpe surface is set, the edges curl up, and the underside is golden, about 45 seconds, turn it over with a thin spatula. Cook for about 45 seconds. Transfer the crêpe to a plate. (Your first couple of crêpes may not be successful, but keep going; you'll get the hang of it.) Repeat with the remaining batter, stacking finished crêpes directly on top of each other.

For the topping, preheat the oven to 500°. Melt a knob of butter in the crêpe pan over medium heat. Add 1 crêpe to the pan and coat it with butter. Lay 1 slice of ham on the crêpe, then crack an egg on top of the ham. Sprinkle ¼ cup of the grated cheese over everything and put the pan in the oven. Cook until the egg white is opaque yet the yolk remains soft, about 5 minutes. Slide the crêpe onto a plate. Sprinkle with some chopped chives. Repeat with the remaining crêpes and toppings.

February 28th, 31°
bright sunshiny day

MELBA TOASTS

Use sliced white sandwich bread or tender-crumbed sweet brioche to make these versatile toasts. Brush both sides of sliced white bread or brioche with melted butter. Lay the slices out on a cookie sheet and set another cookie sheet directly on top. Bake in a preheated 400° oven until golden brown on the bottom, about 10 minutes. Turn the toasts over, cover, and bake until the other side is golden, a few minutes more.

POTTED CRAB

Harissa, a spicy Tunisian red chile paste, is available at specialty food stores and Middle Eastern markets. Heat 3 tablespoons fresh lemon juice and 2 tablespoons sherry in a small saucepan over medium-high heat until reduced to 1 tablespoon, about 3 minutes. Remove from the heat, pour into a food processor, and let cool. Add 8 tablespoons softened salted Irish butter, 2 teaspoons finely grated lemon zest, and 1 teaspoon harissa paste. Purée until smooth. Transfer to a small bowl. Season with salt and pepper to taste. Fold in 8 ounces lump crabmeat (remove any little bits of shell). Pack the crab into a crock or bowl, smoothing the top with a butter knife. Cover and chill for at least 3 hours to allow the flavors to develop. Let the potted crab stand at room temperature for 1 hour to soften before serving. Spread on melba toasts. —— *makes about 1¾ cups*

BLUE CHEESE WITH BLACK PEPPER

This savory butter is great on grilled steaks, lamb chops, roast chicken, and baked potatoes—oh yeah, and melba toasts too. Put 8 ounces softened butter (preferably Irish) into a bowl or a food processor. Add 4 ounces good blue cheese and lots of freshly ground black pepper. Use a fork to blend it together into a coarse mash or pulse it a few times in the food processor for a smoother butter. —— *makes about 1½ cups*

SMOKED SALMON BUTTER

Put 8 ounces softened butter (preferably Irish) into a bowl. Add 4 ounces smoked salmon, 2 pinches cayenne, and the chopped rind of 1 small preserved lemon. Use a fork to blend it together into a coarse mash. Spread on melba toasts. —— *makes about 1½ cups*

ANCHOVY & LEMON BUTTER

On crackers or melba toasts, this is the perfect cocktail crunch as you sip an aperitif. Put 8 ounces softened unsalted butter (preferably Irish) into a bowl or the bowl of a food processor. Add 12 oil-packed anchovy filets, ⅛ teaspoon ground cayenne, and the grated zest of 1 lemon. Use a fork to blend it together by hand into a coarse mash or blend it together in the food processor for a smoother butter. —— *makes 1 cup*

Opposite: clockwise from top, Melba Toasts, Potted Crab, Blue Cheese with Black Pepper, Smoked Salmon Butter, Anchovy & Lemon Butter

❧ March Recipes ❧

fried fish & french-fried potatoes ∾ 322

tartar sauce ∾ 322

roast chicken & bread salad ∾ 324

treviso with mustard vinaigrette ∾ 324

march meatball madness ∾ 328

quick tomato sauce ∾ 328

tetrazzini sauce ∾ 329

dill sauce ∾ 329

watercress soup ∾ 330

crushed potatoes with pancetta, peas & scallions ∾ 330

pork chops with roasted beets & escarole salad ∾ 333

pork cutlets with pickled pearl onions & pancetta ∾ 334

corned beef & cabbage ∾ 338

parsley sauce ∾ 339

irish soda bread ∾339

rabbit stew ∾ 340

"brunette" de veau ∾ 343

old-fashioned baked vanilla custard ∾ 344

thin & crisp chocolate chip cookies ∾ 344

A few years ago while visiting a friend we noticed a wide pretty crock covered with a gauzy linen cloth on her kitchen counter. Intrigued, we inquired about it. "Oh, I am making vinegar. A friend gave me a piece of mother allegedly grown from the original mother that Paula Wolfert brought back from France in the 1970s. (This story did not turn out to be totally accurate but we like to believe it anyway—it makes the vinegar taste better.) Want a piece to start making your own?" Well of course we did.

Good ordinary red-wine vinegar is hard to find. The kind sold in grocery stores is harsh and too acidic. Specialty food stores have fancy balsamicos and flavored vinegars, but often there is no unflavored red-wine variety to be found—guess it's not sexy enough. So we decided to make our own, for the fun and satisfaction of it, and because we love its sparkling bright, fresh flavor.

Our friend fished out the gelatinous vinegar mother from the crock, cut off a piece, and put it in a jar with a splash of wine mixed with water—and we were on our way. The "sainted mother" came with three pages of instructions, including cautionary advice: Don't swamp the mother when feeding it or it will die! If your vinegar smells like furniture polish, throw it away! But we are more intuitive than technical. So we approached vinegar-making our way. And boiled down the instructions to this:

Beg, borrow, steal, or buy a piece of mother. Put it in a clean 1-gallon crock, glass, or plastic container with a wide mouth. Add a bottle of good red wine and 2 cups of water. Drape a double-layered piece of cheesecloth over the top and secure it with a big rubber band, to keep out dirt and bugs and let in air. Stash it in a quiet, cool, dark corner. Then over the next two months, feed every now and then with leftover red wine—we've even used white wine. Take care to gently push the mother aside as you pour in the wine. After about three months of feeding and tending, it should taste like vinegar. Then you can strain it and either pasteurize it, which will keep the mother from growing, or pour it into clean bottles and allow it to age and mellow.

We honored our responsibility and began to leave at least a glass of wine in every bottle to share with the vinegar. Once when we'd forgotten to feed "poor mother" we poured a bottle of 2007 Meredith Estate Pinot Noir in to make up. And we were forgiven; the vinegar kept coming. Since most things are about the same big thing, we try to learn lessons from everything. Making vinegar reminds us of friendship—you pay attention to what it needs and take care of it, and it grows and transforms into something beautiful.

FRIED FISH & FRENCH-FRIED POTATOES
serves 4–6

When we're in a hurry, we use the classic double-fry method to cook frozen French fries—no peeling, no slicing. The resulting crisp golden beauties are the perfect complement to the luscious tender cod. Draining fried food on a wire rack—rather than directly on paper towels—keeps the food crisp on all sides.

Canola oil

One 2-pound bag frozen French fries

Salt

1½ cups milk

2 pounds cod filet, cut into 8 equal pieces

1½ cup all-purpose flour

1½ teaspoons baking powder

1 teaspoon salt

Tartar Sauce

1 lemon, cut into wedges

March 2nd, 37°
rain all day long

Add enough oil to a heavy medium pot to reach a depth of 3 inches. Heat the oil over medium heat until it is hot but not smoking (350° on a candy thermometer). As you fry, adjust the heat to maintain the temperature.

Working in batches, carefully slip the frozen French fries into the hot oil. Fry until pale golden but still limp, about 2 minutes. Transfer the fries with a slotted spatula to a wire rack set over paper towels to drain. When they all have been fried, fry them for a second time in batches, starting with the first batch fried, until deep golden and crisp, 2–3 minutes. Transfer the fries to the rack to drain. Season with salt.

Pour the milk into a shallow pan. Add the fish to the milk, turning the pieces until they are drenched. Sift the flour, baking powder, and salt together onto a platter, then dredge the pieces of fish in the flour, making sure to coat all sides.

Increase the heat slightly so the oil temperature reaches 360°. Working in batches, carefully slip the fish into the hot oil. Fry until golden brown, about 5 minutes, turning the fish over halfway through. Transfer fish with a slotted spatula to the rack. Season with salt. Serve hot with Tartar Sauce, the wedges of lemon and the French fries.

TARTAR SAUCE

We anoint both fish and fries with this perfectly matched mayonnaise.

Mix together 1¼ cups mayonnaise, 5 chopped cornichons, 1 tablespoon chopped capers with a splash of their pickling brine, and 4 finely chopped sprigs each of fresh parsley, dill, and tarragon in a small bowl. Stir in 2 tablespoons lemon juice and salt and pepper to taste. The sauce will keep in the refrigerator for up to 1 week. —— *makes 1½ cups*

ROAST CHICKEN & BREAD SALAD
serves 4

This is a terrific "leftover" lunch. Using some of last night's roast chicken and a half loaf of stale bread, you can eat like a king. Loosely based on *panzanella*, the Italian tomato and bread salad, it's our version for winter, when a good ripe tomato is but a dream.

FOR THE VINAIGRETTE
1 clove garlic
2 tablespoons red wine vinegar
Juice of ½ lemon
½ cup really good extra-virgin olive oil
Salt and pepper

FOR THE SALAD
4 cups roughly torn bite-size pieces good country bread
5 tablespoons extra-virgin olive oil
Salt and pepper
1 pound roasted chicken meat, coarsely shredded
½ cup chopped fresh parsley leaves

March 3rd, 39°
heavy fog
For the vinaigrette, use a Microplane to grate the garlic into a large bowl. Stir in the vinegar and lemon juice. Slowly pour in the olive oil, whisking constantly. Season with salt and pepper, then taste the vinaigrette and adjust the seasonings.

For the salad, preheat the oven to 400°. Toss the bread and the olive oil together in a large bowl until well coated, then season with salt and pepper. Spread the bread out in a single layer on a baking sheet and bake until golden, 10–12 minutes.

Add the toasted bread to the bowl with the vinaigrette and toss together. Add the chicken and parsley, and gently toss. Adjust the seasonings. Divide the salad between 4 plates and drizzle a little really good extra-virgin olive oil over each salad.

TREVISO WITH MUSTARD VINAIGRETTE

We have a taste for deliciously bitter Italian red chicories—round *radicchio di Chioggia*, elongated *radicchio di Treviso*, and the flowerlike *tardivo*, which is only available during the winter months.

March 4th, 40°
extremely hazy
Use a wooden spoon to mash together 1 small garlic clove, salt, and pepper in the bottom of a wooden salad bowl. Stir in 1 tablespoon Dijon mustard and 1 tablespoon red wine vinegar. Whisk in 6–8 tablespoons really good extra-virgin olive oil. Taste the vinaigrette and adjust the seasonings. If the vinaigrette is too thick, add a splash of water.

Halve 2 heads radicchio, *Treviso*, or *tardivo* lengthwise and arrange the leaves on a serving platter. Spoon the dressing over the leaves and garnish with chopped fresh chives. — *serves 4*

MARCH MEATBALL MADNESS
makes 100

Everyone loves good ole meatballs, including us, and this big batch can feed a crowd. We are partial to a delicate diminutive size, so a 1-ounce ice cream scoop works perfectly and keeps everything uniform (a tablespoon works just fine also). We use one of the sauces that follow, depending on our moods.

6 tablespoons olive oil

2 onions, finely chopped

1 clove garlic, minced

Salt and pepper

Freshly grated nutmeg

2 large eggs

1 cup half-and-half

1½ cups fresh bread crumbs

1 pound ground veal

1 pound ground beef

1 pound ground pork

March 7th, 41°
soaking rain

Preheat the oven to 375°. Heat the oil in a large skillet over medium heat. Add the onions and garlic, and cook, stirring often, until the onions are soft and translucent, about 15 minutes. Season to taste with salt, pepper, and lots of nutmeg. Remove from heat and let cool.

Put the eggs and half-and-half into a large bowl and beat together until well mixed. Add the bread crumbs and the cooled onions and mix together. Add the veal, beef, and pork and mix well. Roll the meatballs into 1-ounce balls (they will be very soft but they will hold their shape when cooked) and arrange on 4 large baking pans. Bake in the oven until just cooked, about 20 minutes.

QUICK TOMATO SAUCE
makes 2–3 cups

Add the hot meatballs to the finished sauce and serve over spaghetti for an old-fashioned Italian–American style dinner. Don't forget the candle in the Chianti bottle!

4 tablespoons salted butter

1 onion, minced

1 clove garlic, minced

Salt and pepper

Freshly grated nutmeg

1 bay leaf

Leaves from 1 sprig rosemary, minced

2 cups canned whole
    Italian tomatoes, crushed

⅓ cup minced fresh parsley leaves

Melt the butter in a heavy large pot over medium heat. Add the onions and garlic and cook until soft and translucent, about 15 minutes. Season to taste with salt, pepper, and nutmeg. Add the bay leaf and rosemary. Add the tomatoes, reduce the heat, and gently simmer for about 20 minutes. Add the parsley and adjust the seasonings. Remove the bay leaf before serving.

TETRAZZINI SAUCE
makes 2–3 cups

It seems like no one cooks with sherry anymore—it is a forgotten flavor. Once ladies sipped sherry in tiny stemmed glasses and added a splash of it to sauces to make them taste fancy. This sauce, with its white button mushrooms, is decidedly retro, but we love it spooned over the hot meatballs over creamy mashed potatoes or wide egg noodles.

2 tablespoons butter

1 onion, minced

4 ounces white mushrooms, cleaned and sliced

¼ cup dry sherry

Salt and pepper

1½ tablespoons flour

1 cup chicken stock

1 cup whole milk

¼ cup grated parmigiano-reggiano

Melt the butter in a large skillet over medium heat. Add the onions and cook, stirring often, until just soft, about 10 minutes. Add the mushrooms and cook until they are soft, about 10 minutes. Add the sherry and cook until it has evaporated. Season with salt and pepper.

Sprinkle the flour over the mushrooms, stirring until the flour coats them and absorbs any butter left in the pan, 5–10 minutes (At this point you are cooking the flour to remove that raw floury taste.) Heat the chicken stock along with the milk in a saucepan over medium heat until warm. Add the stock mixture, ½ cup at a time, to the mushrooms, stirring with a wooden spoon until the sauce is smooth and thickened. Stir in the parmigiano.

DILL SAUCE
makes about 3 cups

We serve meatballs in this dill sauce on a bed of fluffy white rice. Sometimes we add a spoonful of sour cream on top and lots of chopped fresh dill.

2 tablespoons butter

1 small onion, minced

Salt and pepper

4 tablespoons flour

4 cups chicken stock

½ cup minced fresh dill

Melt the butter in a heavy large pot over medium heat. Add the onions and cook until soft and translucent, about 15 minutes. Season with salt and pepper. Sprinkle in the flour, stirring often with a wooden spoon, and cook for about 10 minutes. Meanwhile, heat the chicken stock in a saucepan until warm. Add the stock, 1 cup at a time, to the onions, stirring with a wooden spoon until the sauce is smooth and thickened. Stir in the fresh dill.

Overleaf: left, meatballs in Quick Tomato Sauce on spaghetti; right, meatballs in Dill Sauce over white rice

WATERCRESS SOUP
makes 10 cups

Every winter, a patch of watercress grows in a pristine stream deep in the woods not far from our town. We pull on our rubber boots and march through the snowy landscape to forage for the peppery plants. Wading into the cold water, we spot the delicate green stems and leaves of the cress just below the surface, then gather big clumps of them to bring back to Canal House to make this soup. When we don't have time for such an adventure, we buy bunches of small-leafed watercress, with its characteristic bold, spicy taste, from the market. The large-leafed hydroponically grown variety is very pretty, but doesn't deliver much flavor.

2 tablespoons butter
1 medium onion, chopped
2 quarts chicken stock
2 russet potatoes, peeled and cubed
4 bunches watercress, large stems trimmed

1½ teaspoons fresh lemon juice (or more)
Salt and pepper
1½ cups chilled heavy cream
3 tablespoons finely minced fresh chives

March 9th, 40°
showery

Melt the butter in a large pot over medium heat. Add the onions and cook until softened, 10–15 minutes. Add the broth and potatoes. Bring to a boil over medium-high heat. Reduce the heat and simmer until the potatoes are tender, about 20 minutes. Turn off the heat.

Add the watercress to the pot, stirring until the leaves wilt. Working in batches, purée the soup in a blender or food processor until smooth. Return the soup to the pot. Stir in the lemon juice. Season with salt and pepper to taste, and add more lemon juice, if you like.

Whisk the heavy cream with a pinch of salt in a large bowl until soft peaks form. Fold in half of the chives. Serve the soup garnished with a dollop of whipped cream and a sprinkling of chives.

CRUSHED POTATOES WITH PANCETTA, PEAS & SCALLIONS

March 12th, 39°
flooding

Put 2 large Yukon gold potatoes in a pot and cover with cold salted water. Bring to a boil over medium-high heat, then reduce the heat to medium and simmer until tender, about 30 minutes. Drain the potatoes, then peel them while they are still warm.

Meanwhile, heat 1 tablespoon extra-virgin olive oil in a medium skillet over medium heat. Add ¾ cup diced pancetta and cook until crisp, about 8 minutes. Use a slotted spoon to transfer the pancetta to a small plate. Discard the fat from the pan, then add 3 tablespoons butter and 1 cup fresh or frozen peas and cook until the butter has melted and the peas are cooked, about 2 minutes.

Arrange the peeled potatoes on 2 plates and crush lightly with a fork. Spoon the pancetta, peas, and butter over the potatoes. Top each with a scattering of finely chopped scallions and plenty of freshly cracked black pepper. —— *serves 2*

PORK CHOPS WITH ROASTED BEETS & ESCAROLE SALAD
serves 4

It is kind of perverse, what we do to escarole. It reminds us of Morticia from the Addams Family, who used to cut off the heads of the roses, leaving a vase full of spiky stems. Like her, we prefer the crisp, flavorful, slightly bitter ribs of escarole to the pretty green leafy part—so we cut off all the ruffly leaves and feed them to the chickens. In its lemony dressing, the escarole is the perfect foil for the rich pork and sweet, earthy beets.

We pound out the meaty chops so there is more surface to brown and caramelize, which adds lots of flavor. Pork is so lean these days that it can't take overcooking or it will be tough and dry. This fast searing ensures juicy, delicious chops.

FOR THE BEETS

8 small beets, leaves trimmed

2 tablespoons really good extra-virgin olive oil

Salt and pepper

FOR THE PORK CHOPS

4 bone-in center loin pork chops

Salt and pepper

2 tablespoons olive oil

FOR THE ESCAROLE SALAD

1 clove garlic

Juice of ½ lemon

¼ cup really good extra-virgin olive oil

Salt and pepper

4–6 cups trimmed, tender escarole leaves

For the beets, preheat the oven to 400°. Wrap each beet in foil and roast in the oven until tender, about 1 hour. Slip the skins off the beets, cut them into wedges, and put them into a bowl. Toss them with the olive oil and season with salt and pepper.

> March 14th, 33°
> a wet snowy mess

For the pork chops, use a flat-bottomed meat pounder on a sturdy work surface and pound the meat of each chop between two sheets of plastic wrap to ½-inch thickness. Take care not to tear the meat. Discard the plastic wrap. Season both sides with salt and pepper. Heat the oil in a heavy large skillet over medium-high heat and, working in batches if you need to, fry the chops on both sides until golden brown, 6–8 minutes, adding more oil between batches if needed.

For the escarole salad, season the salad bowl by rubbing the inside with the clove of garlic, then discard the garlic. Whisk together the lemon juice and olive oil in the bowl. Season with salt and pepper. Add the escarole and toss until the leaves are well coated with dressing.

To serve, divide the pork chops between 4 dinner plates and serve with the roasted beets and escarole salad.

PORK CUTLETS WITH PICKLED PEARL ONIONS & PANCETTA
serves 4

Sometimes we make a triple batch of these pickled onions—they're so simple and so very good. At the end of the day we add them to a gin Gibson (exactly like a martini, with an onion in place of an olive), or serve them as a condiment with fried chicken or even seared flank steak. Their piquant flavor brightens any rich food.

We first had pork cooked this way at Alice Waters' house. Alice and artist Patricia Curtan were cooking lunch for us. They sliced thick cutlets from a pork loin, gave them a flattening pound, a sprinkle of salt and pepper, and quickly seared them in a hot skillet. Of course, everything they do is just right. Pork used to be much more marbled, but now that it is "the other white meat", this lean cut needs to be cooked more like a chicken breast.

FOR THE PICKLED ONIONS
8 ounces white or yellow pearl onions
Salt
2 bay leaves
8 black peppercorns
1 cup red wine vinegar

FOR THE PORK CUTLETS
Four boneless pork loin cutlets,
    6–8 ounces each
Salt and pepper
2 tablespoons olive oil
1 cup finely diced pancetta

March 15th, 41°
rain—cabin fever

For the pickled onions, bring a medium pot of well-salted water to a boil over high heat. Add the pearl onions and cook until just tender, about 10 minutes. Drain the onions. When they are cool enough to handle, use a paring knife to cut off the root end, then pop the onions out of their skins. Put the peeled onions into a pint canning jar and season with a generous pinch of salt. Tuck the bay leaves and peppercorns into the jar and add enough vinegar to cover the onions. Screw on the lid and refrigerate for at least 24 hours before using.

For the pork cutlets, use a flat-bottomed meat pounder on a sturdy work surface and pound each cutlet between two sheets of plastic wrap to ½-inch thickness. Take care not to tear the meat. Discard the plastic wrap. Season both sides with salt and pepper, and set aside.

Heat the oil in a heavy large skillet over medium heat. Add the pancetta and cook, stirring occasionally, until lightly browned and crisp, 8–10 minutes. Use a slotted spoon to transfer the pancetta to a small plate and set aside. Leave the oil in the skillet.

Increase the heat to medium-high and, working in batches, fry the cutlets until golden brown, about 5 minutes. Transfer to a serving platter. Drain the pickled onions and add to the skillet. Cook until warmed through, 1–2 minutes, then add the pancetta. To serve, spoon the onions and pancetta over the cutlets.

CORNED BEEF & CABBAGE
serves 6

We are a bit balmy, so naturally we like to brine our own corned beef. It's our Saint Paddy's Day tradition. It is actually quite easy and well worth it; you just have to think ahead. But if you're short on time, by all means skip the first step of this recipe and buy a ready-to-go corned beef from your market. We serve our corned-beef dinner with a creamy Parsley Sauce (opposite page) as they do back in the Old Country.

FOR THE CORNED BEEF
¾ cup kosher salt
2 tablespoons brown sugar
1 tablespoon pink curing salt
1 beef brisket, about 5 pounds
2 tablespoons black peppercorns
2 tablespoons mustard seeds
2 tablespoons coriander seeds
6 bay leaves, roughly torn
6 whole cloves

FOR THE VEGETABLES
1 pound small white potatoes, peeled
1 pound carrots, peeled
12 small spring onions, long green
    stems attached
1 small Savoy cabbage, cut into 6 wedges
2–4 tablespoons salted butter, melted
Handful of fresh parsley leaves, chopped

March 17th, 43°
a soft Irish misty day

Stir together the kosher salt, brown sugar, and pink salt in a small bowl, then rub it all over the brisket. Lightly crush the peppercorns, mustard seeds, coriander seeds, bay leaves, and cloves with a mortar and pestle. Sprinkle the spice mixture all over the brisket, pressing it onto the meat as best you can. Put the brisket into a large resealable plastic bag along with any of the loose spices, and seal, squeezing out the air. Refrigerate for 5–7 days, flipping the bag over every day.

The day of the meal, remove the brisket from the bag and rinse off all the spices under cold running water. Put the brisket in a heavy large pot with a lid and cover with water by several inches. Bring to a simmer over medium-high heat, skim off the foam from the surface. Reduce the heat to low, cover, and cook until tender, 3–4 hours. Transfer the meat to a platter and cover with foil.

For the vegetables, strain the broth, and return it to the pot. Add the potatoes to the pot and gently cook over medium heat for 10 minutes. Then add the carrots and spring onions and cook until all the vegetables are tender, 15–20 minutes. Transfer the vegetables as done to a serving platter and cover loosely with foil. Add the cabbage to the pot and cook until tender, 10–15 minutes.

Reheat the corned beef in the simmering broth until warmed through. Transfer the meat to a cutting board and thinly slice across the grain, then arrange on another serving platter. Ladle some of the broth over everything. Pour some melted butter over the potatoes and garnish with the chopped parsley. Serve with Parsley Sauce.

Overleaf: left to right, boiled cabbage and other vegetables, Corned Beef, Parsley Sauce

PARSLEY SAUCE

One winter while driving in Ireland through County Cork, we headed into the heart of Cork City to visit the English Market. Upstairs, in the back of the market, we scored a table at Farmgate Café on the crowded black-and-white–tiled balcony overlooking the Saturday morning shopping scene. We ordered oysters, which were carried up from a fish stall below. Next came classic home-cured corned beef with parsley sauce. We'd never seen this sauce, but now we wouldn't think of serving an Irish boiled dinner without it.

Put 1½ cups whole milk and 1 bay leaf in a small saucepan and cook over medium heat until tiny bubbles form around the sides of the pan, about 5 minutes. Remove from the heat and set aside to infuse for about 20 minutes. Remove and discard the bay leaf. Melt 3 tablespoons butter in a medium saucepan over medium-low heat and whisk in 3 tablespoons flour. Cook, whisking constantly, for about 1 minute. Slowly add the milk and cook, whisking, until thickened, 5–10 minutes. Whisk in 1 cup chicken stock (or the Corned Beef poaching liquid) and cook over medium heat, stirring frequently, until creamy, about 5 minutes. Stir in ¾ cup minced fresh parsley and season with salt and pepper. —— *makes about 2 cups*

IRISH SODA BREAD
makes 1 large loaf

This lovely quick bread was handed down to us long ago by Mrs. Cahill, an Irish neighbor. We eat it warm from the oven, then on the next day we toast slices for breakfast.

4 cups all-purpose flour

2 tablespoons sugar

1 teaspoon baking soda

1 teaspoon salt

4 tablespoons butter

1 cup dried currants

1 teaspoon caraway seeds

2 cups buttermilk

1 large egg, lightly beaten

Preheat the oven to 425°. Butter a large cast-iron skillet. Whisk together the flour, sugar, baking soda, and salt in a large mixing bowl. Blend in the butter with a pastry blender or two knives until it resembles coarse cornmeal. Add the currants and caraway seeds.

Make a well in the center of the flour mixture. Stir in the buttermilk and beaten egg. Dust your hands with a little flour, then gently knead the dough in the bowl just long enough to form a rough ball, adding a little extra flour if the dough is very sticky. Transfer the dough to a floured surface and shape into a round loaf.

Put the dough in the buttered skillet, and use a serrated knife to cut a ½-inch-deep × on top of the dough. Bake until the bread is golden and the bottom sounds hollow when tapped with a knife, about 40 minutes. Allow to cool briefly on a wire rack. Serve warm.

RABBIT STEW
serves 4

Up the river and over the hill at Purely Farm, Marc and Joanna Michini raise pastured pork, lamb, rabbit, and chicken, and they also sell free-range eggs. Their protocol is impeccable and their animals are more than humanely raised on this pretty Bucks County farm. They called us one day to say that they were "harvesting" rabbits, and they thought that we might be interested to see the process. So we went. Americans can be ambivalent about rabbit. But it is delicious (theirs especially) and we do love to cook it. So we girded our loins and drove to the farm. We won't divulge who did what, but in the end, one of us sat in the car listening to Kiri Te Kanawa sing Puccini's "*O mio babbino caro*" while the braver of us witnessed the "harvesting". We took rabbit home that night and honored its gift by making this delicious stew.

1 rabbit, 3–4 pounds
Salt and pepper
1 cup flour
4 tablespoons olive oil
12 ounces button mushrooms, quartered
1 tablespoon tomato paste

¼–⅓ cup white wine
3 cups rich poultry stock
4 carrots, peeled and cut into chunks
4 parsnips, peeled and cut into chunks
1 cup frozen peas, defrosted

March 20th, 48°
mild & muddy

Lay the rabbit on its back. Using a sharp knife, cut off the hind legs at the joint near the backbone. Cut under the shoulder blades to remove the forelegs from the rib cage. Trim off the rib cage on either side of the loin, then trim off the neck and tail ends of the loin. Save the rib cage and end pieces to make stock, or discard. Cut the loin crosswise through the backbone in 2 or 3 pieces. Season the rabbit with salt and pepper. Put the flour in a shallow bowl, and dredge each piece of rabbit (there are 7), in flour.

Heat 2 tablespoons of the olive oil in a heavy large pot with a lid over medium heat. Add the floured rabbit pieces in batches and lightly brown all over, about 10 minutes. Transfer the browned rabbit to a large plate, then add the remaining 2 tablespoons of olive oil to the pot. Add the mushrooms and stir to coat well with oil, scraping up any browned bits from the bottom of the pot. Cook until the mushrooms are golden, about 5 minutes. Transfer the mushrooms to the plate with the rabbit and set aside. Add the tomato paste, and cook, stirring, for about 1 minute. Add the wine and cook for 1 minute.

Return the rabbit and mushrooms to the pot, along with any accumulated juices. Add the stock. Increase the heat to medium-high and bring to a simmer. Reduce the heat to medium-low, cover the pot, and simmer until the rabbit is tender, about 1 hour. Scatter the carrots and parsnips over the rabbit and simmer, covered, until the vegetables are tender, 20–30 minutes. Add the peas and simmer until they are just warmed through, about 5 minutes.

"BRUNETTE" DE VEAU

serves 4

Blanquette de Veau, the basis for this recipe, is—as its name tells you—"veal in a white sauce". In the classic preparation, great care is taken to avoid browning the meat, which could color the delicate pale, creamy sauce. Even though we are usually traditionalists, we prefer the extra flavor that browned meat and the caramelization on the bottom of the pan gives to the sauce. So we call this "brunette" instead. Using veal shank rather than veal stew meat ensures the tenderest, most succulent stew. We like to serve this dish with parsleyed and buttered wide egg noodles.

Four 1-pound veal shank pieces
Salt and pepper
¼ cup flour
3 tablespoons olive oil
2 medium onions, chopped
2 cloves garlic, chopped

3 cups beef stock
5 sprigs fresh thyme
3 bay leaves
¼ cup heavy cream
Juice of ½ lemon

March 22nd, 53°
mild pretty day

Season the veal shanks with salt and pepper, then dust with flour. Heat 2 tablespoons of the olive oil in a heavy large pot over medium heat. Add the veal shanks and brown well, doing it in batches if necessary (if you crowd the pot the shanks will steam and not brown), about 5 minutes per side.

Remove the meat from the pot and reduce the heat to medium. Add the onions and garlic to the pot and cook, stirring and scraping up any brown bits stuck on the bottom, until nice and soft, about 5–10 minutes. Add the remaining 1 tablespoon of olive oil if the pot seems dry.

Return the meat to the pot, then add the stock, thyme, and bay leaves. Bring to a simmer, cover, and cook over low heat until the meat is fork-tender, 2–3 hours. At the early end of the timing, test for tenderness; transfer any shanks that are ready to a large plate and continue cooking until all the shanks are tender.

Simmer the sauce over low heat, uncovered, stirring occasionally, until it has thickened and reduced, about 30 minutes. Remove and discard the thyme and bay leaves. Transfer the sauce to a food processor and purée until smooth. Strain through a fine-mesh sieve into a large clean pot. Stir in the cream, then add the lemon juice, and season the sauce with salt and pepper. Return the veal to the pot and heat through for about 10 minutes.

OLD-FASHIONED BAKED VANILLA CUSTARD

March 27th, 45°
clear & sunny

Preheat the oven to 325°. Butter a 3-cup soufflé dish and set it into a larger baking dish. Whisk together 3 eggs, ⅓ cup sugar, and a pinch of salt in a medium mixing bowl. Heat 1½ cups whole milk in a small saucepan over medium heat until just steaming. Whisk a little of the hot milk into the eggs to temper them, then slowly pour in the remaining milk, whisking constantly. Whisk in ½ teaspoon vanilla bean paste or vanilla extract. Pour the custard mixture through a fine-mesh sieve into the buttered dish. Grate some fresh whole nutmeg over the top of the custard. Put it in the oven and pour boiling water into the larger baking dish until it reaches halfway up the sides of the soufflé dish. Bake until the custard is set around the edges but still trembles in the center, about 40 minutes. Remove from the oven and allow the custard to cool in the water bath for 30 minutes. Serve warm. —— *serves 4*

THIN & CRISP CHOCOLATE CHIP COOKIES
makes about 5 dozen

Our friend Katherine Yang is a New York baker whose exquisite pastries and desserts always balance sweet and savory perfectly. We wanted the best chocolate chip cookie recipe ever, so we asked her advice. Always gracious, she shared her recipe for these delicate, crisp, salty-sweet cookies—just the kind we had in mind. Like most bakers, Katherine relies on measuring her ingredients by weight, not volume, for the most consistent results. We agree, but have included both methods below in case you don't have a scale.

10 ounces room temperature high-fat butter
1¼ cups (298g) dark brown sugar
¾ cup (149g) granulated sugar
1 tablespoon vanilla bean paste or extract
2 teaspoons kosher salt

2 large eggs
1¾ cups plus 2 tablespoons (265g) all-purpose flour
1 teaspoon baking soda
8 ounces chocolate chips

March 30th, 47°
a breezy spring day

Preheat the oven to 375°. Line baking sheets with parchment paper. Combine the butter, brown sugar, granulated sugar, vanilla bean paste, and salt in the bowl of a standing mixer fitted with the paddle attachment. Mix on medium-high speed until light, about 3 minutes. Add the eggs and mix on medium speed until blended, about 2 minutes.

Whisk the flour and baking soda together, then add to the dough, continuing to mix on medium speed for 2 minutes. Stir in the chocolate chips.

Remove the bowl from the mixer. Using a spatula, quickly mix the dough, scraping down the sides and bottom of the bowl. Drop the batter by the well-rounded tablespoon, about 4 inches apart, onto the parchment-lined baking sheets. Bake until golden brown, 10–11 minutes. Let the cookies cool for 5 minutes before transferring them to a wire rack to cool.

INDEX

A

Agee's Pecan Pies, 223

Aïoli, Lemony, Composed Summer Salad with, 115

Allen, Mark, 311

almonds

Apricot & Almond Upside-Down Cake, 88

Classic Tuiles, 116–18

Amante, 52

anchovies

Anchovy & Lemon Butter, 316

Chopped Celery Salad, 284

olives stuffed with, 78

Risotto Cakes with Anchovies (or Not), 10

Tomato "Rollmops," 127

Anderson, Lillie, 7

apples, 174

Apple Galette, 230

Apple Tart, 174

Apples Cooked with Cumin, 258

Duck Breasts with Apples & Caraway, 168

Waldorf Chicken Salad, 314

apricots

Apricot & Almond Upside-Down Cake, 88

Apricot Cooler, 91

Apricot Sparkler, 91

Apricot Syrup, 88

Rummy Apricot, 91

April recipe list, 2

aprons, 180

Artichoke, Pea & Fava Bean Salad, 23

arugula

Open-Faced Sandwiches, 38

Pickled Beets with Horseradish Cream, 27

Shaved Asparagus & Arugula Salad with Bruschetta, 33

Sliced Tomatoes with Arugula, 130

Wild Salmon Crudo with Arugula Salad, 76–77

asparagus, 15

Asparagus on Pasta with a Poached Egg & Lemon Butter, 18

Asparagus with Lemon-Butter Sauce, 17

Birthday Halibut with Beets & Asparagus Vinaigrette, 56

Fritto Misto, 143

Roasted Asparagus, 17

Shaved Asparagus & Arugula Salad with Bruschetta, 33

August recipe list, 122

autumn recipe lists, 178, 206, 232

avocados, 279

Avocado Mash on Multigrain Toast, 279

Cold Avocado & Cucumber Soup, 108

Cold White Corn Soup with Lobster & Avocado, 128

Fire-Toasted Corn Tortilla with Mashed Avocado, 279

Roast Beef Sandwich with Avocado & Tomato, 130

Ruby Red Grapefruit, Avocado & Escarole Salad, 280

B

bacon

Butternut Squash & Candied Bacon on Fresh Pasta, 250

Ham & Bacon with Mustard & Brown Sugar Sauce, 272

Old-Fashioned Layered Potato Salad, 102

Spaghetti alla Carbonara, 45

Baguette, Sliced Ham on, 306

baking powder biscuits, 62

Balsamella, 240

Cannelloni, 248–49

basil

basil syrup, 147

Rolled Flank Steak with Pesto, 78

Tomato "Rollmops," 127

Tomatoes Take a Warm Oil Bath, 130

Bates, Karen, 174

beans, 283. See also beans, green; cannellini beans; fava beans; string beans

Borlotti Beans with Sautéed Baby Kale, 283

Cannellini with Smoked Ham & Rosemary, 43

Cold Leg of Lamb with Cannellini & Lemon Mayonnaise, 166

Cranberry Beans in Olive Oil, 166

Tender Swiss Chard with Cannellini, 84

beans, green

Composed Summer Salad with Lemony Aïoli, 115

Corn, String Bean & Potato Succotash Salad, 164–65

Everyday Vegetable Tonic, 276

Rice Salad, 81

String Beans Vinaigrette with French Feta, 101

beef

Beef Tenderloin with Parsley-Tarragon Butter, 284

Braised Beef Brisket with Onions & Currants, 300

Corned Beef & Cabbage, 338

March Meatball Madness, 328

Pimentón & Caraway Short Ribs with Egg Noodles, 312

Ragù Bolognese, 241

Restorative Beef Broth, 276

Roast Beef Sandwich with Avocado & Tomato, 130

Roast Prime Rib of Beef, 256

Rolled Flank Steak with Pesto, 78

Skirt Steak with Buttered Spinach & French Fries, 214

Sliced Brisket with Onions on a Soft Potato Roll, 300

Two Steaks Feed Four, 134–35

Whole Beef Tenderloin, Peppered & Grilled, 134

beets, 183

Birthday Halibut with Beets & Asparagus Vinaigrette, 56

Composed Summer Salad with Lemony Aïoli, 115

Pickled Beets with Horseradish Cream, 27

Pork Chops with Roasted Beets & Escarole Salad, 333

Warm Beet Soup, 183

Bellini, 121

berries. See also strawberries

Mixed Berry Cobbler, 92

Sugared Berries with Crème Anglaise, 116

Bieler, Henry G., 274, 276

birthdays, 36

Birthday Halibut with Beets & Asparagus Vinaigrette, 56

Birthday Strawberry Pavlova, 57

biscuits, baking powder, 62

blackberries. See also berries

Mixed Berry Cobbler, 92

Blue Cheese with Black Pepper, 316

boiling eggs, 70

Bolognese Ragù, 241

    Lasagne Bolognese, 244–45

Boozy Prunes, Chocolate-Covered, 290

Borlotti Beans with Sautéed Baby Kale, 283

bratwurst

    Bratwurst with Fingerling Potatoes, 210

    Bratwurst with Sautéed Caraway Cabbage, 210

bread. *See also* sandwiches; toast

    baking powder biscuits, 62

    Cornbread, 201

    Irish Soda Bread, 339

    No-Knead Bread, 286

    Roast Chicken & Bread Salad, 324

bread crumbs

    Baked Ham with Golden Bread Crumbs, 306

    Cauliflower with Bread Crumbs, Pancetta &
        Prunes, 213

    Golden Bread Crumbs with Pancetta &
        Prunes, 213

Breast of Veal Braised with Green Olives &
    Tomatoes, 50

Brian's Mashed Potato Trick, 221

brining

    chicken, 112, 158

    Corned Beef & Cabbage, 338

    pork 9

    turkey, 220

brisket

    Braised Beef Brisket with Onions & Currants,
        300

    Corned Beef & Cabbage, 338

    Sliced Brisket with Onions on a Soft Potato
        Roll, 300

broths, 274

    Chicken Broth with Spinach & Little
        Meatballs, 193

    Restorative Beef Broth, 276

    Spinach Tagliatelle & Peas in Golden
        Chicken Broth, 46

Brown Sugar Sauce, Ham & Bacon with
    Mustard &, 272

Brownies, Thick & Chewy, 106

"Brunette" de Veau, 343

Bruschetta, Shaved Asparagus & Arugula Salad
    with, 33

Buckwheat Crêpes with Ham & Cheese, 314

butter

    Anchovy & Lemon Butter, 316

    Asparagus with Lemon-Butter Sauce, 17

    Beef Tenderloin with Parsley-Tarragon Butter, 284

    English Peas in Irish Butter, 84

    Fresh Herb Butter, 135

    Fresh Horseradish Butter, 135

    Irish butter, 17, 38, 135

    Lemon Butter, 135

    Pimentón Butter, 135

    Smoked Salmon Butter, 316

"Buttered" Eggs, 71

Buttermilk Love Cakes, 272–73

Butternut Squash & Candied Bacon on Fresh
    Pasta, 250

Buttery Lobster Capellini, 33

C

cabbage

    Bratwurst with Sautéed Caraway Cabbage, 210

    Corned Beef & Cabbage, 338

    Duck Soup with Cabbage, Ham & Chinese
        Rice Noodles, 173

cakes

    Apricot & Almond Upside-Down Cake, 88

    Chocolate Sponge Cake, 310

    Fallen Chocolate Soufflé Cake, 311

    Ginger Spice Cake with Dried Cherries, 262

    Marmalade Cake, 261

    Red Velvet Cupcakes with Meringue
        Frosting, 308

Candied Bacon & Butternut Squash on Fresh
    Pasta, 250

candied orange peel, 261

cannellini beans

    Cannellini with Smoked Ham & Rosemary, 43

    Cold Leg of Lamb with Cannellini & Lemon
        Mayonnaise, 166

    Tender Swiss Chard with Cannellini, 84

Cannelloni, 248–49

capellini

    Buttery Lobster Capellini, 33

Caperberries, Chicken Thighs with Pancetta &, 299

capers, 299

    Hearts of Romaine with Mimosa Dressing, 299

    Marinated Chicken Salad with Radicchio &
        Iceberg, 186

    Tartar Sauce, 322

    Waldorf Chicken Salad, 314

Caponata, 136

Caprese Salad, Year-Round, 72

Caramel & Gianduia Tart, 204

caraway

    Bratwurst with Sautéed Caraway Cabbage, 210

    Duck Breasts with Apples & Caraway, 168

    Irish Soda Bread, 339

    Pimentón & Caraway Short Ribs with Egg
        Noodles, 312

Carême, 62

Carrot Soup, Cold, 140

Cassis Ice Cream, 87

cauliflower

    Cauliflower with Bread Crumbs, Pancetta &
        Prunes, 213

    Cauliflower with Brown Butter, 84

    Fennel & Ginger–Rubbed Chicken with
        Cauliflower, 12–13

celery

    Chilled Potato & Celery Soup, 140

    Chopped Celery Salad, 284

    Everyday Vegetable Tonic, 276

    Pickled Shrimp & Celery, 254–55

chanterelles, 152, 160

    Chanterelle Salad, 162

    Fricassée of Chanterelles, 162

    Roast Chicken Smothered in Chanterelles, 158

    Soft Scrambled Eggs & Chanterelles, 160

cheese. *See also specific types*

    Blue Cheese with Black Pepper, 316

    Buckwheat Crêpes with Ham & Cheese, 314

    Cheese Straws, 252

    Ham & Cheese Omelet, 13

    Roasted Pumpkin Soup, 189

Cherries, Dried, Ginger Spice Cake with, 262

chestnuts

    Chestnut & Pearl Onion Stuffing, 222

    Grilled Quail with Braised Chestnuts &
        Kabocha Squash, 194

Chèvre & Smoked Salmon on Crax, 77

chicken

    Cannelloni, 248–49

    Chicken en Gelée Sandwiches, 158

    Chicken Roasted Over Potatoes & Lemon, 184

    Chicken Soup with Ditalini, 186

    Chicken Thighs with Pancetta &
        Caperberries, 299

    Cleansing Ginger-Chicken Soup, 277

Fennel & Ginger–Rubbed Chicken with
    Cauliflower, 12–13
The Fry Queen's Fried Chicken, 112
Marinated Chicken Salad with Radicchio &
    Iceberg, 186
Pan-Fried Chicken Thighs with Little
    Zucchini, 38
Poached Chicken with Tarragon & Chive
    Mayonnaise, 31
Roast Chicken, 158
Roast Chicken & Bread Salad, 324
Roast Chicken Smothered in Chanterelles, 158
Roasted Chicken in a Pot with Spring
    Onions, 82
spatchcocking, 184
Waldorf Chicken Salad, 314
chicken broth
    Chicken Broth with Spinach & Little
        Meatballs, 193
    Spinach Tagliatelle & Peas in Golden Chicken
        Broth, 46
chiles
    Curd Rice, 296
    Pork Stewed in Guajillo Chile Mole, 198
    Shrimp Roast, 296
Chinese Rice Noodles, Duck Soup with
    Cabbage, Ham &, 173
chives, 66
    Canal House Year-Round Caprese Salad, 72
    Poached Chicken with Tarragon & Chive
        Mayonnaise, 31
    Sole Meunière with Peas, Parsley & Chives, 20
chocolate, 311
    Chocolate-Covered Boozy Prunes, 290
    Chocolate Sponge Cake, 310
    Fallen Chocolate Soufflé Cake, 311
    Gianduia, 203
    Gianduia & Caramel Tart, 204
    Little Chocolate Turnovers, 289
    Little Gianduia Turnovers, 289
    Thick & Chewy Brownies, 106
    Thin & Crisp Chocolate Chip Cookies, 344
Chorizo & Potato Frittata, 10
Christmas, in Italy, 234
Cipolline, Kabocha Squash & Yukon Gold
    Potatoes, 196
citrus syrup, 147

clams
    Sausage & Clam Stew, 188–89
    White Clam Pizza, 305
Classic Tuiles, 116–18
Classic Vanilla Ice Cream, 86
cleansing foods, 274
    Cleansing Ginger-Chicken Soup, 277
    Everyday Vegetable Tonic, 276
    Restorative Beef Broth, 276
Cobbler, Mixed Berry, 92
cocktails. See drinks
cod
    Fried Fish & French-Fried Potatoes, 322
coffee
    Coffee Ice Cream, 87
    Roast Leg of Lamb for Easter, 26
    Strong Coffee Granita, 148
Composed Summer Salad with Lemony Aïoli, 115
compound butters
    Beef Tenderloin with Parsley-Tarragon
        Butter, 284
    Fresh Herb Butter, 135
    Fresh Horseradish Butter, 135
    Lemon Butter, 135
    Pimentón Butter, 135
Confit of Duck Legs with Potatoes Sarladaise, 172
Conserves, Strawberry, 60
    Preserved Strawberries & Jamón Serrano on
        Little Toasts, 60
cookies. See also brownies
    Classic Tuiles, 116–18
    Thin & Crisp Chocolate Chip Cookies, 344
Cooler, Apricot, 91
corn
    Chilled Corn Soup, 108
    Cold White Corn Soup with Lobster &
        Avocado, 128
    Corn, String Bean & Potato Succotash Salad,
        164–65
Corn Tortilla, Fire-Toasted, with Mashed
    Avocado, 279
Cornbread, 201
Corned Beef & Cabbage, 338
crab
    Canal House Crab Louis, 101
    Potted Crab, 316
crackers, 77
    Smoked Salmon with Chèvre on Crax, 77

Cranberry Beans in Olive Oil, 166
Cranberry-Port Gelée, 221
cream
    Pappardelle with Peas & Scallions Bathed in
        Cream, 7
    Pickled Beets with Horseradish Cream, 27
Crème Anglaise, Sugared Berries with, 116
Crêpes, Buckwheat, with Ham & Cheese, 314
Crushed Potatoes with Pancetta, Peas &
    Scallions, 330
cucumbers
    Cold Avocado & Cucumber Soup, 108
    Cool Cucumber & Mint Salad with Sichuan
        Pepper, 103
Cumin, Apples Cooked with, 258
Cupcakes, Red Velvet, with Meringue Frosting, 308
Curd Rice, 296
currants
    Braised Beef Brisket with Onions &
        Currants, 300
    Caponata, 136
    Irish Soda Bread, 339
    Marmalade Cake, 261
    Red Currant Jelly, 91
    Waldorf Chicken Salad, 314
curry
    Shrimp Roast, 296
Curtan, Patricia, 334
custards
    Old-Fashioned Baked Vanilla Custard, 344
    Sugared Berries with Crème Anglaise, 116

D
Day-After-Thanksgiving Turkey Sandwich, 228
December recipe list, 232
Deconstructed Carbonara, 201
desserts
    Agee's Pecan Pies, 223
    Apple Galette, 230
    Apricot & Almond Upside-Down Cake, 88
    Birthday Strawberry Pavlova, 57
    Cassis Ice Cream, 87
    Chocolate-Covered Boozy Prunes, 290
    Chocolate icing, 310
    Chocolate Sponge Cake, 310
    Classic Tuiles, 116–18
    Classic Vanilla Ice Cream, 86
    Coffee Ice Cream, 87

Fallen Chocolate Soufflé Cake, 311

Gianduia, 203

Gianduia & Caramel Tart, 204

Ginger Spice Cake with Dried Cherries, 262

Kabocha Squash Pie, 226

Lemon Meringue Tart, 29–31

Little Chocolate Turnovers, 289

Little Gianduia Turnovers, 289

Marmalade Cake, 261

Mixed Berry Cobbler, 92

Old-Fashioned Baked Vanilla Custard, 344

Peppermint Crunch Ice Cream, 87

Pink Lemon Granita, 148

Poached White Peaches in Lemon Verbena
   Syrup, 118

Puff Pastry Jam Tartlets, 290

Pumpkin Chiffon Pie, 227

Red Velvet Cupcakes with Meringue
   Frosting, 308

Strawberries Romanoff, 62

Strawberry Ice Cream, 87

Strawberry Shortcake, 62

Strong Coffee Granita, 148

Sugared Berries with Crème Anglaise, 116

Thick & Chewy Brownies, 106

Thin & Crisp Chocolate Chip Cookies, 344

Vin Santo–Roasted Pears, 203

Deviled Eggs, 71

dill

   Dill Sauce, 329

   Tartar Sauce, 322

Ditalini, Chicken Soup with, 186

Dried Cherries, Ginger Spice Cake with, 262

drinks

   Amante, 52

   Apricot Cooler, 91

   Apricot Sparkler, 91

   Bellini, 121

   Lemonade, 121

   Limonada, 270

   Melon Water, 147

   Milk Punch, 252

   Rummy Apricot, 91

   Simple Syrup, 147

   Tisane of Fresh or Dried Lemon Verbena, 146

   Winter Margarita, 270

dry brining, 9, 158

duck

   Confit of Duck Legs with Potatoes
      Sarladaise, 172

   Duck Breasts with Apples & Caraway, 168

   Duck Soup with Cabbage, Ham & Chinese
      Rice Noodles, 173

E

Easter, Roast Leg of Lamb for, 26

Egg Noodles, Pimentón & Caraway Short Ribs
   with, 312

eggplant

   Caponata, 136

   Fritto Misto, 143

eggs

   Asparagus on Pasta with a Poached Egg &
      Lemon Butter, 18

   "Buttered" Eggs, 71

   Chorizo & Potato Frittata, 10

   Composed Summer Salad with Lemony
      Aïoli, 115

   Deconstructed Carbonara, 201

   Deviled Eggs, 71

   Ham & Cheese Omelet, 13

   Hearts of Romaine with Mimosa Dressing, 299

   How to Boil an Egg, 70

   Old-Fashioned Layered Potato Salad, 102

   Open-Faced Sandwiches, 38

   Open-Faced Zucchini Omelet, 72

   Pickled Beets with Horseradish Cream, 27

   Soft Scrambled Eggs & Chanterelles, 160

   Spaghetti alla Carbonara, 45

English Peas in Irish Butter, 84

escarole, 333

   Escarole, Fontina & Black Olive Pizza, 305

   Escarole Salad with Lemon & Parmigiano, 228

   Pork Chops with Roasted Beets & Escarole
      Salad, 333

   Ruby Red Grapefruit, Avocado & Escarole
      Salad, 280

Everyday Vegetable Tonic, 274, 276

F

Fallen Chocolate Soufflé Cake, 311

fava beans

   Artichoke, Pea & Fava Bean Salad, 23

   Raviolini with Fava Beans & Parmigiano, 81

   Rice Salad, 81

February recipe list, 292

fennel

   Fennel & Ginger–Rubbed Chicken with
      Cauliflower, 12–13

   fennel seed syrup, 147

Feta, French, String Beans Vinaigrette with, 101

Fingerling Potatoes, Bratwurst with, 210

Fire-Toasted Corn Tortilla with Mashed
   Avocado, 279

fish

   Birthday Halibut with Beets & Asparagus
      Vinaigrette, 56

   Fried Fish & French-Fried Potatoes, 322

   Fritto Misto, 143

   Grilled Salmon, 139

   Poached Wild Salmon with Fresh English
      Peas & Morels, 76

   Sole Meunière with Peas, Parsley & Chives, 20

   Wild Salmon Crudo with Arugula Salad, 76–77

Flank Steak, Rolled, with Pesto, 78

Fontina, Escarole, & Black Olive Pizza, 305

Food Is Your Best Medicine (Bieler), 274, 276

Fourth of July, Hoisin-Ful Spareribs for, 102

fraises des bois, 58

French-Fried Potatoes, Fried Fish &, 322

French Fries, Skirt Steak with Buttered Spinach
   &, 214

Fresh Pasta, 236

   Butternut Squash & Candied Bacon on Fresh
      Pasta, 250

   Spinach Pasta, 238

Fricassée of Chanterelles, 162

Fried Chicken, The Fry Queen's, 112

Fried Fish & French-Fried Potatoes, 322

Frittata, Chorizo & Potato, 10

Fritto Misto, 143

   Tiny Zucchini with their Blossoms Fritto
      Misto, 84

G

Galantine of Turkey & Pork with Peas, 40

Galette, Apple, 230

garden produce, 84, 124

Gazpacho, Roasted Red Pepper & Tomato, 107

gelée

   Chicken en Gelée Sandwiches, 158

   Cranberry-Port Gelée, 221

Gianduia, 203

   Gianduia & Caramel Tart, 204

   Little Gianduia Turnovers, 289

ginger, 277
    Cleansing Ginger-Chicken Soup, 277
    Cool Cucumber & Mint Salad with Sichuan
        Pepper, 103
    Curd Rice, 296
    Duck Soup with Cabbage, Ham & Chinese
        Rice Noodles, 173
    Fennel & Ginger–Rubbed Chicken with
        Cauliflower, 12–13
    Ginger Spice Cake with Dried Cherries, 262
    Shrimp Roast, 296
    White Sweet Potato Soup with Pickled
        Scallions, 280
goat cheese
    Smoked Salmon with Chèvre on Crax, 77
Golden Bread Crumbs with Pancetta &
    Prunes, 213
Goose, Roast, with Ten Legs, 258
granita
    Pink Lemon Granita, 148
    Strong Coffee Granita, 148
grapefruit
    Ruby Red Grapefruit, Avocado & Escarole
        Salad, 280
Gravy, Turkey, 220–21
green beans
    Composed Summer Salad with Lemony
        Aïoli, 115
    Corn, String Bean & Potato Succotash Salad,
        164–65
    Everyday Vegetable Tonic, 276
    Rice Salad, 81
    String Beans Vinaigrette with French Feta, 101
Green Lasagne with Tomato Sauce & Fresh
    Ricotta, 244
Green Lentil & Smoked Ham Hock Salad, 165
Green Sauce with Mint & Parsley, 26
Guajillo Chile Mole, Pork Stewed in, 198

H
Halibut with Beets & Asparagus Vinaigrette, 56
ham. *See also* prosciutto
    Baked Ham with Golden Bread Crumbs, 306
    Buckwheat Crêpes with Ham & Cheese, 314
    Cannellini with Smoked Ham & Rosemary, 43
    Duck Soup with Cabbage, Ham & Chinese
        Rice Noodles, 173
    Green Lentil & Smoked Ham Hock Salad, 165
    Ham & Bacon with Mustard & Brown Sugar
        Sauce, 272

    Ham & Cheese Omelet, 13
    Preserved Strawberries & Jamón Serrano on
        Little Toasts, 60
    Sliced Ham on Baguette, 306
hard-boiled eggs
    "Buttered" Eggs, 71
    Composed Summer Salad with Lemony
        Aïoli, 115
    Deviled Eggs, 71
    Galantine of Turkey & Pork with Peas, 40
    Hearts of Romaine with Mimosa Dressing, 299
    How to Boil an Egg, 70
    Old-Fashioned Layered Potato Salad, 102
    Open-Faced Sandwiches, 38
    Pickled Beets with Horseradish Cream, 27
hazelnuts
    Gianduia, 203
    Gianduia & Caramel Tart, 204
    Little Gianduia Turnovers, 289
Healthy Pancakes, Ian's, 273
Hearts of Romaine with Mimosa Dressing, 299
Heatter, Maida, 311
herbs, 66. *See also* specific types
    Fresh Herb Butter, 135
    Fritto Misto, 143
    herb mayonnaise, 56
    herb syrup, 147
    Roast Pork with Salmoriglio, 9
    Tartar Sauce, 322
Hoisin-Ful Spareribs for the Fourth of July, 102
hollandaise sauce
    Asparagus with Lemon-Butter Sauce, 17
horseradish
    Fresh Horseradish Butter, 135
    Pickled Beets with Horseradish Cream, 27
How to Boil an Egg, 70

I
Ian's Healthy Pancakes, 273
ice cream
    Cassis Ice Cream, 87
    Classic Vanilla Ice Cream, 86
    Coffee Ice Cream, 87
    Peppermint Crunch Ice Cream, 87
    Strawberry Ice Cream, 87
Iceberg, Marinated Chicken Salad with
    Radicchio &, 186
icing, chocolate, 310

Irish butter, 17, 38, 135
    compound butters, 135
    English Peas in Irish Butter, 84
Irish Soda Bread, 339
Italy, Christmas in, 234

J
jam
    Puff Pastry Jam Tartlets, 290
    Strawberry Conserves, 60
January recipe list, 266
Jelly, Red Currant, 91
Jerre Anne Bake Shoppe, 223
July recipe list, 96
June recipe list, 64

K
kabocha squash
    Grilled Quail with Braised Chestnuts &
        Kabocha Squash, 194
    Kabocha Squash Pie, 226
    Kabocha Squash, Yukon Gold Potatoes &
        Cipolline, 196
    Roasted Kabocha Squash, 196
Kaimal, Maya, 296
kale
    Borlotti Beans with Sautéed Baby Kale, 283
Kennedy, Diana, 43
King, Niloufer Ichaporia, 147

L
Lahey, Jim, 286
lamb, 4
    Cold Leg of Lamb with Cannellini & Lemon
        Mayonnaise, 166
    Lamb Shoulder Chops with Rosemary
        Potatoes, 216
    Roast Leg of Lamb for Easter, 26
lasagne, 234
    Green Lasagne with Tomato Sauce & Fresh
        Ricotta, 244
    Lasagne Bolognese, 244–45
Layered Potato Salad, Old-Fashioned, 102
Lee, Julia, 112
lemon(s)
    about Meyer lemons, 103, 294
    Anchovy & Lemon Butter, 316
    Asparagus on Pasta with a Poached Egg &
        Lemon Butter, 18
    Asparagus with Lemon-Butter Sauce, 17

Chicken Roasted Over Potatoes & Lemon, 184

Cold Leg of Lamb with Cannellini & Lemon
    Mayonnaise, 166

Composed Summer Salad with Lemony
    Aïoli, 115

Escarole Salad with Lemon & Parmigiano, 228

Fritto Misto, 143

Lemon Butter, 135

Lemon Meringue Tart, 29–31

lemon syrup, 121, 147

Lemonade, 121

Pink Lemon Granita, 148

Potato Salad "Buttered" & Lemoned, 103

Prosciutto, Lemon & Green Olive Pizza, 304

lemon verbena, 118

    lemon verbena syrup, 147

    Poached White Peaches in Lemon Verbena
        Syrup, 118

    Tisane of Fresh or Dried Lemon Verbena, 146

lentils

    Green Lentil & Smoked Ham Hock Salad, 165

lettuces. See also salads

    Marinated Chicken Salad with Radicchio &
        Iceberg, 186

    Salad of Head & Leaf Lettuces, 84

limes

    Limonada, 270

Lineberry, Afra, 223

lobster

    Buttery Lobster Capellini, 33

    Cold White Corn Soup with Lobster &
        Avocado, 128

    Lobster Stew, 255

Love Cakes, Buttermilk, 272–73

M

March Meatball Madness, 328

March recipe list, 318

Margarita, Winter, 270

Marmalade Cake, 261

Mashed Potato Trick, Brian's, 221

May recipe list, 34

mayonnaise

    "Buttered" Eggs, 71

    Cold Leg of Lamb with Cannellini & Lemon
        Mayonnaise, 166

    Composed Summer Salad with Lemony
        Aïoli, 115

    herb mayonnaise, 56

Poached Chicken with Tarragon & Chive
    Mayonnaise, 31

Tartar Sauce, 322

meat. See also beef; lamb; pork; veal

    brining, 9

    for flavor, 43

meatballs

    Chicken Broth with Spinach & Little
        Meatballs, 193

    March Meatball Madness, 328

    sauces for, 328–29

Melba Toasts, 316

Melon Water, 147

meringue

    Birthday Strawberry Pavlova, 57

    Lemon Meringue Tart, 29–31

    Red Velvet Cupcakes with Meringue
        Frosting, 308

Meyer lemons, 103, 294. See also lemon(s)

Michini, Marc & Joanna, 340

Milk Punch, 252

Mimosa Dressing, Hearts of Romaine with, 299

mint

    Cool Cucumber & Mint Salad with Sichuan
        Pepper, 103

    Green Sauce with Mint & Parsley, 26

    mint syrup, 147

Mixed Berry Cobbler, 92

Mole, Guajillo Chile, Pork Stewed in, 198

Morels, Poached Wild Salmon with Fresh
    English Peas &, 76

mozzarella

    Canal House Year-Round Caprese Salad, 72

    Sautéed Zucchini with Scallions & Fresh
        Mozzarella, 144

Multigrain Toast, Avocado Mash on, 279

mushrooms, 152. See also chanterelles

    Fritto Misto, 143

    Pappardelle & Mushrooms, 245

    Poached Wild Salmon with Fresh English
        Peas & Morels, 76

    Tetrazzini Sauce, 329

mustard

    Ham & Bacon with Mustard & Brown Sugar
        Sauce, 272

    Treviso with Mustard Vinaigrette, 324

N

nettles

    Stinging Nettle Soup, 7

New Year's, 270, 273, 274

No-Knead Bread, 286

noodles. See also pasta

    Duck Soup with Cabbage, Ham & Chinese
        Rice Noodles, 173

    Pimentón & Caraway Short Ribs with Egg
        Noodles, 312

November recipe list, 206

O

October recipe list, 178

okra

    Fritto Misto, 143

Old-Fashioned Baked Vanilla Custard, 344

Old-Fashioned Layered Potato Salad, 102

olive oil

    Cranberry Beans in Olive Oil, 166

    Olive Oil-Poached Zucchini & Raw
        Tomatoes, 144

    Tomatoes Take a Warm Oil Bath, 130

olives

    anchovy-stuffed, 78

    Breast of Veal Braised with Green Olives &
        Tomatoes, 50

    Caponata, 136

    Escarole, Fontina & Black Olive Pizza, 305

    Prosciutto, Lemon & Green Olive Pizza, 304

omelets

    Ham & Cheese Omelet, 13

    Open-Faced Zucchini Omelet, 72

onions. See also scallions

    Braised Beef Brisket with Onions &
        Currants, 300

    Chestnut & Pearl Onion Stuffing, 222

    Everyday Vegetable Tonic, 276

    Kabocha Squash, Yukon Gold Potatoes &
        Cipolline, 196

    Pork Cutlets with Pickled Pearl Onions &
        Pancetta, 334

    Potato & Onion Pizza, 305

    Roasted Chicken in a Pot with Spring
        Onions, 82

    Roasted Spring Onions, 23

    Sliced Brisket with Onions on a Soft Potato
        Roll, 300

Open-Faced Sandwiches, 38

Open-Faced Zucchini Omelet, 72
orange
    candied orange peel, 261
    Marmalade Cake, 261
    Rhubarb Syrup, 52
oregano
    Roast Pork with Salmoriglio, 9
outdoor refrigeration, 268

P
pancakes
    Buttermilk Love Cakes, 272–73
    Ian's Healthy Pancakes, 273
pancetta, 43
    Cauliflower with Bread Crumbs, Pancetta &
        Prunes, 213
    Chestnut & Pearl Onion Stuffing, 222
    Chicken Thighs with Pancetta &
        Caperberries, 299
    Crushed Potatoes with Pancetta, Peas &
        Scallions, 330
    Deconstructed Carbonara, 201
    Golden Bread Crumbs with Pancetta &
        Prunes, 213
    Pork Cutlets with Pickled Pearl Onions &
        Pancetta, 334
    Rice Salad, 81
    Spaghetti alla Carbonara, 45
pappardelle
    Pappardelle & Mushrooms, 245
    Pappardelle Bolognese, 241
    Pappardelle with Peas & Scallions Bathed in
        Cream, 7
paprika. See pimentón
parmigiano
    Cheese Straws, 252
    Escarole Salad with Lemon & Parmigiano, 228
    Raviolini with Fava Beans & Parmigiano, 81
    Rigatoni with Passato & Parmigiano-
        Reggiano, 188
parsley
    Beef Tenderloin with Parsley-Tarragon
        Butter, 284
    Fritto Misto, 143
    Green Sauce with Mint & Parsley, 26
    Parsley Sauce, 339
    Roast Chicken & Bread Salad, 324
    Roast Pork with Salmoriglio, 9
    Rolled Flank Steak with Pesto, 78
    Sole Meunière with Peas, Parsley & Chives, 20

Passato & Parmigiano-Reggiano, Rigatoni
    with, 188
pasta, 234. See also noodles; pasta sauces
    Asparagus on Pasta with a Poached Egg &
        Lemon Butter, 18
    Butternut Squash & Candied Bacon on Fresh
        Pasta, 250
    Buttery Lobster Capellini, 33
    Cannelloni, 248–49
    Chicken Soup with Ditalini, 186
    cutting, 236
    Deconstructed Carbonara, 201
    Fresh Pasta, 236
    Fricassée of Chanterelles, 162
    Green Lasagne with Tomato Sauce & Fresh
        Ricotta, 244
    Hot Spaghetti Tossed with Raw Tomato
        Sauce, 128
    Lasagne Bolognese, 244–45
    Pappardelle & Mushrooms, 245
    Pappardelle Bolognese, 241
    Pappardelle with Peas & Scallions Bathed in
        Cream, 7
    Raviolini with Fava Beans & Parmigiano, 81
    Rigatoni with Passato & Parmigiano-
        Reggiano, 188
    Spaghetti alla Carbonara, 45
    Spaghetti with Tomato Sauce & Ricotta, 44
    Spinach Pasta, 238
    Spinach Tagliatelle & Peas in Golden
        Chicken Broth, 46
    Spinach Tagliatelle Bolognese, 241
    Spinach Tagliatelle with Tomato Sauce &
        Ricotta, 250
pasta sauces. See also tomato sauces
    Balsamella, 240
    Ragù Bolognese, 241
    Simple Tomato Sauce, 240
pastries. See pies; puff pastry; tarts
Pavlova, Birthday Strawberry, 57
peaches
    Bellini, 121
    Poached White Peaches in Lemon Verbena
        Syrup, 118
    Pears, Vin Santo–Roasted, 203
peas
    Artichoke, Pea & Fava Bean Salad, 23
    Crushed Potatoes with Pancetta, Peas &
        Scallions, 330

English Peas in Irish Butter, 84
Galantine of Turkey & Pork with Peas, 40
Pappardelle with Peas & Scallions Bathed in
    Cream, 7
Poached Wild Salmon with Fresh English
    Peas & Morels, 76
Rice Salad, 81
Sole Meunière with Peas, Parsley &
    Chives, 20
Spinach Tagliatelle & Peas in Golden
    Chicken Broth, 46
pecans
    Agee's Pecan Pies, 223
    Waldorf Chicken Salad, 314
Pepper, Black, Blue Cheese with, 316
Pepper, Sichuan, Cool Cucumber & Mint Salad
    with, 103
Peppermint Crunch Ice Cream, 87
peppers
    Roasted Red Pepper & Tomato Gazpacho, 107
Pesto, Rolled Flank Steak with, 78
pickles
    Pickled Beets with Horseradish Cream, 27
    Pickled Shrimp & Celery, 254–55
    Pork Cutlets with Pickled Pearl Onions &
        Pancetta, 334
    White Sweet Potato Soup with Pickled
        Scallions, 280
pies
    Agee's Pecan Pies, 223
    Kabocha Squash Pie, 226
    Pumpkin Chiffon Pie, 227
pimentón
    Pimentón & Caraway Short Ribs with Egg
        Noodles, 312
    Pimentón Butter, 135
Pink Lemon Granita, 148
pizza
    Escarole, Fontina & Black Olive Pizza, 305
    Pizza Dough, 304
    Potato & Onion Pizza, 305
    Prosciutto, Lemon & Green Olive Pizza, 304
    White Clam Pizza, 305
Poached White Peaches in Lemon Verbena
    Syrup, 118
    Bellini, 121
porcini, 245
    Pappardelle & Mushrooms, 245

pork. *See also* ham; pancetta; prosciutto; sausage
    Cannelloni, 248–49
    Chicken Broth with Spinach & Little
        Meatballs, 193
    for flavor, 43
    Galantine of Turkey & Pork with Peas, 40
    Hoisin-Ful Spareribs for the Fourth of July, 102
    March Meatball Madness, 328
    Pork Chops with Roasted Beets & Escarole
        Salad, 333
    Pork Cutlets with Pickled Pearl Onions &
        Pancetta, 334
    Pork Stewed in Guajillo Chile Mole, 198
    Ragù Bolognese, 241
    Roast Pork with Salmoriglio, 9
port
    Cranberry-Port Gelée, 221
potatoes
    Bratwurst with Fingerling Potatoes, 210
    Brian's Mashed Potato Trick, 221
    Chicken Roasted Over Potatoes & Lemon, 184
    Chilled Potato & Celery Soup, 140
    Chorizo & Potato Frittata, 10
    Composed Summer Salad with Lemony
        Aïoli, 115
    Confit of Duck Legs with Potatoes
        Sarladaise, 172
    Corn, String Bean & Potato Succotash
        Salad, 164–65
    Crushed Potatoes with Pancetta, Peas &
        Scallions, 330
    Fried Fish & French-Fried Potatoes, 322
    Kabocha Squash, Yukon Gold Potatoes &
        Cipolline, 196
    Lamb Shoulder Chops with Rosemary
        Potatoes, 216
    Lobster Stew, 255
    Old-Fashioned Layered Potato Salad, 102
    Potato & Onion Pizza, 305
    Potato Salad "Buttered" & Lemoned, 103
    Sister Frances's Potatoes, 27
    Skirt Steak with Buttered Spinach & French
        Fries, 214
    Turkey & Potato Soup, 228
Potted Crab, 316
poultry. *See* chicken; duck; quail; turkey
preserved lemons, 103, 294
    Chopped Celery Salad, 284
    Potato Salad "Buttered" & Lemoned, 103

preserves
    Cassis Ice Cream, 87
    Marmalade Cake, 261
    Preserved Strawberries & Jamón Serrano on
        Little Toasts, 60
    Puff Pastry Jam Tartlets, 290
    Red Currant Jelly, 91
    Strawberry Conserves, 60
Prime Rib of Beef, Roast, 256
prosciutto, 43
    Chicken Broth with Spinach & Little
        Meatballs, 193
    Open-Faced Sandwiches, 38
    Prosciutto, Lemon & Green Olive Pizza, 304
prunes
    Cauliflower with Bread Crumbs, Pancetta &
        Prunes, 213
    Chocolate-Covered Boozy Prunes, 290
    Golden Bread Crumbs with Pancetta &
        Prunes, 213
    Restorative Beef Broth, 276
pudding
    Little Yorkshire Puddings, 256
puff pastry, 155, 156, 289
    Cheese Straws, 252
    Little Chocolate Turnovers, 289
    Little Gianduia Turnovers, 289
    Puff Pastry Jam Tartlets, 290
    Simple Puff Pastry, 155
pumpkin
    Pumpkin Chiffon Pie, 227
    Roasted Pumpkin Soup, 189
Punch, Milk, 252
Purely Farm, 340

Q
Quail, Grilled, with Braised Chestnuts &
    Kabocha Squash, 194
Quick Tomato Sauce, 328

R
Rabbit Stew, 340
radicchio, 324
    Marinated Chicken Salad with Radicchio &
        Iceberg, 186
    Treviso with Mustard Vinaigrette, 324
radishes
    Open-Faced Sandwiches, 38
Ragù Bolognese, 241
    Lasagne Bolognese, 244–45

raisins
    Braised Beef Brisket with Onions & Raisins, 300
    Marinated Chicken Salad with Radicchio &
        Iceberg, 186
    Pork Stewed in Guajillo Chile Mole, 198
raspberries. *See also* berries
    Mixed Berry Cobbler, 92
Raviolini with Fava Beans & Parmigiano, 81
Raw Tomato Sauce, Hot Spaghetti Tossed
    With, 128
Red Currant Jelly, 91
red peppers
    Roasted Red Pepper & Tomato Gazpacho, 107
Red Velvet Cupcakes with Meringue Frosting, 308
refrigeration, outdoor, 268
Restorative Beef Broth, 276
rhubarb
    Amante, 52
    Rhubarb Syrup, 52
    Roasted Rhubarb, 52
ribs
    Hoisin-Ful Spareribs for the Fourth of July, 102
    Pimentón & Caraway Short Ribs with Egg
        Noodles, 312
rice, 46, 81. *See also* risotto
    Curd Rice, 296
    Rice Salad, 81
Rice Noodles, Chinese, Duck Soup with
    Cabbage, Ham &, 173
ricotta
    Green Lasagne with Tomato Sauce & Fresh
        Ricotta, 244
    Spaghetti with Tomato Sauce & Ricotta, 44
    Spinach Tagliatelle with Tomato Sauce &
        Ricotta, 250
Rigatoni with Passato & Parmigiano-
    Reggiano, 188
risotto
    Risotto Cakes with Anchovies (or Not), 10
    risotto sandwiches, 38
    Shrimp Risotto, 46
Roast Prime Rib of Beef, 256
Rolled Flank Steak with Pesto, 78
"Rollmops," Tomato, 127
rosemary
    Cannellini with Smoked Ham & Rosemary, 43
    Lamb Shoulder Chops with Rosemary
        Potatoes, 216
    rosemary syrup, 147

Ruby Red Grapefruit, Avocado & Escarole
Salad, 280
Rummy Apricot, 91
S
sage
Fritto Misto, 143
Saint Patrick's Day, 338
Corned Beef & Cabbage with Parsley
Sauce, 338–39
Irish Soda Bread, 339
salads
Artichoke, Pea & Fava Bean Salad, 23
Canal House Crab Louis, 101
Canal House Year-Round Caprese Salad, 72
Chanterelle Salad, 162
Chopped Celery Salad, 284
Composed Summer Salad with Lemony
Aïoli, 115
Cool Cucumber & Mint Salad with Sichuan
Pepper, 103
Corn, String Bean & Potato Succotash
Salad, 164–65
Escarole Salad with Lemon & Parmigiano, 228
Green Lentil & Smoked Ham Hock Salad, 165
Hearts of Romaine with Mimosa Dressing, 299
Marinated Chicken Salad with Radicchio &
Iceberg, 186
Old-Fashioned Layered Potato Salad, 102
Pickled Beets with Horseradish Cream, 27
Pork Chops with Roasted Beets & Escarole
Salad, 333
Potato Salad "Buttered" & Lemoned, 103
Rice Salad, 81
Roast Chicken & Bread Salad, 324
Ruby Red Grapefruit, Avocado & Escarole
Salad, 280
Salad of Head & Leaf Lettuces, 84
Shaved Asparagus & Arugula Salad with
Bruschetta, 33
Sliced Tomatoes with Arugula, 130
String Beans Vinaigrette with French Feta, 101
Tomatoes with Tonnato Sauce, 111
Treviso with Mustard Vinaigrette, 324
Waldorf Chicken Salad, 314
Wild Salmon Crudo with Arugula Salad, 76–77
salmon, 76
Grilled Salmon, 139

Poached Wild Salmon with Fresh English
Peas & Morels, 76
Smoked Salmon Butter, 316
Smoked Salmon with Chèvre on Crax, 77
Wild Salmon Crudo with Arugula Salad, 76–77
Salmoriglio, Roast Pork with, 9
sandwiches
Chicken en Gelée Sandwiches, 158
Day-After-Thanksgiving Turkey Sandwich,
228
Open-Faced Sandwiches, 38
Roast Beef Sandwich with Avocado &
Tomato, 130
Sliced Brisket with Onions on a Soft Potato
Roll, 300
Sliced Ham on Baguette, 306
The Splendid Summer Tomato Sandwich, 127
Tomatoes All Dressed Up for Summer, 127
sauces. *See also* mayonnaise; tomato sauces
Asparagus with Lemon-Butter Sauce, 17
Balsamella, 240
compound butters, 135
Dill Sauce, 329
Green Sauce with Mint & Parsley, 26
Ham & Bacon with Mustard & Brown Sugar
Sauce, 272
Parsley Sauce, 339
Tartar Sauce, 322
Tetrazzini Sauce, 329
Tomatoes with Tonnato Sauce, 111
sausage
Bratwurst with Fingerling Potatoes, 210
Bratwurst with Sautéed Caraway Cabbage, 210
Chorizo & Potato Frittata, 10
Sausage & Clam Stew, 188–89
scallions
Crushed Potatoes with Pancetta, Peas &
Scallions, 330
Fritto Misto, 143
Pappardelle with Peas & Scallions Bathed in
Cream, 7
Sautéed Zucchini with Scallions & Fresh
Mozzarella, 144
White Sweet Potato Soup with Pickled
Scallions, 280
Schiltz Goose Farm, 258
Scrambled Eggs & Chanterelles, Soft, 160
seafood. *See* clams; fish; lobster; shrimp

September recipe list, 150
Serrano Ham & Preserved Strawberries on Little
Toasts, 60
sherry, 329
Tetrazzini Sauce, 329
short ribs
Pimentón & Caraway Short Ribs with Egg
Noodles, 312
Shortcake, Strawberry, 62
shrimp
Fritto Misto, 143
Pickled Shrimp & Celery, 254–55
Shrimp Roast, 296
Shrimp Risotto, 46
Sichuan pepper, Cool Cucumber & Mint Salad with, 103
Simili, Margherita, 234
Simili, Valeria, 234
Simple Puff Pastry, 155
Simple Syrup, 147. *See also* syrups
Sister Frances's Potatoes, 27
Skirt Steak with Buttered Spinach & French
Fries, 214
Smoked Salmon Butter, 316
Smoked Salmon with Chèvre on Crax, 77
Soda Bread, Irish, 339
Sole Meunière with Peas, Parsley & Chives, 20
soups, 274. *See also* broths
Chicken Soup with Ditalini, 186
Chilled Corn Soup, 108
Chilled Potato & Celery Soup, 140
Cleansing Ginger-Chicken Soup, 277
Cold Avocado & Cucumber Soup, 108
Cold Carrot Soup, 140
Cold White Corn Soup with Lobster &
Avocado, 128
Duck Soup with Cabbage, Ham & Chinese
Rice Noodles, 173
Everyday Vegetable Tonic, 276
Restorative Beef Broth, 276
Roasted Pumpkin Soup, 189
Roasted Red Pepper & Tomato Gazpacho, 107
Stinging Nettle Soup, 7
Turkey & Potato Soup, 228
Warm Beet Soup, 183
Watercress Soup, 330
White Sweet Potato Soup with Pickled
Scallions, 280

spaghetti
    Hot Spaghetti Tossed with Raw Tomato
        Sauce, 128
    Spaghetti alla Carbonara, 45
    Spaghetti with Tomato Sauce & Ricotta, 44
Spareribs, Hoisin-Ful, for the Fourth of July, 102
sparklers
    Apricot Sparkler, 91
    Bellini, 121
spinach
    Chicken Broth with Spinach & Little
        Meatballs, 193
    Skirt Steak with Buttered Spinach & French
        Fries, 214
    Spinach Pasta, 238
spinach tagliatelle
    Spinach Tagliatelle & Peas in Golden
        Chicken Broth, 46
    Spinach Tagliatelle Bolognese, 241
    Spinach Tagliatelle with Tomato Sauce &
        Ricotta, 250
Splendid Summer Tomato Sandwich, The, 127
Sponge Cake, Chocolate, 310
spreads. *See also* mayonnaise
    Anchovy & Lemon Butter, 316
    Blue Cheese with Black Pepper, 316
    compound butters, 135
    Potted Crab, 316
    Smoked Salmon Butter, 316
spring garden lunch, 84
spring onions
    Roasted Chicken in a Pot with Spring
        Onions, 82
    Roasted Spring Onions, 23
spring recipe lists, 2, 34, 64
squash. *See also* kabocha squash; pumpkin; zucchini
    Butternut Squash & Candied Bacon on Fresh
        Pasta, 250
steak
    Rolled Flank Steak with Pesto, 78
    Skirt Steak with Buttered Spinach & French
        Fries, 214
    Two Steaks Feed Four, 134–35
stews
    Lobster Stew, 255
    Pork Stewed in Guajillo Chile Mole, 198
    Rabbit Stew, 340
    Sausage & Clam Stew, 188–89

Stinging Nettle Soup, 7
stock. *See also* broths
    Turkey Stock, 221
strawberries, 58. *See also* berries
    Birthday Strawberry Pavlova, 57
    Preserved Strawberries & Jamón Serrano on
        Little Toasts, 60
    Strawberries Romanoff, 62
    Strawberry Conserves, 60
    Strawberry Ice Cream, 87
    Strawberry Shortcake, 62
string beans. *See also* green beans
    Composed Summer Salad with Lemony
        Aïoli, 115
    Corn, String Bean & Potato Succotash
        Salad, 164–65
    Everyday Vegetable Tonic, 276
    Rice Salad, 81
    String Beans Vinaigrette with French Feta, 101
Strong Coffee Granita, 148
stuffing a turkey, 220
    Chestnut & Pearl Onion Stuffing, 222
Succotash Salad, Corn, String Bean, &
    Potato, 164–65
Sugared Berries with Crème Anglaise, 116
summer recipe lists, 96, 122, 150
Summer Salad with Lemony Aïoli, 115
sweet potatoes
    White Sweet Potato Soup with Pickled
        Scallions, 280
Swiss chard with Cannellini, 84
syrups
    apricot syrup drinks, 91
    lemon syrup, 121
    Poached White Peaches in Lemon Verbena
        Syrup, 118
    Rhubarb Syrup, 52
    Simple Syrup with variations, 147

T
tagliatelle. *See* spinach tagliatelle
tarragon
    Beef Tenderloin with Parsley-Tarragon
        Butter, 284
    Poached Chicken with Tarragon & Chive
        Mayonnaise, 31
    tarragon syrup, 147
    Tartar Sauce, 322
Tartlets, Puff Pastry Jam, 290

tarts
    Apple Galette, 230
    Apple Tart, 174
    Gianduia & Caramel Tart, 204
    Lemon Meringue Tart, 29–31
    Simple Puff Pastry, 155
    Tomato Tart, 156
Tetrazzini Sauce, 329
Thanksgiving, 208
    Agee's Pecan Pies, 223
    Brian's Mashed Potato Trick, 221
    Chestnut & Pearl Onion Stuffing, 222
    Cranberry-Port Gelée, 221
    Day-After-Thanksgiving Turkey Sandwich,
        228
    Kabocha Squash Pie, 226
    Pumpkin Chiffon Pie, 227
    Roast Turkey, 220
    Turkey Gravy, 220–21
Thick & Chewy Brownies, 106
Thin & Crisp Chocolate Chip Cookies, 344
thyme syrup, 147
Tisane of Fresh or Dried Lemon Verbena, 146
toast. *See also* spreads
    Avocado Mash on Multigrain Toast, 279
    Melba Toasts, 316
    Preserved Strawberries & Jamón Serrano on
        Little Toasts, 60
    Shaved Asparagus & Arugula Salad with
        Bruschetta, 33
    The Splendid Summer Tomato Sandwich, 127
    Tomatoes All Dressed Up for Summer, 127
tomato sauces
    Green Lasagne with Tomato Sauce & Fresh
        Ricotta, 244
    Hot Spaghetti Tossed with Raw Tomato
        Sauce, 128
    Quick Tomato Sauce, 328
    Ragù Bolognese, 241
    Rigatoni with Passato & Parmigiano-
        Reggiano, 188
    Simple Tomato Sauce, 240
    Spaghetti with Tomato Sauce & Ricotta, 44
    Spinach Tagliatelle with Tomato Sauce &
        Ricotta, 250
tomatoes, 124. *See also* tomato sauces
    Breast of Veal Braised with Green Olives &
        Tomatoes, 50

Canal House Year-Round Caprese Salad, 72

Caponata, 136

Kabocha Squash, Yukon Gold Potatoes & Cipolline, 196

Olive Oil–Poached Zucchini & Raw Tomatoes, 144

Roast Beef Sandwich with Avocado & Tomato, 130

Roasted Red Pepper & Tomato Gazpacho, 107

Sliced Tomatoes with Arugula, 130

The Splendid Summer Tomato Sandwich, 127

Tomato "Rollmops," 127

Tomato Tart, 156

Tomatoes All Dressed Up for Summer, 127

Tomatoes Take a Warm Oil Bath, 130

Tomatoes with Tonnato Sauce, 111

tonics. *See* cleansing foods

Tonnato Sauce, Tomatoes with, 111

tortillas

Fire-Toasted Corn Tortilla with Mashed Avocado, 279

Treviso with Mustard Vinaigrette, 324

Tuiles, Classic, 116–18

tuna

Tomatoes with Tonnato Sauce, 111

turkey, 208, 220

Day-After-Thanksgiving Turkey Sandwich, 228

Galantine of Turkey & Pork with Peas, 40

Roast Turkey, 220

Turkey & Potato Soup, 228

Turkey Gravy, 220–21

Turnips with Brown Butter, 84

turnovers

Little Chocolate Turnovers, 289

Little Gianduia Turnovers, 289

U

Upside-Down Cake, Apricot & Almond, 88

V

vanilla

Classic Vanilla Ice Cream, 86

Old-Fashioned Baked Vanilla Custard, 344

vanilla syrup, 147

veal

Breast of Veal Braised with Green Olives & Tomatoes, 50

"Brunette" de Veau, 343

Cannelloni, 248–49

Chicken Broth with Spinach & Little Meatballs, 193

March Meatball Madness, 328

Vegetable Tonic, Everyday, 276

Vin Santo–Roasted Pears, 203

vinaigrette

Birthday Halibut with Beets & Asparagus Vinaigrette, 56

String Beans Vinaigrette with French Feta, 101

Treviso with Mustard Vinaigrette, 324

vinegar, making your own, 320

W

Waldorf Chicken Salad, 314

walnuts

Thick & Chewy Brownies, 106

watercress, 330

Pickled Beets with Horseradish Cream, 27

Watercress Soup, 330

watermelon

Melon Water, 147

Waters, Alice, 334

Welch, Raquel, 274

White Clam Pizza, 305

White Sweet Potato Soup with Pickled Scallions, 280

wild mushrooms. *See also* chanterelles

Pappardelle & Mushrooms, 245

Poached Wild Salmon with Fresh English Peas & Morels, 76

wild salmon. *See* salmon

wine vinegar, 320

Winter Margarita, 270

winter recipe lists, 266, 292, 318

winter squash. *See also* kabocha squash; pumpkin

Butternut Squash & Candied Bacon on Fresh Pasta, 250

Y

Yang, Katherine, 344

yogurt

Curd Rice, 296

Yorkshire Puddings, Little, 256

Yukon Gold Potatoes, Kabocha Squash & Cipolline, 196

Z

zucchini

Everyday Vegetable Tonic, 276

Fritto Misto, 143

Olive Oil-Poached Zucchini & Raw Tomatoes, 144

Open-Faced Zucchini Omelet, 72

Pan-Fried Chicken Thighs with Little Zucchini, 38

Sautéed Zucchini with Scallions & Fresh Mozzarella, 144

Tiny Zucchini with their Blossoms Fritto Misto, 84

METRIC CONVERSIONS AND EQUIVALENTS

APPROXIMATE METRIC EQUIVALENTS

WEIGHT

¼ ounce	7 grams
½ ounce	14 grams
¾ ounce	21 grams
1 ounce	28 grams
1¼ ounces	35 grams
1½ ounces	42.5 grams
1⅔ ounces	45 grams
2 ounces	57 grams
3 ounces	85 grams
4 ounces (¼ pound)	113 grams
5 ounces	142 grams
6 ounces	170 grams
7 ounces	198 grams
8 ounces (½ pound)	227 grams
16 ounces (1 pound)	454 grams
35.25 ounces (2.2 pounds)	1 kilogram

LENGTH

⅛ inch	3 millimeters
¼ inch	6 millimeters
½ inch	1¼ centimeters
1 inch	2½ centimeters
2 inches	5 centimeters
2½ inches	6 centimeters
4 inches	10 centimeters
5 inches	13 centimeters
6 inches	15¼ centimeters
12 inches (1 foot)	30 centimeters

VOLUME

¼ teaspoon	1 milliliter
½ teaspoon	2.5 milliliters
¾ teaspoon	4 milliliters
1 teaspoon	5 milliliters
1¼ teaspoon	6 milliliters
1½ teaspoon	7.5 milliliters
1¾ teaspoon	8.5 milliliters
2 teaspoons	10 milliliters
1 tablespoon (½ fluid ounce)	15 milliliters
2 tablespoons (1 fluid ounce)	30 milliliters
¼ cup	60 milliliters
⅓ cup	80 milliliters
½ cup (4 fluid ounces)	120 milliliters
⅔ cup	160 milliliters
¾ cup	180 milliliters
1 cup (8 fluid ounces)	240 milliliters
1¼ cups	300 milliliters
1½ cups (12 fluid ounces)	360 milliliters
1⅔ cups	400 milliliters
2 cups (1 pint)	460 milliliters
3 cups	700 milliliters
4 cups (1 quart)	.95 liter
1 quart plus ¼ cup	1 liter
4 quarts (1 gallon)	3.8 liters

OVEN TEMPERATURES

To convert Fahrenheit to Celsius, subtract 32 from Fahrenheit, multiply the result by 5, then divide by 9.

Description	Fahrenheit	Celsius	British Gas Mark
Very cool	200°	95°	0
Very cool	225°	110°	¼
Very cool	250°	120°	½
Cool	275°	135°	1
Cool	300°	150°	2
Warm	325°	165°	3
Moderate	350°	175°	4
Moderately hot	375°	190°	5
Fairly hot	400°	200°	6
Hot	425°	220°	7
Very hot	450°	230°	8
Very hot	475°	245°	9

METRIC CONVERSION FORMULAS

To Convert	Multiply
Ounces to grams	Ounces by 28.35
Pounds to kilograms	Pounds by .454
Teaspoons to milliliters	Teaspoons by 4.93
Tablespoons to milliliters	Tablespoons by 14.79
Fluid ounces to milliliters	Fluid ounces by 29.57
Cups to milliliters	Cups by 236.59
Cups to liters	Cups by .236
Pints to liters	Pints by .473
Quarts to liters	Quarts by .946
Gallons to liters	Gallons by 3.785
Inches to centimeters	Inches by 2.54

COMMON INGREDIENTS AND THEIR APPROXIMATE EQUIVALENTS

1 cup uncooked rice = 225 grams

1 cup all-purpose flour = 140 grams

1 stick butter (4 ounces • ½ cup • 8 tablespoons) = 110 grams

1 cup butter (8 ounces • 2 sticks • 16 tablespoons) = 220 grams

1 cup brown sugar, firmly packed = 225 grams

1 cup granulated sugar = 200 grams

Information compiled from a variety of sources, including *Recipes into Type* by Joan Whitman and Dolores Simon (Newton, MA: Biscuit Books, 2000); *The New Food Lover's Companion* by Sharon Tyler Herbst (Hauppauge, NY: Barron's, 1995); and *Rosemary Brown's Big Kitchen Instruction Book* (Kansas City, MO: Andrews McMeel, 1998).

ACKNOWLEDGMENTS

WE STAND ON THE SHOULDERS OF GIANTS. We are grateful to this wonderful collection of food-loving souls who worked with us to bring this book into the world:

Amanda Hesser, for channeling the fun-loving, home-cooking spirit of Julia Child.

Margo True, our wise editor and gentle guide. She hears our voices through the words that we write and always knows just what we mean. Best friends forever.

Valerie Saint-Rossy, our cultured, food-centric copy editor, for her great knowledge of the English (and French, Italian, Spanish, Japanese, and Chinese) language.

Teresa Hopkins, who knows all things technical, answers every call with grace and good cheer, and reminds us to check that the computer is plugged in.

Frani Beadle, for her eagle eye, kind, friendly manner, and her fine home cooking skills.

Patricia Curtan is always in our minds as we work. Nothing is designed at Canal House without us considering, "Would Patty like this?"

Michelle Fuerst and Kate Winslow, for sharing their intelligence, fine organized minds, and their devotion to delicious food. They both arrived at Canal House with impressive culinary portfolios, and then slipped into the kitchen and cooked their way through this book and right into our hearts.

Stephen Sheppard, our advocate/agent, who understands our vision for Canal House and through his wise ways helps us get there.

Kirsty Melville, who told us to just do it—so we did. Thank you for believing in us.

Chris Schillig, for gracefully guiding us through the layers of printers and publishers and keeping us on schedule (and looking the other way when we weren't).

The great Andrews McMeel team: Amy Worley, Tammie Barker, Carol Coe, and Lynne McAdoo.

CH thanks MH, and MH thanks CH. It has been an honor. And we both thank Henry the studio dog for his patience and constant good nature.

CHRISTOPHER HIRSHEIMER (left) is a home cook, writer, award-winning photographer, and cofounder of Canal House, whose facets include a publishing venture, culinary and design studio, and an annual series of three seasonal cookbooks titled *Canal House Cooking*. Before starting Canal House in 2007 in Lambertville, New Jersey, Hirsheimer was one of the founders of *Saveur*, where she was executive editor. She cowrote the award-winning *Saveur Cooks* series and *The San Francisco Ferry Plaza Farmers' Market Cookbook* (Chronicle, 2006), and her photographs have appeared in more than fifty cookbooks by such notables as Colman Andrews, Lidia Bastianich, Mario Batali, Julia Child, Jacques Pépin, David Tanis, and Alice Waters; and in numerous magazines, including *Bon Appétit*, *Food & Wine*, *InStyle*, and *Town & Country*.

MELISSA HAMILTON (right) is a home cook, writer, painter, food stylist, and cofounder of Canal House. She previously worked at *Saveur* as test kitchen director, and was its food editor for many years. Hamilton also worked at *Martha Stewart Living* and *Cook's Illustrated*, and was cofounder and the first executive chef of Hamilton's Grill Room in Lambertville, New Jersey. She has developed and tested recipes and styled food for both magazines and cookbooks, including those by acclaimed chefs and cookbook authors Colman Andrews, Lidia Bastianich, John Besh, Jonathan Waxman, David Tanis, and Alice Waters.

Hamilton and Hirsheimer currently collaborate on *Canal House Cooking*, for which they do all the writing, recipes, photography, design, and production. To see more of what these two women are up to, visit their website, thecanalhouse.com.

"The Canal House itself seems like a foodie fantasy—leave the big city, start a small food business with your best cooking pal, sit around inventing cocktails and snacks at the end of every day—but both are resolutely real cooks."
—*Julia Moskin, The New York Times*

"Christopher Hirsheimer and Melissa Hamilton are brilliant."—*Sheryl Julian, The Boston Globe*

"If there were a hall of fame for the culinary arts, these two women would surely be among the inducted." —Diana Cercone, *Edible Jersey*

"Leafing through the recipes is like looking through the old Chez Panisse books, or maybe Deborah Madison or Richard Olney. Every other page, you think, 'Oh, I want to make that.' And the pictures are so perfect that you just know you can."
— *Russ Parsons, L.A. Times*

"Beautifully shot and filled with simple produce-driven recipes…*Canal House Cooking* makes me jealous. They sure make it look fun."—*Lessley Anderson,* Chow.com

"This is just the kind of cooking that will inspire you, satisfy you, and compel you into the kitchen time and again."
—*Denise Mickelsen, Fine Cooking*

"With gorgeous pictures and watercolors, just because. Hard to believe that something this useful could be this lovable. But the evidence that this is true is on each and every page." —*Jesse Kornbluth,* HeadButler.com

"Once you see the summer volume, you'll want them all."
—*Elaine McCardel, theItaliandishblog.com*

"Halfway between a cookbook and a food magazine, *Canal House Cooking,* a gorgeous, unpretentious new periodical, arrives every four months filled with just enough irresistible seasonal recipes to keep you cooking until the next issue turns up." —*O, The Oprah Magazine*

"Usually when I see "charming" and "self-published" in the same sentence, I run quickly in the opposite direction. But *Canal House Cooking,* a charming new self-published cookbook by Christopher Hirsheimer and Melissa Hamilton, has me running to the kitchen instead."
—*John Willoughby, Gourmet*

"Wonderful, marvelous, fabulous, and we love the color. I couldn't wait to line all the books up in the bookcase. You have done it again and now I have a million things I am dying to cook."
—*Peggy Knickerbocker,* award-winning cookbook author

"Ever been in the kitchen cooking with a friend and thought, if only I did this for a living? Food-world vets Melissa Hamilton and Christopher Hirsheimer live that dream." —*Glamour Magazine*